Qualifications and Credit Framework (QCF)

AQ2013
LEVEL 4 DIPLOMA IN ACCOUNTING

(QCF)

QUESTION BANK

Financial Performance

2015 Edition

For assessments from September 2015

Third edition June 2015
ISBN 9781 4727 2203 4

Previous edition
ISBN 9781 4727 0937 0

British Library Cataloguing-in-Publication Data
A catalogue record for this book is available from the British Library

Published by
BPP Learning Media Ltd
BPP House
Aldine Place
London W12 8AA

www.bpp.com/learningmedia

Printed in the United Kingdom by Martins of Berwick
Sea View Works
Spittal
Berwick-Upon-Tweed
TD15 1RS

We are grateful to the AAT for permission to reproduce the sample
assessment(s). The answers to the sample assessment(s) have been
published by the AAT. All other answers have been prepared by BPP
Learning Media Ltd.

CONTENTS

Introduction   v

Question and answer bank

A NOTE ABOUT COPYRIGHT

Dear Customer

What does the little © mean and why does it matter?

Your market-leading BPP books, course materials and e-learning materials do not write and update themselves. People write them on their own behalf or as employees of an organisation that invests in this activity. Copyright law protects their livelihoods. It does so by creating rights over the use of the content.

Breach of copyright is a form of theft – as well being a criminal offence in some jurisdictions, it is potentially a serious breach of professional ethics.

With current technology, things might seem a bit hazy but, basically, without the express permission of BPP Learning Media:

- Photocopying our materials is a breach of copyright

- Scanning, ripcasting or conversion of our digital materials into different file formats, uploading them to facebook or emailing them to your friends is a breach of copyright

You can, of course, sell your books, in the form in which you have bought them – once you have finished with them. (Is this fair to your fellow students? We update for a reason). Please note the e-products are sold on a single user licence basis: we do not supply 'unlock' codes to people who have bought them secondhand.

And what about outside the UK? BPP Learning Media strives to make our materials available at prices students can afford by local printing arrangements, pricing policies and partnerships which are clearly listed on our website. A tiny minority ignore this and indulge in criminal activity by illegally photocopying our material or supporting organisations that do. If they act illegally and unethically in one area, can you really trust them?

INTRODUCTION

This is BPP Learning Media's AAT Question Bank for Financial Performance. It is part of a suite of ground-breaking resources produced by BPP Learning Media for the AAT's assessments under the Qualification and Credit Framework.

The Financial Performance assessment will be **computer assessed**. As well as being available in the traditional paper format, this **Question Bank is available in an online environment** containing tasks similar to those you will encounter in the AAT's testing environment. BPP Learning Media believe that the best way to practise for an online assessment is in an online environment. However, if you are unable to practise in the online environment you will find that all tasks in the paper Question Bank have been written in a style that is as close as possible to the style that you will be presented with in your online assessment.

This Question Bank has been written in conjunction with the BPP Text, and has been carefully designed to enable students to practise all of the learning outcomes and assessment criteria for the units that make up Financial Performance. It is fully up to date as at June 2015 and reflects both the AAT's unit guide and the sample assessment(s) provided by the AAT.

This Question Bank contains these key features:

- Tasks corresponding to each chapter of the Text. Some tasks are designed for learning purposes, others are of assessment standard

- AAT's AQ2013 sample assessments and answers for Financial Performance and further BPP practice assessments

The emphasis in all tasks and assessments is on the practical application of the skills acquired.

VAT

You may find tasks throughout this Question Bank that need you to calculate or be aware of a rate of VAT. This is stated at 20% in these examples and questions.

Approaching the assessment

When you sit the assessment it is very important that you follow the on screen instructions. This means you need to carefully read the instructions, both on the introduction screens and during specific tasks.

When you access the assessment you should be presented with an introductory screen with information similar to that shown below (taken from the introductory screen from one of the AAT's AQ2013 Sample Assessments for Financial Performance).

We have provided the following assessment to help you familiarise yourself with AAT's e-assessment environment. It is designed to demonstrate as many as possible of the question types you may find in a live assessment. It is not designed to be used on its own to determine whether you are ready for a live assessment.

Please note that in this sample test only your responses to tasks 1-5 and 7-9 are marked. Equivalents of tasks 6 and 10 will be human marked in the live assessment.

This assessment contains <u>10 tasks</u> and you should attempt and aim to complete EVERY task. Each task is independent. You will not need to refer to your answers to previous tasks. Read every task carefully to make sure you understand what is required.

Where the date is relevant, it is given in the task data.

Both minus signs and brackets can be used to indicate negative numbers UNLESS task instructions say otherwise.

You must use a full stop to indicate a decimal point. For example, write 100.57 NOT 100,57 or 100 57

You may use a comma to indicate a number in the thousands, but you don't have to. For example, 10000 and 10,000 are both OK.

Other indicators are not compatible with the computer-marked system.

Complete all 10 tasks

The actual instructions will vary depending on the subject you are studying for. It is very important you read the instructions on the introductory screen and apply them in the assessment. You don't want to lose marks when you know the correct answer just because you have not entered it in the right format.

In general, the rules set out in the AAT Sample Assessments for the subject you are studying for will apply in the real assessment, but you should carefully read the information on this screen again in the real assessment, just to make sure. This screen may also confirm the VAT rate used if applicable.

A full stop is needed to indicate a decimal point. We would recommend using minus signs to indicate negative numbers and leaving out the comma signs to indicate thousands, as this results in a lower number of key strokes and less margin for error when working under time pressure. Having said that, you can use whatever is easiest for you as long as you operate within the rules set out for your particular assessment.

You have to show competence throughout the assessment and you should therefore complete all of the tasks. Don't leave questions unanswered.

In some assessments, written or complex tasks may be human marked. In this case you are given a blank space or table to enter your answer into. You are told in the assessments which tasks these are (note: there may be none if all answers are marked by the computer).

If these involve calculations, it is a good idea to decide in advance how you are going to lay out your answers to such tasks by practising answering them on a word document, and certainly you should try all such tasks in this Question Bank and in the AAT's environment using the sample/practice assessments.

When asked to fill in tables, or gaps, never leave any blank even if you are unsure of the answer. Fill in your best estimate.

Note that for some assessments where there is a lot of scenario information or tables of data provided (eg tax tables), you may need to access these via 'pop-ups'. Instructions will be provided on how you can bring up the necessary data during the assessment.

Finally, take note of any task specific instructions once you are in the assessment. For example you may be asked to enter a date in a certain format or to enter a number to a certain number of decimal places.

Remember you can practise the BPP questions in this Question Bank in an online environment on our dedicated AAT Online page. On the same page is a link to the current AAT Sample Assessments as well.

If you have any comments about this book, please email nisarahmed@bpp.com or write to Nisar Ahmed, AAT Head of Programme, BPP Learning Media Ltd, BPP House, Aldine Place, London W12 8AA.

Question bank

Chapter 1 – Costs

Task 1.1

At a production level of 16,000 units the production cost incurred totals £54,400. At a production level of 22,000 units the same cost totals £68,200.

This is a variable cost. True or false? Tick the correct box.

True ☐

False ☐

Task 1.2

The following details are available for four types of costs at two activity levels:

Cost type	Cost at 1,000 units	Cost at 1,500 units
I	£7,000	£10,500
II	£11,000	£12,500
III	£12,000	£12,000
IV	£3,800	£5,700

Complete the table to classify each cost by behaviour:

Cost	Behaviour
Cost I	
Cost II	
Cost III	
Cost IV	

Task 1.3

A manufacturing business anticipates that its variable costs and fixed costs will be £32,000 and £25,000 respectively at a production level of 10,000 units.

Complete the table to show the total production cost and the cost per unit at each of the activity levels.

Activity level – units	Total production cost £	Cost per unit £
8,000		
12,000		
15,000		

Task 1.4

The costs of a supervisor at a manufacturing company are £20,000. One supervisor is required per 750 units produced.

Complete the table to show the total supervisors cost and the supervisors cost per unit at each of the activity levels.

Activity level – units	Total supervisors cost £	Supervisors cost per unit £
500		
1,000		
1,500		

Task 1.5

Given below are a number of types of cost – classify each one according to its behaviour:

		Cost behaviour
(i)	Maintenance department costs which are made up of £25,000 of salaries and an average of £500 cost per call out.	
(ii)	Machinery depreciation based upon machine hours used.	
(iii)	Salary costs of nursery school teachers, where one teacher is required for every six children in the nursery.	
(iv)	Rent for a building that houses the factory, stores and maintenance departments.	

Task 1.6

A business produces one product which requires the following inputs:

Direct materials	6 kg @ £4.80 per kg
Direct labour	4 hours @ £7.00 per hour
Building costs	£18,000 per quarter
Leased machines	£600 for every 500 units of production
Stores costs	£3,000 per quarter plus £3.00 per unit

(i) **Complete the table to show the total cost of production and the cost per unit at each of the quarterly production levels.**

Production level – units	Total cost of production £	Cost per unit £
1,000		
1,500		
2,000		

(ii) **Explain why the cost per unit is different at each level of production.**

....

Task 1.7

The costs of a factory maintenance department appear to be partially dependent upon the number of machine hours operated each month. The machine hours and the maintenance department costs for the last six months are given below:

	Machine hours	Maintenance cost £
June	14,200	285,000
July	14,800	293,000
August	15,200	300,000
September	14,500	290,000
October	15,000	298,000
November	14,700	292,000

The variable cost per machine hour is £ [ ]

The fixed costs of the maintenance department are £ [ ]

....

Task 1.8

The activity levels and related production costs for the last six months of 20X8 for a business have been as follows:

	Activity level	Production cost
	Units	£
July	63,000	608,000
August	70,000	642,000
September	76,000	699,000
October	73,000	677,000
November	71,000	652,000
December	68,000	623,000

(a) **The fixed element of the production costs is £** [   ]

The variable element of the production costs per unit is £ [   ]

(b) **Complete the table to show the estimated production costs at each of the levels of production.**

Level of production – units	Production cost – £
74,000	
90,000	

(c) **Comment upon which of the two estimates of production costs calculated in (b) is likely to be most accurate and why.**

Task 1.9

The costs of the factory maintenance department for DF Ltd appear to have a variable element dependent upon the number of units produced. The fixed element of the costs steps up by £50,000 when 45,000 or more units are produced. The variable cost per unit is constant.

Production volume (units)	£
40,000	205,000
48,000	279,000

(a) **The variable element of the production costs per unit is £** ☐

(b) **Complete the table to show the fixed costs at each of the levels of production.**

Level of production – units	Fixed cost – £
40,000	
48,000	

Task 1.10

The costs of the factory maintenance department for JEB Ltd appear to have a variable element dependent upon the number of units produced. The fixed element of the costs steps up when 10,000 or more units are produced. At an activity level of 12,000 units, the fixed element of the cost is £15,000. The variable cost per unit is constant.

Production volume (units)	£
8,000	58,000
13,000	93,000

(a) **What would be the total cost for 9,000 units? £** ☐

(b) **What would be the total cost for 11,000 units? £** ☐

Task 1.11

The costs of the factory maintenance department for HM Ltd appear to have a variable element dependent upon the number of units produced. The fixed element of the costs steps up when 20,000 or more units are produced. The variable cost per unit is constant at £25.

Production volume (units)	£
18,000	468,000
22,000	570,000

(a) **What would be the total cost for 19,000 units? £** ☐

(b) **What would be the total cost for 21,000 units? £** ☐

Chapter 2 – Methods of costing

Task 2.1

The budgeted overheads of a manufacturing business have been allocated and apportioned to the two production cost centres as follows:

Cutting £58,600

Finishing £42,400

The two production cost centres are budgeted to produce 10,000 units in the next period.

You are also provided with the following further information:

	Cutting	Finishing
Direct labour hours	4,000	24,000
Machine hours	12,000	2,000
Direct labour cost	£24,500	£168,000
Direct materials cost	£180,000	£25,000
Prime cost	£204,500	£193,000

Complete the following table to calculate overhead absorption rates for each of the two production cost centres. Choose from the picklist when each absorption rate would be appropriate.

Absorption rate method	Cutting rate £	Finishing rate £	Most appropriate 1, 2 or 3
Rate per unit			▼
Rate per direct labour hour			▼
Rate per machine hour			▼

Picklist

1   Most appropriate in a largely mechanised department where most of the overhead relates to machinery costs.

2   Most appropriate where all products are of similar size and require a similar input in terms of time and resources of the departments.

3   Most appropriate in labour intensive departments where most of the overhead relates to labour.

Task 2.2

The budgeted overheads apportioned to a business's two production cost centres, C and D, together with the budgeted labour hours and machine hours, are given below:

	C	D
Overheads	£125,000	£180,000
Direct labour hours	12,000	80,000
Machine hours	100,000	10,000

Production cost centre C is a highly mechanised department with only a few machine operatives whereas production cost centre D is a highly labour intensive department.

(a) **Complete the table to calculate separate departmental overhead absorption rates for each production cost centre using an appropriate basis.**

Department	Overhead absorption rate £
C	
D	

(b) Each unit of Product P spends the following hours in each production department:

	C	D
Direct labour hours	1	7
Machine hours	5	2

The overhead to be included in the cost of each unit of product P is £ ☐

Task 2.3

The costs of the canteen department of a manufacturing business are estimated to be £20,000 for the following quarter. Both the packaging and assembly departments use the canteen. They have 20 and 30 employees respectively, but 50% of the assembly department work nights, when the canteen is not open. The packaging department employees do not work nights.

Complete the table below to show how much canteen overhead will be apportioned to each of the packaging and assembly departments.

Overhead apportioned to packaging department	£
Overhead apportioned to assembly department	£

Task 2.4

In each of the following situations calculate any under- or over-absorption of overheads and state whether this would be a debit or a credit in the statement of profit or loss (income statement):

	Under-absorption £	Over-absorption £	Debit/Credit
Budgeted production was 1,200 units and budgeted overheads were £5,400. Overheads are to be absorbed on a unit basis. The actual production was 1,000 units and the overheads incurred were £5,000.			
Budgeted production was 600 units to be produced in 1,800 labour hours. Budgeted overheads of £5,040 are to be absorbed on a direct labour hour basis. The actual production for the period was 700 units in 2,200 labour hours and the actual overheads were £5,100.			
Budgeted production was 40,000 units and the budgeted machine hours were 2 hours per unit. Budgeted overheads were £320,000 and were to be absorbed on a machine hour basis. The actual overheads incurred were £320,000 and the production was 42,000 units. The total machine hours were 82,000.			

Task 2.5

A business produces a single product in its factory which has two production departments, cutting and finishing. In the following quarter it is anticipated that 120,000 units of the product will be produced. The expected costs are:

Direct materials		£12 per unit
Direct labour		2 hours cutting @ £7.40 per hour
		1 hour finishing @ £6.80 per hour
Variable overheads	cutting	£336,000
	finishing	£132,000
Fixed overheads	cutting	£144,000
	finishing	£96,000

Overheads are absorbed on the basis of direct labour hours.

10

BPP
LEARNING MEDIA

The unit cost under absorption costing will be £ [   ]

The unit cost under marginal costing will be £ [   ]

Task 2.6

Given below are the budgeted production and sales figures for the single product that a business makes and sells for the months of July and August.

	July	August
Production	24,000 units	24,000 units
Sales	22,000 units	25,000 units

There was inventory of 1,500 units of the product at the start of July.

The expected production costs for each of the two months are as follows:

Direct materials	£6.80 per unit
Direct labour	£3.60 per unit
Variable production costs	£32,400
Fixed production costs	£44,400

Overheads are absorbed on the basis of the budgeted production level and the product is sold for £16 per unit.

(a) **The absorption costing profit for July was** £ [   ]

   The absorption costing profit for August was £ [   ]

   The marginal costing profit for July was £ [   ]

   The marginal costing profit for August was £ [   ]

(b) **Prepare a reconciliation explaining any difference in the two profit figures in each of the two months.**

Task 2.7

You are given the budgeted data about the production of a business's single product for the following quarter:

Opening inventory	840 units
Production	8,000 units
Sales	8,200 units
Direct materials	£23.60
Direct labour	4 hours @ £5.80 per hour
Variable overheads	£88,000
Fixed overheads	£51,200

Overheads are absorbed on the basis of units of production. The product has a selling price of £70 per unit.

(a) **The profit for the quarter under absorption costing is** £ [   ]

The profit for the quarter under marginal costing is £ [   ]

(b) **Prepare a reconciliation explaining any difference in the profit using absorption costing and profit using marginal costing.**

Task 2.8

Charleroi Aircon Ltd design and install industrial air-conditioning systems. The company is based in Birmingham.

Charleroi's usual pricing policy is to use direct costs (equipment and installation labour) plus a mark-up of 50% to establish the selling price for an air-conditioning installation.

The company is about to tender for two contracts, quotation HMG/012 and quotation CFG/013.

The company is in the process of designing an Activity Based Costing system and the following information has been obtained about the two jobs.

Estimates related to contracts HMG/012 and CFG/013		
Contract number:	HMG/012	CFG/013
Equipment: cost	£175,000	£120,000
number of items purchased	650	410
Direct labour: hours	10,000	6,000
hourly rate	£13	£11
Design hours	1,280	620
Distance from Birmingham office (miles round-trip)	320	90
Engineer site visits required	30	10

The following overhead information is also available in relation to ABC costs.

ABC details for overhead activities connected with air conditioning installation contracts			
Activity	Budgeted cost pool £pa	Cost driver	Cost driver units pa
Design department	675,000	Design hours	25,000
Site engineers	370,000	Miles travelled	185,000
Purchasing department	105,000	Items purchased	15,000
Payroll department	75,000	Direct hours	300,000
Site management	750,000	Direct hours	300,000
Post-installation inspection	80,000	Items purchased	20,000

(a) Usual pricing policy

The price of job HMG/012 based upon direct costs plus 50% mark-up is

£ ☐

The price of job CFG/013 based upon direct costs plus 50% mark-up is

£ ☐

(b) **Complete the tables to show the activity-based overhead costs for each of jobs HMG/012 and CFG/013.**

Activity	Budgeted cost pool	Cost driver	Cost driver units pa	Cost per unit of cost driver
	£			£
Design department				
Site engineers				
Purchasing department				
Payroll dept				
Site management				
Post-installation inspection				

Cost pool	Total cost HMG/012	Total cost CFG/013
	£	£
Design department		
Site engineers		
Purchasing department		
Payroll dept		
Site management		
Post-installation inspection		
Total cost		

Task 2.9

You are employed as a financial analyst at Drampton plc, a computer retailer. Drampton plc has recently taken over Little Ltd, a small company making personal computers and servers. Little appears to make all of its profits from servers. Drampton's finance director tells you that Little's fixed overheads are currently charged to production using standard labour hours and gives you their standard cost of making PCs and servers. These are shown below.

Little Ltd: Standard cost per computer

Model	Server	PC
Annual budgeted volume	5	5,000
Unit standard cost		
	£	£
Material and labour	50,000	500
Fixed overhead	4,000	40
Standard cost per unit	54,000	540

The finance director asks for your help and suggests you reclassify the fixed overheads between the two models using activity-based costing. You are given the following information.

- **Budgeted total annual fixed overheads**

	£
Set-up costs	10,000
Rent and power (production area)	120,000
Rent (stores area)	50,000
Salaries of store issue staff	40,000
Total	220,000

Every time Little makes a server, it has to stop making PCs and rearrange the factory layout. The cost of this is shown as set-up costs. If the factory did not make any servers these costs would be eliminated.

- **Cost drivers**

	Server	PC	Total
Number of set-ups	5	0	5
Number of weeks of production	10	40	50
Floor area of stores (square metres)	400	400	800
Number of issues of inventory	2,000	8,000	10,000

Complete the table to show how to reallocate Little's budgeted total fixed annual overheads between server and PC production on an Activity Based Costing basis.

	Server allocated overheads £	PC allocated overheads £
Set-up costs		
Rent and power (production area)		
Rent (stores area)		
Salaries of stores issue staff		
Total overheads		

Task 2.10

You are the management accountant at a manufacturing company which makes two products, the Plastic and the Metal. Standard costing information for direct material and labour costs are given for the two products below.

Product	Plastic	Metal
Budgeted production units	5,000	1,000
Unit standard cost		
	£	£
Material	10	25
Labour	2	4

The company has the following budgeted overheads.

	£
Power for machinery	110,000
Rent of factory	120,000
Canteen costs	40,000
Total	270,000

The cost drivers for these costs are given below, for the different products.

Cost drivers

	Plastic	Metal	Total
Machine hours	2,500	3,000	5,500
Floor space (square metres)	1,000	200	1,200
Number of employees	200	50	250

Complete the table to show how to reallocate the budgeted total overheads between the two products on an Activity Based Costing basis.

	Plastic allocated overheads £	Metal allocated overheads £
Power for machinery		
Rent of factory		
Canteen costs		
Total overheads		

Chapter 3 – Decision making

Task 3.1

A business sells a single product and has budgeted sales of 115,000 units for the next period. The selling price per unit is £28 and the variable costs of production are £17. The fixed costs of the business are £1,100,000.

The breakeven point in units is [　　　] **units**

The margin of safety in units is [　　　] **units**

The margin of safety as a percentage of budgeted sales is [　　　　　]

· ·

Task 3.2

The following information relates to one period for Product D which is manufactured by Mild Ltd.

Expected sales revenue = £160,000

Selling price per unit = £16 per unit

Variable cost = £8 per unit

Fixed costs = £40,000

The breakeven point both in terms of units and sales revenue is:

Breakeven point in units		Breakeven point in sales revenue	
5,000 units	☐	£40,000	☐
5,000 units	☐	£80,000	☐
10,000 units	☐	£40,000	☐
10,000 units	☐	£80,000	☐

· ·

Task 3.3

The following information relates to one period for Product V which is manufactured by Hay-on-Wye Ltd.

Selling price per unit = £80

Variable cost per unit = £25

Budgeted fixed costs = £110,000

Budgeted sales = 2,500 units

The margin of safety, in terms of both units and sales revenue is:

Units		Sales revenue	
500	☐	£12,500	☐
2,000	☐	£160,000	☐
1,900	☐	£152,000	☐
500	☐	£40,000	☐

Task 3.4

A business sells a single product at a selling price of £83 and the variable costs of production and sales are £65 per unit. The fixed costs of the business are £540,000.

The number of units of the product that the business must sell in order to make a target profit of £300,000 is ⬚ **units.**

Task 3.5

A business sells its single product for £40. The variable costs of this product total £28. The fixed costs of the business are £518,000.

The sales revenue required in order to make a target profit of £250,000 is £ ⬚

Task 3.6

Three products are produced by a business. There is a shortage of the material which is used to make each product, with only 3,000 kg available in the coming period.

	Product		
	A	B	C
Direct materials @ £4 per kg	£8	£4	£16
Direct labour @ £10 per hour	£20	£5	£15
Selling price	£40	£25	£47
Maximum sales demand	1,000 units	800 units	600 units

Complete the table to determine the production plan which will maximise contribution.

Product	Units

....

Task 3.7

A business produces three products. Production and sales details are given below:

	Product		
	R	S	T
Direct materials @ £5 per kg	£20	£25	£15
Direct labour @ £7 per hour	£14	£21	£21
Selling price	£45	£60	£55
Machine hours per unit	4	3	2
Maximum sales demand	20,000 units	25,000 units	8,000 units

During the next period the supply of materials is limited to 250,000 kgs, the labour hours available are 100,000 and the machine hours available are 180,000.

Complete the table to determine the production plan which will maximise contribution.

Product	Units

The contribution that will be earned under this production plan is £ [   ]

....

Task 3.8

A company is considering the purchase of a small sole trader's business for a cost of £84,000 on 30 June 20X5. The estimated cash inflows from the purchased business are:

	£
30 June 20X6	26,000
30 June 20X7	30,000
30 June 20X8	21,000
30 June 20X9	14,000

Thereafter the purchased business will be closed down and its operations merged with the other operations of the company.

The company has a cost of capital of 7% and analyses potential investments using the net present value method.

The discount factors at 7% are as follows:

Year	Discount factor
0	1.000
1	0.935
2	0.873
3	0.816
4	0.763

The net present value of the investment is £ [   ]

....

Task 3.9

The managers of a business are considering investing in a new factory. It has been estimated that the cost now would total £355,000. The anticipated profit for the factory for each of the next five years are as follows:

	Profit £
Year 1	47,000
Year 2	55,000
Year 3	68,000
Year 4	53,000
Year 5	22,000

The profit figures given are after charging depreciation of £60,000 in each year. The business has a cost of capital of 12%.

The discount factors at 12% are as follows:

Year	Discount factor
0	1.000
1	0.893
2	0.797
3	0.712
4	0.635
5	0.567

The net present value of the potential investment is £ ☐

....

Task 3.10

A company is to invest in a project with an immediate cash outflow of £200,000. The receipts from this project are £90,000 in one year's time, £130,000 in two years' time and finally £70,000 in three years' time.

The interest rate applicable to the company is 7%.

Calculate the net terminal value of the project.

....

Task 3.11

An organisation makes two products, X and Y. The following information is available for the next month.

	Product X £ per unit	Product Y £ per unit
Selling prices	100	135
Variable costs		
Material cost (£5 per kilogram)	30	40
Labour cost	25	38
Total variable costs	55	78
Fixed costs		
Fixed production costs	12	15
Fixed administration costs	8	8
Total fixed costs	20	23
Profit per unit	25	34
Monthly demand	3,500	4,250

The materials are in short supply in the coming month and only 22,500 kilograms of material will be available.

(a) **Complete the following table, rounding to the nearest penny.**

	Product X	Product Y
The contribution per unit is		
The contribution per kilogram of materials		

(b) **The optimal production order for products X, and Y is** [▼]

Picklist:

Product Y then Product X
Product X then Product Y

(c) **Complete the table below for the optimal production mix**

	Product X	Product Y
Production in units		

(d) **Complete the table below for the total contribution for each product.**

	Product X	Product Y
Total contribution		

Chapter 4 – Statistical methods

Task 4.1

Given below are the production cost figures for the last ten months. **Calculate a three month moving average for these figures.**

	Production costs	Three month moving total	Three month moving average
	£	£	£
March	104,500		
April	110,300		
May	112,800		
June	109,400		
July	117,600		
August	116,000		
September	119,200		
October	122,300		
November	120,500		
December	119,300		

Task 4.2

A new restaurant has recently been opened which only trades for five days a week. The takings have been increasing rapidly over the first four weeks since opening, as given below.

Complete the table to calculate the five day moving average and the daily seasonal variations in accordance with the additive model.

		Actual	5-day moving average – trend	Seasonal variation (actual – trend)
		£	£	£
Week 1	Day 1	600		
	Day 2	700		
	Day 3	1,000		
	Day 4	1,200		
	Day 5	1,500		
Week 2	Day 1	680		
	Day 2	750		
	Day 3	1,250		
	Day 4	1,400		
	Day 5	1,860		
Week 3	Day 1	820		
	Day 2	1,030		
	Day 3	1,940		
	Day 4	2,100		
	Day 5	2,500		
Week 4	Day 1	1,000		
	Day 2	1,320		
	Day 3	1,560		
	Day 4	2,290		
	Day 5	2,670		

Task 4.3

Given below are the quarterly sales figures for a small business.

(i)   **Complete the table to calculate the trend using a four month centred moving average and the seasonal variations using the additive model.**

		Actual	4-quarter moving average	Centred moving average – trend	Seasonal variations
		£	£	£	£
20X5	Quarter 3	50,600			
	Quarter 4	52,800			
20X6	Quarter 1	55,600			
	Quarter 2	48,600			
	Quarter 3	51,200			
	Quarter 4	53,900			
20X7	Quarter 1	58,000			
	Quarter 2	49,800			
	Quarter 3	53,000			
	Quarter 4	54,600			
20X8	Quarter 1	60,100			
	Quarter 2	50,700			
	Quarter 3	54,200			
	Quarter 4	55,200			

(ii)   **Complete the following table to average the seasonal variations.**

	Quarter 1	Quarter 2	Quarter 3	Quarter 4
	£	£	£	£
20X6				
20X7				
20X8				

Task 4.4

A business uses time series analysis and has found that the predicted trend of sales for the next four quarters and historical seasonal variations are as follows:

	Predicted trend	Seasonal variation
	£	£
Quarter 1	418,500	+21,500
Quarter 2	420,400	+30,400
Quarter 3	422,500	−16,700
Quarter 4	423,800	−35,200

What are the predicted actual sales figures for these four quarters?

	Predicted trend
	£
Quarter 1	
Quarter 2	
Quarter 3	
Quarter 4	

Task 4.5

Given below are the production cost figures for a business and the Retail Price Index for the last six months.

(a) **Complete the table to show the production cost figures in terms of January's prices.**

	Actual costs	RPI	Workings	Costs at January prices
	£			£
January	129,600	171.1		
February	129,700	172.0		
March	130,400	172.2		
April	131,600	173.0		
May	130,500	174.1		
June	131,600	174.3		

(b) **Complete the table to show the production cost figures in terms of June's prices.**

	Actual costs	RPI	Workings	Costs at June prices
	£			£
January	129,600	171.1		
February	129,700	172.0		
March	130,400	172.2		
April	131,600	173.0		
May	130,500	174.1		
June	131,600	174.3		

Task 4.6

Given below are the quarterly sales figures for a business for the last two years. **Complete the table in order to calculate an index for these sales with quarter 1 20X7 as the base period.**

		Actual	Workings	Index
		£		
20X7	Quarter 1	126,500		
	Quarter 2	130,500		
	Quarter 3	131,400		
	Quarter 4	132,500		
20X8	Quarter 1	133,100		
	Quarter 2	135,600		
	Quarter 3	136,500		
	Quarter 4	137,100		

Task 4.7

AB Ltd set the standard cost of material C at £3.50 per litre when an index of material prices stood at 115. The index now stands at 145.

The updated standard cost for material C is £ ☐

Task 4.8

The direct materials cost for quarter 1 and quarter 2 of next year have been estimated in terms of current prices at £657,000 and £692,500 respectively. The current price index for these materials is 126.4 and the price index is estimated as 128.4 for quarter 1 of next year and 131.9 for quarter 2.

What are the forecast direct materials costs for quarters 1 and 2 of next year?

Quarter 1 £ ☐

Quarter 2 £ ☐

Task 4.9

You have been given an equation and information to estimate the cost of a raw material for January and February 20X9.

The equation is Y = a + bX, where:

- X is the time period in months
- The value for X in November 20X8 is 29
- The value for X in December 20X8 is 30
- Y is the cost of the raw material
- The constant 'a' is 9 and constant 'b' is 0.1

Complete the table to calculate the expected price of the raw material per kilogram for January and February 20X9.

January 20X9	£
February 20X9	£

Task 4.10

The total production cost varies linearly with the volume of production, and so can be described by the linear regression equation:

$$y = a + bx$$

where x is the volume of production.

If the total production cost of 100 units is £2,500, and the total production cost of 1,000 units is £7,000, what are the values of a and b?

a £ _____

b £ _____

The total production cost for 750 units is £ _____

Task 4.11

The linear regression equation for production costs for a business is:

$$y = 138,000 + 6.4x$$

where x is the number of units.

If production is expected to be 105,000 units in the next quarter the anticipated production costs are £ _____

Task 4.12

The linear regression equation for the power costs of a factory is given as follows:

$y = 80,000 + 0.5x$

where x is the number of machine hours used in a period.

The anticipated machine hours for April are 380,000 hours.

The anticipated power costs for April are £ ☐

Task 4.13

The linear regression equation for the trend of sales in thousands of units per month based upon time series analysis of the figures for the last two years is:

$y = 3.1 + 0.9x$

What is the estimated sales trend for each of the first three months of next year?

Month 1 ☐ units

Month 2 ☐ units

Month 3 ☐ units

Task 4.14

A time series analysis of sales volumes each quarter for the last three years, 20X6 to 20X8, has identified the trend equation as follows:

$y = 400 + 105x$

where y is the sales volume and x is the time period.

The seasonal variations for each quarter have been calculated as:

Quarter 1	−175
Quarter 2	+225
Quarter 3	+150
Quarter 4	−200

Estimate the actual sales volume for each quarter of 20X9.

Quarter 1 ☐ units

Quarter 2 ☐ units

Quarter 3 ☐ units

Quarter 4 ☐ units

Task 4.15

You have been given an equation and information to estimate the cost of raw materials for the coming two months.

The equation is Y = a + bX, where

- X is the time period in months
- The value for X in May 20X8 is 25
- Y is the cost of raw materials
- The constant 'a' is 125 and constant 'b' is 2

The cost of raw materials is set on the first day of each month and is not changed during the month. The cost of the raw materials in May 20X8 was £175 per tonne.

(a) **Calculate the expected price of the raw material per tonne for June and July 20X8.**

June cost per tonne (£)	
July cost per tonne (£)	

(b) **Convert the raw materials prices per tonne for June and July to index numbers using May 20X8 as the base (correct to two decimal places).**

June index	
July index	

Task 4.16

The relationship between distribution costs (y) and output of production and sales (x) can be described by the equation:

y = a + bx

You are given the following distribution costs at two different levels of output:

Output (x)	Distribution costs (y)
1,500	14,500
3,000	19,000

(a) **Calculate the values of a and b, using the two activity levels.**

	£
a	
b	

(b) **Use the values of a and b in the equation to determine the distribution costs at the following activity levels.**

Output	£
2,000 units	
4,000 units	

(c) **Complete the following sentence:**

The value of distribution costs for [▼] units is most accurate.

Picklist

2,000

4,000

Chapter 5 – Standard costing

Task 5.1

Write a brief memo to a new accounts assistant explaining what factors should be taken into account when setting the standard cost of labour for a product.

MEMORANDUM

To:	New Accounts Assistant
From:	Accountant
Date:	xx/xx/xx
Subject:	**Setting the standard cost of labour**

Task 5.2

A business budgeted to produce 2,680 units of one of its products during the month of May. The product uses 5 kg of raw material with a standard cost of £4.00 per kg. During the month the actual production was 2,800 units using 14,400 kg of raw materials costing £60,480.

Calculate the following variances:

	Variance £	Adverse/Favourable
Total materials cost variance		
Materials price variance		
Materials usage variance		

Task 5.3

A business has the following standard cost card for one unit of its product:

Direct materials	4 kg @ £3 per kg	£12
Direct labour	3 hours @ £9 per hour	£27
Fixed overheads	3 hours @ £4 per hour	£12

The budgeted production level is 12,000 units.

The actual results for the period are:

Production   11,400 units

Materials 44,800 kgs   £150,480

Calculate the following variances:

	Variance £	Adverse/Favourable
Total materials cost variance		
Materials price variance		
Materials usage variance		

Task 5.4

Production of product Z1 for the month of November in a manufacturing business was 12,100 units using 54,900 hours of direct labour costing £410,200. The standard cost card shows that the standard labour input for a unit of Z1 is 4.5 hours at a rate of £7.30 per hour.

Calculate the following variances:

	Variance £	Adverse/Favourable
Total labour cost variance		
Labour rate variance		
Labour efficiency variance		

Task 5.5

Production of product X for the month of January was 10,680 units using 53,600 hours of direct labour costing £531,800. The standard cost card shows that the standard labour input for a unit of X is 5 hours at a rate of £10 per hour.

Calculate the following variances:

	Variance £	Adverse/Favourable
Total labour cost variance		
Labour rate variance		
Labour efficiency variance		

Task 5.6

A business has the following standard cost card for one unit of its product:

Direct materials	4 kg @ £3 per kg	£12
Direct labour	3 hours @ £9 per hour	£27
Fixed overheads	3 hours @ £4 per hour	£12

The budgeted production level is 12,000 units.

The actual results for the period are:

| Production | 11,400 units |
| Labour 34,700 hours | £316,400 |

Calculate the following variances:

	Variance £	Adverse/Favourable
Total labour cost variance		
Labour rate variance		
Labour efficiency variance		

Task 5.7

A business has budgeted to produce and sell 10,000 units of its single product. The standard cost per unit is as follows:

Direct materials	£18
Direct labour	£13
Fixed production overhead	£7

During the period the actual results were:

| Production and sales | 11,500 units |
| Fixed production overheads | £75,000 |

The fixed overhead expenditure variance is £ [   ]

The fixed overhead volume variance is £ [   ]

Task 5.8

A business has a single product into which fixed overheads are absorbed on the basis of labour hours. The standard cost card shows that fixed overheads are to be absorbed on the basis of 6 labour hours per unit at a rate of £7.60 per hour. The budgeted level of production is 50,000 units.

The actual results for the period were that fixed overheads were £2,200,000, the actual hours worked were 310,000 and the actual units produced were 52,000.

Calculate the following variances:

	Variance £	Adverse/Favourable
Fixed overhead expenditure variance		
Fixed overhead volume variance		
Fixed overhead efficiency variance		
Fixed overhead capacity variance		

Task 5.9

A business incurred fixed overheads of £203,000 in the month of May. The fixed overheads are absorbed into units of production at the rate of £3.60 per direct labour hour. The actual production during the month was 13,200 units although the budget had been for 14,000 units. The standard labour cost for the production is 4 hours per unit at an hourly rate of £8.00. During the month 50,000 labour hours were worked at a total cost of £403,600.

Calculate the following figures:

(i)   **The budgeted fixed overhead for the month was** £ ☐

(ii) **The fixed overhead expenditure variance was** £ ☐

(iii) **The fixed overhead volume variance was** £ ☐

(iv) **The fixed overhead efficiency variance was** £ ☐

(v)   **The fixed overhead capacity variance was** £ ☐

Task 5.10

The standard cost card for a business's product is shown below:

	£
Direct materials 4.8 kg at £2.80 per kg	13.44
Direct labour 2.5 hours at £8.50 per hour	21.25
Fixed overheads 2.5 hours at £1.60 per hour	4.00
	38.69

The budgeted production was for 1,100 units in the month of July. The actual costs during the month of July for the production of 1,240 units were as follows:

	£
Direct materials 5,800 kg	17,100
Direct labour 3,280 hours	27,060
Fixed overheads	4,650

The following variances have been calculated:

Materials price	£860 Adv
Materials usage	£426 Fav
Labour rate	£820 Fav
Labour efficiency	£1,530 Adv
Fixed overhead expenditure	£250 Adv
Fixed overhead efficiency	£288 Adv
Fixed overhead capacity	£848 Fav

Calculate the budgeted cost of 1,240 units of production and insert the variances in the correct place in the following operating statement. Total the variances and reconcile the budgeted cost of actual production to the actual cost of actual production.

	Favourable £	Adverse £	Total £
Budgeted cost of actual production			
Variances			
Materials price			
Materials usage			
Labour rate			
Labour efficiency			
Fixed overhead expenditure			
Fixed overhead efficiency			
Fixed overhead capacity	_____	_____	_____
Total variances			
Actual cost of actual production			

Task 5.11

XYZ Ltd is planning to make 120,000 units per period of a new product. The following standards have been set.

		Per unit
Direct material A		1.2 kgs at £11 per kg
Direct material B		4.7 kgs at £6 per kg
Direct labour:	Operation 1	42 minutes
	Operation 2	37 minutes
	Operation 3	11 minutes

Overheads are absorbed at the rate of £30 per labour hour. All direct operatives are paid at the rate of £8 per hour.

What is the standard cost of one unit?

£41.40 ☐

£53.40 ☐

£83.40 ☐

£98.40 ☐

Task 5.12

A manufacturing company has provided you with the following data which relates to component RYX, for the period which has just ended.

	Budget	Actual
Number of labour hours	8,400	7,980
Production units	1,200	1,100
Overhead cost (all fixed)	£22,260	£25,536

Overheads are absorbed at a rate per standard labour hour.

Which of the following is the overhead capacity variance?

£5,131 Adverse ☐

£3,276 Adverse ☐

£742 Adverse ☐

£1,113 Adverse ☐

Task 5.13

You are employed as part of the management accounting team in a large industrial company which operates a four-weekly system of management reporting. Your division makes a single product, the Omega, and, because of the nature of the production process, there is no work in progress at any time.

The group management accountant has completed the calculation of the material and labour standard costing variances for the current period to 1 April but has not had the time to complete any other variances. Details of the variances already calculated are reproduced in the working papers below, along with other standard costing data.

Standard costing and budget data – four weeks ended 1 April			
	Quantity	Unit price £	Cost per unit £
Material (kgs)	7	25.00	175
Labour (hours)	40	7.50	300
Fixed overheads (hours)	40	12.50	500
			975
	Units	Standard unit cost	Standard cost of production
Budgeted production for the four weeks	4,100	£975	£3,997,500

Working papers

Actual production and expenditure for the four weeks ended 1 April

Units produced	3,850
Cost of 30,000 kgs of materials consumed	£795,000
Cost of 159,000 labour hours worked	£1,225,000
Expenditure on fixed overheads	£2,195,000

Calculate the following variances.

(i)   The fixed overhead expenditure variance
(ii)   The fixed overhead volume variance
(iii)   The fixed overhead capacity variance
(iv)   The fixed overhead efficiency variance

Task 5.14

Choose from the picklist below to show which account the material usage variance will be included in.

Picklist

Stores control
Work in progress control
Production overhead control
Wages control

Task 5.15

The variable production overhead cost of product X is as follows:

2 hours at £1.50 = £3 per unit

During period 6, 400 units of product X were made. The labour force worked 820 hours, of which 60 hours were recorded as idle time. The variable overhead cost was £1,230.

Calculate the following variances:

	Variance £	Adverse/Favourable
Total variable production overhead total variance		
Variable production overhead expenditure variance		
Variable production overhead efficiency variance		

Task 5.16

P Co, a manufacturing firm, operates a standard marginal costing system. It makes a single product, PG, using a single raw material.

Standard costs relating to PG have been calculated as follows.

Standard cost schedule – PG	Per unit £
Direct material, 100 kg at £5 per kg	500
Direct labour, 10 hours at £8 per hour	80
Variable production overhead, 10 hours at £2 per hour	20
	600

The standard selling price of a PG is £900 and P Co plan to produce and sell 1,020 units a month.

During December 20X0, 1,000 units of PG were produced and sold. Relevant details of this production are as follows.

Direct material

90,000 kgs costing £720,000 were bought and used.

Direct labour

8,200 hours were worked during the month and total wages were £63,000.

Variable production overhead

The actual cost for the month was £25,000.

Inventories of the direct material are valued at the standard price of £5 per kg.

Each PG was sold for £975.

(a) The variable production cost variance for December 20X0 is £ [   ]

(b) (i) The direct labour rate variance is £ [   ]

(ii) The direct labour efficiency variance is £ [   ]

(c) (i) The direct material price variance is £ [   ]

(ii) The direct material usage variance is £ [   ]

(d) (i) The variable production overhead expenditure variance is £ [   ]

(ii) The variable production overhead efficiency variance is £ [   ]

Task 5.17

You are employed as a management accountant in the head office of Travel Holdings plc. Travel Holdings owns a number of transport businesses. One of them is Travel Ferries Ltd. Travel Ferries operates ferries which carry passengers and vehicles across a large river. Each year, standard costs are used to develop the budget for Travel Ferries Ltd. The latest budgeted and actual operating results are reproduced below.

Travel Ferries Ltd				
Budgeted and actual operating results for the year to 30 November 20X8				
Operating data		*Budget*		*Actual*
Number of ferry crossings		6,480		5,760
Operating hours of ferries		7,776		7,488
Cost data		£		£
Fuel	1,244,160 litres	497,664	1,232,800 litres	567,088
Labour	93,312 hours	699,840	89,856 hours	696,384
Fixed overheads		466,560		472,440
Cost of operations		1,664,064		1,735,912

Other accounting information

- Fuel and labour are variable costs.
- Fixed overheads are absorbed on the basis of budgeted operating hours.

One of your duties is to prepare costing information and a standard costing reconciliation statement for the chief executive of Travel Holdings.

(a) **Calculate the following information.**

(1) The standard price of fuel per litre
(2) The standard litres of fuel for 5,760 ferry crossings
(3) The standard labour rate per hour

(4) The standard labour hours for 5,760 ferry crossings
(5) The standard fixed overhead cost per budgeted operating hour
(6) The standard operating hours for 5,760 crossings
(7) The standard fixed overhead cost absorbed by the actual 5,760 ferry crossings

(b) **Using the data provided in the operating results and your answers to part (i), calculate the following variances.**

(1) The material price variance for the fuel
(2) The material usage variance for the fuel
(3) The labour rate variance
(4) The labour efficiency variance
(5) The fixed overhead expenditure variance
(6) The fixed overhead volume variance
(7) The fixed overhead capacity variance
(8) The fixed overhead efficiency variance

(c) **Prepare a statement reconciling the actual cost of operations to the standard cost of operations for the year to 30 November 20X8.**

Statement reconciling the actual cost of operations to the standard cost of operations for year ended 30 November 20X8

Number of ferry crossings		
	£	£
Actual cost of operations		
Cost variances		
Material price for fuel		
Material usage for fuel		
Labour rate		
Labour efficiency		
Fixed overhead expenditure		
Fixed overhead capacity		
Fixed overhead efficiency		
Standard cost of operations		

Task 5.18

Bedworth Co has the following cost card for unit of product C.

Direct materials	5kg @ £2 per kg	£10
Direct labour	2 hours @ £8 per hour	£16
Fixed overheads	2 hours @ £4 per hour	£8

The budgeted level of production is 12,000 units. The actual results for the period are:

Production	11,400 units
Materials	45,600 kg costing £136,800
Labour	11,400 hours costing £79,800
Fixed overheads	£95,000

(a) **Prepare a reconciliation of the budgeted material cost with the actual material cost using the material cost variances.**

Standard cost of materials for actual production			
Variances	Favourable	Adverse	
Direct material price variance			
Direct material usage variance			
Total variance			
Actual cost of materials for actual production			

(b) **Prepare a reconciliation of the budgeted labour cost with the actual labour cost using the labour cost variances.**

Standard cost of labour for actual production			
Variances	Favourable	Adverse	
Direct labour rate variance			
Direct labour efficiency variance			
Total variance			
Actual cost of labour for actual production			

(c) **Prepare a reconciliation of the budgeted fixed overhead cost with the actual fixed overhead cost using the fixed overhead cost variances.**

Standard cost of fixed overhead for actual production			
Variances	Favourable	Adverse	
Fixed overhead expenditure variance			
Fixed overhead volume variance			
Total variance			
Actual cost of fixed overhead for actual production			

Task 5.19

You are given the following information about a manufacturing company.

Budgeted overheads	£810,000
Budgeted output	27,000 units
Budgeted hours	108,000 hours
Actual output	29,000 units
Actual hours	118,000 hours
Actual overheads	£834,500

Calculate the fixed overhead capacity and efficiency variances from the information in the table above.

Chapter 6 – Standard costing – further aspects

Task 6.1

State possible reasons for each of the following variances which are all independent of each other.

Variance	Possible causes
Favourable materials price variance	
Favourable materials usage variance	
Adverse labour rate variance	
Adverse labour efficiency variance	

Task 6.2

What possible effect will the following scenarios have on the variances?

Scenario	Possible effects
A business has had to use a less-skilled grade of labour in its production process.	
A factory had a machine breakdown which resulted in three days of production delays last month.	

Task 6.3

The standard direct materials cost for a business's product is:

6 kg @ £8.00 per kg = £48.00

During the month of October production was 7,400 units of the product and the actual materials cost was £397,400 for 45,100 kgs. The price of the materials has been unexpectedly increased to £8.50 per kg for the whole month.

The total materials price variance is £ ☐

The non-controllable element of the materials price variance that has been caused by the price increase is £ ☐

The controllable element of the materials price variance caused by other factors is

£ ☐

Task 6.4

A business's product has a standard direct material cost of £26.00 (4 kgs @ £6.50 per kg). During the month of March the total production of the product was 2,500 units using 10,600 kgs of materials at a total cost of £73,140. During the month the price was unexpectedly increased due to a shortage of the material to £7.00 per kg.

The total materials price variance is £ ☐

The non-controllable variance due to price increase is £ ☐

The controllable variance due to other factors is £ ☐

Task 6.5

A business makes a product which uses a raw material which has a standard cost of £7.00 per kg. Each unit of the product requires 5 kgs of this material. The price of the materials for the last few years has been subjected to a time series analysis and the following seasonal variations have been seen to occur.

Jan – Mar	–£0.42
Apr – June	+£0.56
July – Aug	+£0.77
Sept – Dec	–£0.91

During March 18,000 units of the product were made and the price paid for the 92,000 kgs of material was £631,200.

The total materials price variance is £ [ ]

The non-controllable variance due to the season is £ [ ]

The controllable variance due to other factors is £ [ ]

Task 6.6

The standard cost of direct materials for a product is made up of 8 kgs of material at an average standard cost of £4.00 per kg. It has been noted over the years that the cost of the material fluctuates on a seasonal basis around the average standard cost as follows:

Jan – Mar	+£0.48
Apr – June	+£0.72
July – Sept	–£0.64
Oct – Dec	–£0.56

In the month of June the actual production was 5,000 units and 42,300 kgs of material were used at a cost of £194,580.

The total materials price variance is £ [ ]

The non-controllable variance caused by the seasonal price change is

£ [ ]

The controllable variance caused by other factors is £ [ ]

Task 6.7

A business sets the standard cost of its materials at 5kg per unit at a price of £20 per kg, when the index for this particular materials price was 120. During January, 9,000 units were produced using 46,000 kg of material at a total cost of £946,000. In January, the index of the materials price stood at 130.

The total materials price variance is £ [ ]

The non-controllable variance caused by the index change is £ [ ]

The controllable variance caused by other factors is £ [ ]

Task 6.8

You are employed as the assistant management accountant in the group accountant's office of Hampstead plc. Hampstead recently acquired Finchley Ltd, a small company making a specialist product called the Alpha. Standard marginal costing is used by all the companies within the group and, from 1 August 20X8, Finchley Ltd will also be required to use standard marginal costing in its management reports. Part of your job is to manage the implementation of standard marginal costing at Finchley Ltd.

John Wade, the managing director of Finchley, is not clear how the change will help him as a manager. He has always found Finchley's existing absorption costing system sufficient. By way of example, he shows you a summary of his management accounts for the three months to 31 May 20X8. These are reproduced below.

Statement of budgeted and actual cost of Alpha production – 3 months ended 31 May 20X8					
	Actual		*Budget*		*Variance*
Alpha production (units)		10,000		12,000	
	Inputs	£	*Inputs*	£	£
Materials	32,000 m	377,600	36,000 m	432,000	54,400
Labour	70,000 hrs	422,800	72,000 hrs	450,000	27,200
Fixed overhead absorbed		330,000		396,000	66,000
Fixed overhead unabsorbed		75,000		0	(75,000)
		1,205,400		1,278,000	72,600

John Wade is not convinced that standard marginal costing will help him to manage Finchley. 'My current system tells me all I need to know,' he said. 'As you can see, we are £72,600 below budget which is really excellent given that we lost production as a result of a serious machine breakdown.'

To help John Wade understand the benefits of standard marginal costing, you agree to prepare a statement for the three months ended 31 May 20X8 reconciling the standard cost of production to the actual cost of production.

(a) **Write a short memo to John Wade:**

Your memo should:

(i) **Use the budget data to determine the following.**

(1) The standard marginal cost per Alpha.

(2) The standard cost of actual Alpha production for the three months to 31 May 20X8.

(ii) **Calculate the following variances.**

    (1) Material price variance
    (2) Material usage variance
    (3) Labour rate variance
    (4) Labour efficiency variance
    (5) Fixed overhead expenditure variance

(iii) **Include a statement reconciling the actual cost of production to the standard cost of production.**

(iv) **Give TWO reasons why your variances might differ from those in his original management accounting statement, despite using the same basic data.**

(v) **Briefly discuss ONE further reason why your reconciliation statement provides improved management information.**

MEMO

To: Managing Director
From: Assistant Management Accountant
Date: xx/xx/xx

Subject: The use of standard marginal costing at Finchley Ltd

(i)   (1) Standard marginal cost of a unit of Alpha

       (2) Standard cost of producing 10,000 units of Alpha

(ii)   Variance calculations

    (1) Material price variance
    (2) Material usage variance
    (3) Labour rate variance
    (4) Labour efficiency variance
    (5) Fixed overhead expenditure variance

(iii)

Reconciliation statement			£
Standard cost of output			
Variances	*Fav*	*Adv*	
	£	£	
Materials price			
Materials usage			
Labour rate			
Labour efficiency			
Fixed overhead expenditure			
Actual cost of output			

(b) On receiving your memo, John Wade informs you that the machine breakdown resulted in the workforce having to be paid for 12,000 hours even though no production took place, and that an index of material prices stood at 466.70 when the budget was prepared but at 420.03 when the material was purchased.

Using this new information, prepare a revised statement reconciling the standard cost of production to the actual cost of production. Your statement should subdivide both the labour variances into those parts arising from the machine breakdown and those parts arising from normal production, and the material price variance into that part due to the change in the index and that part arising for other reasons.

Task 6.9

Croxton Ltd makes a specialised chemical, X14, in barrels at its factory. The factory has two departments: the processing department and the finishing department. Because of the technology involved, Croxton apportions both budgeted and actual total factory fixed overheads between the two departments on the basis of budgeted machine hours.

The standard absorption cost per barrel of X14 in the processing department, and the budgeted production for the five weeks ended 31 May 20X8, are shown below.

Processing department: standard cost per barrel of X14			
Input	Quantity	Standard price/rate	Cost £
Material	10 litres	£60 per litre	600
Labour	8 labour hrs	£8 per labour hr	64
Fixed overheads	16 machine hrs	£20 per machine hr	320
Standard absorption cost per barrel			984
Budgeted production 5 weeks ending 31 May 20X8			45 barrels

You are employed by Croxton Ltd as an accounting technician. One of your duties is to prepare standard costing reconciliation statements. Croxton's finance director gives you the following information for the five weeks ended 31 May 20X8.

Total factory budgeted and actual data

- Factory budgeted machine hours   1,152 machine hours
- Factory budgeted fixed overheads   £23,040
- Factory actual fixed overheads   £26,000

- Budgeted **and** actual factory fixed overheads are apportioned between the processing and finishing departments **on the basis of budgeted machine hours**.

Processing department actual data

- Actual costs

Materials at £58.50 per litre	£23,985
Labour (328 hours)	£2,788

- Actual production output   40 barrels
- Actual machine hours worked   656 hours
- There was no work in progress at any stage

(a) **Calculate the following information for the processing department.**

    (i)   Actual litres of material used

    (ii)   Standard litres of material required for 40 barrels of X14

    (iii)   Average actual labour rate per hour

    (iv)   Standard labour hours required for 40 barrels of X14

    (v)   Budgeted number of machine hours

    (vi)   Budgeted fixed overheads

    (vii) Actual fixed overheads (based on its share of actual factory overhead)

    (viii) Standard machine hours for actual production

    (ix)   Standard absorption cost of actual production

    (x)   Actual absorption cost of actual production

(b) **Using data given and your answers to part (a), calculate the following variances for the processing department.**

    (i)   Material price variance

    (ii)   Material usage variance

    (iii)   Labour rate variance

    (iv)   Labour efficiency variance

    (v)   Fixed overhead expenditure variance

    (vi)   Fixed overhead volume variance

    (vii) Fixed overhead efficiency variance

    (viii) Fixed overhead capacity variance

(c) **Prepare a statement for the five weeks ended 31 May 20X8 reconciling the standard absorption cost of actual production with the actual absorption cost of actual production.**

Reconciliation statement – five weeks ended 31 May 20X8			
			£
Standard absorption cost of actual production			
	£	£	
	(F)	(A)	
Variances			
Material price			
Material usage			
Labour rate			
Labour efficiency			
Fixed overhead expenditure			
Fixed overhead efficiency			
Fixed overhead capacity			
Actual absorption cost of actual production			

(d) Judith Green is the production manager of the processing department. You show her the statement reconciling the actual and standard costs of actual production. Judith then gives you the following additional information.

- When the standard costs were agreed, a price index for the material used in making the X14 was 140, but during the five weeks ended 31 May it was 133.

- Actual production output was 40 barrels but Croxton had to make 41 barrels of X14 as one barrel had to be scrapped on completion. This was because the barrel was damaged. The scrapped barrel had no value.

- If labour hours worked exceed 320 hours per five weeks, overtime is incurred. The overtime premium is £8.00 per hour of overtime.

- There is just one customer for the X14. The customer purchased 40 barrels during the five weeks ended 31 May 20X8.

Judith believes there is no need to examine the variances any further, for a number of reasons.

- The material price variance clearly shows that the purchasing department is efficient.

- The labour rate, labour efficiency and material usage variances were entirely due to the one scrapped barrel.

- Fixed overheads are not controllable by the processing department.

Write a memo to Judith Green. In your memo you should do the following.

(i) Use the material price index to identify a revised standard price for the materials used in X14.

(ii) Subdivide the material price variance calculated in task (b) (i) into that part due to the change in the price index and that part due to other reasons.

(iii) Briefly explain whether the material price variance calculated in task (b) (i) arose from efficiencies in the purchasing department.

(iv) Explain whether the one scrapped barrel might fully account for the following.

  (1) Material usage variance

  (2) Labour efficiency variance

  (3) Labour rate variance

(v) Give ONE reason why the fixed overheads might not be controllable by the processing department.

MEMO

To: Judith Green, production manager

From: Accounting technician

Date: 7 August 20X5

Subject: **Croxton Ltd – analysis of variances for 5 weeks ended 31 May 20X8**

Task 6.10

(a) You are the assistant management accountant at the Bare Foot Hotel complex on the tropical island of St Nicolas. The hotel complex is a luxury development. All meals and entertainment are included in the price of the holiday and guests only have to pay for drinks.

The Bare Foot Hotel complex aims to create a relaxing atmosphere. Because of this, meals are available throughout the day and guests can eat as many times as they wish.

The draft performance report for the hotel for the seven days ended 27 November 20X8 is reproduced below.

	Notes	Budget		Actual	
Bare Foot Hotel Complex					
Draft performance report for seven days ended 27 November 20X8					
Guests		540		648	
		£	£	£	£
Variable costs					
Meal costs	1		34,020		49,896
Catering staff costs	2,3		3,780		5,280
Total variable costs			37,800		55,176
Fixed overhead costs					
Salaries of other staff		5,840		6,000	
Local taxes		4,500		4,200	
Light, heat and power		2,500		2,600	
Depreciation of buildings and equipment		5,000		4,000	
Entertainment		20,500		21,000	
Total fixed overheads			38,340		37,800
Total cost of providing for guests			76,140		92,976

Notes

1 Budgeted cost of meals: number of guests × 3 meals per day × 7 days × £3 per meal

2 Budgeted cost of catering staff: each member of the catering staff is to prepare and serve 12 meals per hour. Cost = (number of guests × 3 meals per day × 7 days ÷ 12 meals per hour) × £4 per hour.

3 Actual hours worked by catering staff = 1,200 hours

Other notes

The amount of food per meal has been kept under strict portion control. Since preparing the draft performance report, however, it has been discovered that guests have eaten, on average, four meals per day.

You report to Alice Groves, the general manager of the hotel, who feels that the format of the draft performance report could be improved to provide her with more meaningful management information. She suggests that the budgeted and actual data given in the existing draft performance report is rearranged in the form of a standard costing report, using absorption costing.

(i) **Use the budget data, the actual data and the notes to the performance report to calculate the following for the seven days ended 27 November 20X8.**

    (1) The actual number of meals served

    (2) The standard number of meals which should have been served for the actual number of guests

    (3) The actual hourly rate paid to catering staff

    (4) The standard hours allowed for catering staff to serve three meals per day for the actual number of guests

    (5) The standard fixed overhead per guest

    (6) The total standard cost for the actual number of guests

(ii) **Use the data given in the task and your answers to part (a) (i) to calculate the following variances for the seven days ended 27 November 20X8.**

    (1) The material price variance for meals served

    (2) The material usage variance for meals served

    (3) The labour rate variance for catering staff

    (4) The labour efficiency variance for catering staff, based on a standard of three meals served per guest per day

    (5) The fixed overhead expenditure variance

    (6) The fixed overhead volume variance on the assumption that the fixed overhead absorption rate is based on the budgeted number of guests per seven days

(iii) **Prepare a statement reconciling the standard cost for the actual number of guests to the actual cost for the actual number of guests for the seven days ended 27 November 20X8.**

(b) On receiving your reconciliation statement, Alice Groves asks the following questions.

    • How much of the labour efficiency variance is due to guests taking, on average, four meals per day rather than the three provided for in the budget and how much is due to other reasons?

    • Would it be feasible to subdivide the fixed overhead volume variance into a capacity and efficiency variance?

Write a memo to Alice Groves. Your memo should do the following.

(i) Divide the labour efficiency variance into that part due to guests taking more meals than planned and that part due to other efficiency reasons.

(ii) Explain the meaning of the fixed overhead capacity and efficiency variances.

(iii) Briefly discuss whether or not it is feasible to calculate the fixed overhead capacity and efficiency variances for the Bare Foot Hotel complex.

MEMO

To: Alice Groves, general manager

From: Assistant management accountant

Date: xx.xx.xx

Subject: **Performance report** for seven days ended 27 November 20X8

(i) Subdivision of the catering labour efficiency variance

(ii) The meaning of the fixed overhead capacity and efficiency variances

(iii) Calculating the fixed overhead capacity and efficiency variances for the Bare Foot Hotel complex

---

Chapter 7 – Performance indicators

Task 7.1

Suggest possible measures of productivity for each of the following types of organisation:

Organisation	Possible productivity measures
Taxi firm	
Hospital	
Motorbike courier service	
Firm of accountants	
Retail store	
Maker of hand-made pottery	

Task 7.2

You are given the following information about a small manufacturing business for the year ending 31 March:

Sales revenue	£1,447,600
Cost of materials used	£736,500
Cost of bought in services	£316,900
Number of employees	15

The total value added is £ ☐

The value added per employee is £ ☐

Task 7.3

Given below is the summarised production information for a manufacturing organisation for the last month:

Budgeted production in units	15,000
Actual production in units	14,200
Labour hours worked	46,000
Standard hours for each unit	3

(a) **Complete the table to calculate the following performance indicators and briefly explain what each one means:**

	Calculation	Explanation
Efficiency ratio		
Capacity ratio		
Production volume ratio		

(b) **If the workforce had operated at 95% efficiency how many labour hours would have been saved last month?**

Task 7.4

Given below is the statement of profit or loss (income statement) for a business for the year ending 31 March 20X9 and a statement of financial position at that date.

Statement of profit or loss (income statement)

	£	£
Revenue		2,650,400
Cost of sales		
Opening inventory	180,000	
Purchases	1,654,400	
	1,834,400	
Less closing inventory	191,200	
		1,643,200
Gross profit		1,007,200
Less expenses		
Selling and distribution costs	328,400	
Administration expenses	342,200	
		670,600
Operating profit		336,600
Interest payable		36,000
Profit after interest		300,600

Statement of financial position

	£	£
Non-current assets		1,920,400
Current assets:		
Inventory	191,200	
Receivables	399,400	
Bank	16,800	
	607,400	
Payables	(190,300)	
Net current assets		417,100
		2,337,500
Less long term loan		600,000
		1,737,500
Share capital		1,000,000
Other reserves		150,000
Retained earnings		587,500
		1,737,500

(a) **Using the statement of profit or loss (income statement) and statement of financial position complete the table to calculate the performance indicators:**

Gross profit margin	
Operating profit margin	
Return on capital employed	
Asset turnover	
Non-current asset turnover	
Current ratio	
Quick ratio	
Receivables' collection period	
Inventory holding period in days	
Payables' payment period	
Interest cover	
Gearing ratio	

(b) **If the payables' payment period was increased to 60 days what effect would this have on the cash balance?**

Task 7.5

Given below is a summary of a business's performance for the last six months:

	July	Aug	Sept	Oct	Nov	Dec
	£'000	£'000	£'000	£'000	£'000	£'000
Sales	560	540	500	550	580	600
Cost of sales	370	356	330	374	400	415
Expenses	123	119	110	116	122	131
Interest payable	–	–	–	3	3	3
Shareholders' funds	440	445	458	468	480	490
Loan	–	–	–	50	50	50

(a) **For each month of the year complete the table to calculate the performance indicators:**

	July	Aug	Sept	Oct	Nov	Dec
Gross profit margin						
Operating profit margin						
% of expenses to sales						
Return on capital employed						
Asset turnover						

(b) **Comment on what the figures calculated in part (a) show about the performance of the business over the last six months.**

Task 7.6

A manufacturing business has three small divisions, North, South and Central. The figures for the last three months of 20X6 for each division are given below:

	North	South	Central
	£	£	£
Financial details			
Sales	870,000	560,000	640,000
Opening inventory	34,000	41,000	34,000
Closing inventory	32,000	29,000	38,000
Purchases	590,000	380,000	420,000

	North	South	Central
	£	£	£
Expenses	121,000	106,000	138,000
Share capital and reserves	980,000	690,000	615,000
Payables	103,400	42,600	66,700
Receivables	100,100	107,300	87,600
Non-financial details			
Factory floor area	500 sq m	400 sq m	420 sq m
Factory employees	18	12	15
Hours worked	8,500	5,800	7,000
Units produced	17,000	10,200	12,300

(a) **Complete the table to calculate the performance indicators for each division:**

	North	South	Central
Gross profit margin			
Operating profit margin			
Return on capital employed			
Asset turnover			
Inventory holding in months (using average inventory)			
Receivables' collection period in months			
Payables' collection period in months			
Units produced per square metre of floor area			
Units produced per employee			
Units produced per hour			

(b) **Use the performance indicators calculated in (a) to compare the performances of the three divisions for the three-month period.**

Task 7.7

(i) A business operates on a gross profit margin of 48% and sales for the period were £380,000. **The gross profit is** £ ☐

(ii) A business operates on a gross profit margin of 34% and the gross profit made in the period was £425,000.

The sales for the period were £ ☐

(iii) A business had sales of £85,000 in a month and with a gross profit margin of 40% and an operating profit margin of 11.5%.

The expenses for the month were £ ☐

(iv) A business has a return on capital employed of 11.6% and made an operating profit for the period of £100,000.

The capital employed is £ ☐

(v) A business has a net profit percentage of 8% and a return on capital employed of 10%.

The asset turnover of the business is ☐

(vi) A business has opening inventory and closing inventory of £158,000 and £182,000 and made purchases during the year totalling £560,000.

Inventory turned over ☐ **times during the year.**

(vii) A business has a receivables' collection period of 48 days and the closing receivables figure is £96,000.

The sales for the year are £ ☐

Task 7.8

Given below are the summarised statements of profit or loss (income statements) and statements of financial position of a business for the last two years.

Summarised statements of profit or loss (income statements)

	Y/e 31 Dec	Y/e 31 Dec
	20X8	20X7
	£'000	£'000
Revenue	602	564
Cost of sales	329	325
Gross profit	273	239
Expenses	163	143
Operating profit	110	96
Interest payable	10	10
Profit before tax	100	86

Summarised statements of financial position

	31 Dec 20X8		31 Dec 20X7	
	£	£	£	£
Non-current assets		709		632
Current assets:				
Inventory	28		32	
Receivables	66		68	
Cash	2		3	
	96		103	
Payables	55		45	
Net current assets		41		58
		750		690
Long term loan		150		150
		600		540
Share capital		300		300
Retained earnings		300		240
		600		540

(a) **Complete the table for each of the two years to calculate the performance indicators, based on total capital employed when relevant.**

	31 Dec 20X8	31 Dec 20X7
Gross profit margin		
Operating profit margin		
Return on capital employed		
Asset turnover		
Non-current asset turnover		
Current ratio		
Quick ratio		
Receivables' collection period		
Inventory holding in days		
Payables' payment period		
Interest cover		
Gearing ratio		

(b) **Comment upon the performance of the business for the last two years basing your comments on the performance indicators calculated in part (a).**

Task 7.9

Middle plc owns two subsidiaries, East Ltd and West Ltd, producing soft drinks. Both companies rent their premises and both use plant of similar size and technology. Middle plc requires the plant in the subsidiaries to be written off over ten years using straight-line depreciation and assuming zero residual values.

East Ltd was established five years ago but West Ltd has only been established for two years. Goods returned by customers generally arise from quality failures and are destroyed. Financial and other data relating to the two companies are reproduced below.

Statements of profit or loss (Income statements) year to 30 November 20X8			Statements of financial position extracts at 30 November 20X8		
	West Ltd	East Ltd		West Ltd	East Ltd
	£'000	£'000		£'000	£'000
Revenue	18,000	17,600	Plant	16,000	10,000
Less Returns			Depreciation to date	3,200	5,000
	90	176			
Net revenue	17,910	17,424	Non-current assets	12,800	5,000
Material	2,000	2,640	Current assets	4,860	3,000
Labour	4,000	4,840	Current liabilities	(2,320)	(1,500)
Production overheads*	3,000	3,080	Net assets	15,340	6,500
Gross profit	8,910	6,864			
Marketing	2,342	1,454			
Research & development	1,650	1,010			
Training	950	450			
Administration	900	1,155			
Operating profit	3,068	2,795			

*Includes plant depreciation of £1,600,000 for West Ltd and £1,000,000 for East Ltd

Other data (000's litres)	West Ltd	East Ltd
Gross sales	20,000	22,000
Returns	100	220
Net sales	19,900	21,780
Orders received in year	20,173	22,854

You are employed by Middle plc as a member of a team monitoring the performance of subsidiaries within the group. Middle plc aims to provide its shareholders with the best possible return for their investment and to meet customers' expectations. It does this by comparing the performance of subsidiaries and using the more efficient ones for benchmarking.

Your team leader, Angela Wade, has asked you to prepare a report evaluating the performance of West Ltd and East Ltd. Your report should do the following.

(a) **Calculate and explain the meaning of the following financial ratios for each company.**

    (i)   **The return on net assets**
    (ii)   **The net asset turnover**
    (iii) **The operating profit margin**

(b) **Calculate the percentage of faulty sales as a measure of the level of customer service for each company.**

(c) **Identify ONE other possible measure of the level of customer service which could be derived from the accounting data.**

(d) **Identify TWO limitations to your analysis in task (a), using the data in the accounts.**

(a) **Angela Wade**

From: A Technician

Date: xx.xx.xx

Subject: West Ltd and East Ltd – Performance Report

(i)   **Return on net assets (RONA)**

(ii)   **Net asset turnover**

(iii)   **Operating profit margin**

(b) **Measure of customer service: faulty sales**

(c) **Further measure of customer service**

(d) **Limitations of financial ratios**

....

Task 7.10

(a) You are employed by Micro Circuits Ltd as a financial analyst reporting to Angela Frear, the Director of Corporate Strategy. One of your responsibilities is to monitor the performance of subsidiaries within the group. Financial and other data relating to subsidiary A is reproduced below.

Subsidiary A					
Statement of profit or loss (Income statement) year to 30 November 20X8			**Extract from statement of financial position at 30 November 20X8**		
	£'000	£'000		£'000	£'000	£'000

Statement of profit or loss	£'000	£'000
Revenue		4,000
less returns		100
Net revenue[1]		3,900
Material	230	
Labour	400	
Production overheads[2]	300	
Cost of production	930	
Opening finished inventory	50	
Closing finished inventory	(140)	
Cost of sales		840
Gross profit		3,060
Marketing	500	
Customer support	400	
Research and development	750	
Training	140	
Administration	295	2,085
Operating profit		975

Non-current assets	Land and buildings £'000	Plant and machinery £'000	Total £'000
Cost	2,000	2,500	4,500
Additions	–	1,800	1,800
	2,000	4,300	6,300
Accumulated dep'n	160	1,700	1,860
	1,840	2,600	4,440

	£'000	
Raw material inventory	15	
Finished goods inventory	140	
	155	
Receivables	325	
Cash and bank	40	
Payables	(85)	
		435
Net assets		4,875

Other information

Notes
(1) **Analysis of revenue**

	£'000		£'000
Regular customers	3,120	New products	1,560
New customers	780	Existing products	2,340
	3,900		3,900

(2) Production overheads include £37,200 of reworked faulty production.

(3) Orders received in the year totalled £4,550,000.

(a) **Angela Frear asks you to calculate the following performance indicators in preparation for a board meeting.**

Performance indicator	Workings	
Return on net assets		
Net asset turnover		
Operating profit margin		
Average age of receivables in months		
Average age of finished inventory in months		

(b) One of the issues to be discussed at the board meeting is the usefulness of performance indicators. Angela Frear has recently attended a conference on creating and enhancing value.

Three criticisms were made of financial performance indicators.

- They could give misleading signals.

- They could be manipulated.

- They focus on the short term and do not take account of other key, non-financial performance indicators.

At the conference, Angela was introduced to the idea of the balanced scorecard. The balanced scorecard looks at performance measurement from four perspectives.

The financial perspective

This is concerned with satisfying shareholders. Examples include the return on net assets and operating profit margin.

The customer perspective

This asks how customers view the business and is concerned with measures of customer satisfaction. Examples include speed of delivery and customer loyalty.

The internal perspective

This looks at the quality of the company's output in terms of technical excellence and customer needs. Examples would be striving towards total quality management and flexible production as well as unit cost.

The innovation and learning perspective

This is concerned with the continual improvement of existing products and the ability to develop new products as customers' needs change. An example would be the percentage of revenue attributable to new products.

Angela Frear asks you to prepare briefing notes for the board meeting. Using the data from part (a) where necessary, your notes should do the following.

(i)   **Suggest ONE reason why the return on net assets calculated in (a) might be misleading.**

(ii) **Identify ONE way of manipulating the operating profit margin.**

(iii) **Calculate the average delay in fulfilling orders.**

(iv) **Identify ONE other possible measure of customer satisfaction other than the delay in fulfilling orders.**

(v)   **Calculate TWO indicators which may help to measure performance from an internal perspective.**

(vi) **Calculate ONE performance indicator which would help to measure the innovation and learning perspective.**

Briefing notes on the usefulness of performance indicators

Prepared for Angela Frear

Prepared by Financial Analyst

Dated: xx.xx.xx

(i)   **Return on net assets**

(ii) **Operating profit margin**

(iii) **Average delay in fulfilling orders**

(iv) **Measures of customer satisfaction**

(v) **Measuring performance from an internal perspective**

(vi) **Measuring the innovation and learning perspective**

Task 7.11

(a) Travel Bus Ltd is owned by Travel Holdings plc. It operates in the town of Camford. Camford is an old town with few parking facilities for motorists. Several years ago, the Town Council built a car park on the edge of the town and awarded Travel Bus the contract to carry motorists and their passengers between the car park and the centre of the town.

Originally, the Council charged motorists £4.00 per day for the use of the car park but, to encourage motorists not to take their cars into the town centre, parking has been free since 1 December 20X7.

The journey between the car park and the town centre is the only service operated by Travel Bus Ltd in Camford. A summary of the results for the first two years of operations, together with the net assets associated with the route and other operating data, is reproduced below.

Statement of profit or loss (Income statement) year ended 30 November			Extract from statement of financial position at 30 November		
	20X7 £	20X8 £		20X7 £	20X8 £
Revenue	432,000	633,600	Buses	240,000	240,000
			Accumulated		
Fuel	129,600	185,328	depreciation	168,000	180,000
Wages	112,000	142,000	Non-current assets	72,000	60,000
Other variable costs	86,720	84,512	Net current assets	14,400	35,040
Gross profit	103,680	221,760		86,400	95,040
Bus road tax and insurance	22,000	24,000			
Depreciation of buses	12,000	12,000			
Maintenance of buses	32,400	28,512			
Fixed garaging costs	29,840	32,140			
Administration	42,000	49,076			
Operating profit/(loss)	(34,560)	76,032			

Other operating data	20X7	20X8
Fare per passenger journey	£0.80	£1.00
Miles per year	324,000	356,400
Miles per journey	18.0	18.0
Days per year	360	360
Wages per driver	£14,000	£14,200

Throughout the two years, the drivers were paid a basic wage per week, no bonuses were paid and no overtime was incurred.

In two weeks there will be a meeting between officials of the Town Council and the chief executive of Travel Holdings to discuss the performance of Travel Bus for the year to 30 November 20X8. The previous year's performance indicators were as follows.

Gross profit margin	24%
Operating profit margin	−8%
Return on capital employed	−40%
Asset turnover	5 times
Number of passengers in the year	540,000
Total cost per mile	£1.44
Number of journeys per day	50
Maintenance cost per mile	£0.10
Passengers per day	1,500
Passengers per journey	30
Number of drivers	8

In preparation for the meeting, you have been asked to calculate the following performance indicators for the year to 30 November 20X8.

		Performance indicator for year to 30 November 20X8
(i)	Gross profit margin	
(ii)	Operating profit margin	
(iii)	Return on capital employed	
(iv)	Asset turnover	
(v)	Number of passengers in the year	
(vi)	Total cost per mile	
(vii)	Number of journeys per day	
(viii)	Maintenance cost per mile	
(ix)	Passengers per day	
(x)	Passengers per journey	
(xi)	Number of drivers	

(b) On receiving your performance indicators, the chief executive of Travel Holdings raises the following issues with you.

- The drivers are claiming that the improved profitability of Travel Bus reflects their increased productivity.

- The managers believe that the change in performance is due to improved motivation arising from the introduction of performance related pay for managers during the year to 30 November 20X8.

- The officials from the Town Council are concerned that Travel Bus is paying insufficient attention to satisfying passenger needs and safety.

The chief executive asks for your advice.

Write a memo to the chief executive of Travel Holdings plc. Where relevant, you should make use of the data and answers to task a) to do the following.

(i) Briefly discuss whether or not increased productivity always leads to increased profitability.

(ii) Develop ONE possible measure of driver productivity and suggest whether or not the drivers' claim is valid.

(iii) Suggest ONE reason, other than improved motivation, why the profitability of Travel Bus might have improved.

(iv) (1) Suggest ONE existing performance indicator which might measure the satisfaction of passenger needs.

    (2) Suggest ONE other possible performance indicator of passenger needs which cannot be measured from the existing performance data collected by Travel Bus.

(v) (1) Suggest ONE existing performance indicator which might measure the safety aspect of Travel Bus's operations.

    (2) Suggest ONE other possible performance indicator which cannot be measured from the existing performance data collected by Travel Bus.

MEMO

To: Chief executive

From: Management accountant

Date: xx.xx.xx

Subject: **Performance of Travel Bus Ltd for the year to 30 November 20X8**

This memo addresses a number of issues concerning the productivity and profitability of Travel Bus Ltd.

(i)   Productivity and profitability

(ii) Driver productivity

(iii) Reason for improved profitability

(iv) Performance indicators to measure the satisfaction of passenger needs

(v) Monitoring the safety aspect of Travel Bus's operations

Task 7.12

TeesRus Ltd makes and packs tea bags. The company currently has 8 Pickmaster machines, which are coming to the end of their useful life. The company is considering replacing all 8 machines with either new Pickmaster machines or new Pickmaster 2 machines.

Each new Pickmaster machine costs £20,000 and requires 10 operators per day for the 100 days of the harvest. The machine will have a life of 10 years and a depreciation charge of £2,000 per year.

A new Pickmaster 2 machine requires only 1 operator per day for the 100 days. This machine costs £90,000 to purchase and will have a life of 10 years. The depreciation charge will be £9,000 per year.

Other budgeted information for 20X8 is as follows:

- The forecast harvest will last 100 days and produce 2.5 million kilograms of tea.

- The selling price of tea will be 45 pence per kilogram.

- Budgeted revenue is £1,125,000.

- Tea picker costs will be £150,000.

- Tea processor operators currently earn £6 per day.

- The tea pickers and tea processor operators are employed as and when needed on temporary contracts.

- Seed and fertiliser costs will be £75,000.

- Administration costs will be £150,000 if the Pickmaster machines are purchased.

- Administration costs will be £135,000 if the Pickmaster 2 machines are purchased.

- Distribution costs will be £350,000.

- The net assets at the end of the period will be £935,500 plus the budgeted operating profit.

- Disposing of the old machines will incur no profit, loss or any depreciation charge during 20X8.

(a) **Prepare TWO budgeted statements of profit or loss (income statements) and net asset workings assuming that the business purchases either 8 Pickmaster or 8 Pickmaster 2 machines.**

Budgeted statements of profit or loss (income statements)

	Pickmaster	Pickmaster 2
	£	£
Revenue		
Cost of sales		
Tea pickers		
Tea processor operators		
Depreciation		
Seed and fertiliser costs		
Total cost of sales		
Gross profit		
Administration costs		
Distribution costs		
Operating profit		

Net assets at year end

	Pickmaster	Pickmaster 2
	£	£
Budgeted net assets		
Operating profit		

(b) **Complete the table to calculate the following indicators for each option:**

	Pickmaster	Pickmaster 2
Gross profit margin		
Operating profit margin		
Return on net assets		

(c) **Prepare a report for the managing director to include the following:**

(i) Comments on the indicators calculated in part (b) above.

(ii) Two other considerations.

(iii) A recommendation whether to purchase the Pickmaster or Pickmaster 2 machines.

REPORT

To: Managing Director

From: Accounting technician

Date: December 20X7

Subject: Purchase of new machinery

Performance indicators

Other considerations

Conclusion

....

Task 7.13

BeThere Airlines is reviewing its catering division and has provided the following information for the previous three months. The division has no administration or distribution costs. All costs are treated as costs of sales. All production has to be used in that day.

Catering Division

Cost report for the three-month period

	September £	October £	November £
Revenue	690,000	697,200	672,000
Cost of production			
Direct materials	185,000	185,100	185,220
Direct labour	274,313	275,975	279,300
Fixed production overheads	82,000	82,000	82,000
Total cost of sales	541,313	543,075	546,520
Profit	148,687	154,125	125,480

Catering Division statement of financial position

	September	October	November
Non-current assets			
Land and buildings	800,000	795,000	790,000
Machinery	480,000	460,000	420,000
Current assets			
Inventory of raw materials	231,000	251,500	307,800
Amounts due from Airlines Division	690,000	697,200	672,000
Current liabilities			
Trade payables	190,000	185,000	185,100
Net current assets	731,000	763,700	794,700
Non-current liabilities	800,000	800,000	800,000
Net assets	1,211,000	1,218,700	1,204,700

	Units	Units	Units
Capacity (meals per month)	125,000	125,000	125,000
Meals ordered by Flights Division	115,000	117,000	112,000
Budgeted meals	115,000	117,000	112,000
Meals produced	115,500	116,200	117,600

(a) **Calculate the following performance indicators for each month, expressing each answer to two decimal places:**

(i) Profit margin
(ii) Direct material cost as a percentage of revenue
(iii) Direct labour cost as a percentage of revenue
(iv) Return on capital employed (ROCE)
(v) Meals produced as a percentage of orders
(vi) Meals produced as a percentage of capacity

(b) **Draft a brief report to the managing director commenting on the performance of the division in November.** You should base your report on your calculations above.

REPORT

To: Managing Director

From: Accounting Technician

Subject: Performance of the Catering Division

Date: 7 December 20X6

(c) The operations director is now reviewing various alternatives to determine whether it is possible to reduce monthly costs.

She is considering whether to invest in a new machine which:

- Will mechanise part of the process and reduce the labour cost per meal from the current rate of £2.375 to £1.50

- Could either be purchased for £3 million or rented for £50,000 per month

- Is expected to have a life of 10 years and a scrap value of £900,000.

If the company purchases the machine, the division's net assets as at the end of November will increase by £1 million plus the profit for the period.

If the company rents the machine, the division's net assets will only increase by the profit for the period.

The operations director's performance is measured on ROCE, which she would like to see improved.

(i) **Prepare a forecast statement of profit or loss (income statement) and net asset calculation (a full statement of financial position is not required) for both options (renting and purchasing) for one month.**

   Note: Assume that the number of meals produced and sold will be 120,000 per month at a cost of £6 per meal. The material cost will remain as standard at £2 per meal, and monthly overheads will stay at £82,000 before any additional costs of the new machine. Ignore the time value of money.

(ii) **Calculate the profit margin and the ROCE for both options.**

(iii) **What action would you recommend to the operations director?**

81

Task 7.14

A company makes two products, S1 and S2. The following information is available for the year.

	S1	S2
Sales volume (units)	50,000	100,000
	£	£
Sales price per unit	20	16
Total sales revenue	1,000,000	1,600,000
Material costs	300,000	600,000
Labour costs	300,000	600,000
Fixed production costs	250,000	250,000
Total cost of sales	850,000	1,450,000
Gross profit	150,000	150,000
Material cost per unit	£6.00	£6.00
Labour cost per unit	£6.00	£6.00
Fixed production cost per unit	£5.00	£2.50
Gross profit margin	15.00%	9.38%

Explain why the gross profit margin is different between S1 and S2 by considering the following:

(a) Sales price and sales volume
(b) Material cost
(c) Fixed production cost

Chapter 8 – Cost management

Task 8.1

For each of the following state which type of cost of quality it is (prevention, appraisal, internal failure or external failure):

		Type of cost
(i)	Lost contribution on defective products sold as seconds	
(ii)	Cost of replacing faulty products	
(iii)	Claims from customers relating to defective products	
(iv)	Products scrapped due to faulty raw materials	
(v)	Training for quality control staff	
(vi)	Maintenance of quality control equipment	
(vii)	Performance testing of finished goods	
(viii)	Costs of customer after sales service department	
(ix)	Costs of inspection of raw materials	
(x)	Costs of production delays due to re-working defective products discovered in quality inspection	

Task 8.2

A clothing manufacturer has had a number of events occurring recently:

(i) The internal designers have designed a new type of zipper that should last much longer than normal zippers and should reduce returns of products.

(ii) One line of jumpers produced over the last few months were produced on a faulty machine and have been returned by all the retailers who purchased them as the seams have come apart. Some of the retailers are considering suing the company for losses caused and it is almost certain that they will never purchase from the manufacturer again.

(iii) It has been discovered that the fabric used to make a large quantity of men's suits was flawed and these can now only be sold at a drastically reduced price as seconds.

As a result of this discovery the manufacturer has introduced new inspection controls for raw materials.

Analyse each of these events and determine what effects they are likely to have on the various categories of quality costs – prevention, appraisal, internal failure and external failure – by completing the table.

	Prevention	Appraisal	Internal failure	External failure
(i) Zippers				
(ii) Jumpers				
(iii) Men's suits				

Task 8.3

Give three examples of explicit costs of quality and three examples of implicit costs of quality.

Explicit costs of quality

•

•

•

Implicit costs of quality

•

•

•

Task 8.4

A manufacturing business estimates that 3 out of every 1,000 of its products that is sold is defective in some way. When the goods are returned by customers they are replaced free of charge. It is estimated that 70% of customers who buy a faulty product will return it but that all customers who buy a faulty product will not buy from the business again. Each unit costs £10 to manufacture and is sold at a price of £15.

Due to quality inspections it is also estimated that 4,000 defective units a year are discovered before they are sold and these can then be sold as 'seconds' at a price of £11. The quality inspections cost £35,000 each year.

The unit sales of the product are 10 million each year.

Analyse and calculate the explicit costs of quality.

Prevention costs	
Appraisal costs	
Internal failure costs	
External failure costs	

Task 8.5

A manufacturing organisation carries out quality inspections on its product and in the last year 5,200 defective units were discovered and had to be sold as seconds at a price of £108 compared with the normal selling price of £200. The costs of the quality inspections totalled £340,000 for the year.

Sales of the product are 1 million units each year and it is estimated that a further 1 in every 2,000 sales will be defective. Of these it is expected that 60% will be returned by customers and will be replaced free of charge. The cost of producing a unit of the product is £120. The customers who do not return their products are unlikely to buy the company's products again; the company expects satisfied customers to make a repeat purchase annually.

List all of the costs of quality incurred by the business and the amount of that cost if possible. State which type of cost of quality each cost is and whether it is an explicit cost or an implicit cost.

....

Task 8.6

What is life cycle costing?

....

Task 8.7

Barnet Ltd is a small company owned by Hampstead plc. Barnet operates a job costing system making a specialist, expensive piece of hospital equipment.

Existing system

Currently, employees are assigned to individual jobs and materials are requisitioned from stores as needed. The standard and actual costs of labour and materials are recorded for each job. These job costs are totalled to produce the marginal cost of production. Fixed production costs – including the cost of storekeeping and inspection of deliveries and finished equipment – are then added to determine the standard and actual cost of production. Any costs of remedial work are included in the materials and labour for each job.

Proposed system

Carol Johnson, the chief executive of Barnet, has recently been to a seminar on modern manufacturing techniques. As a result, she is considering introducing a Total Quality Management. Barnet would offer suppliers a long-term contract at a fixed price but suppliers would have to guarantee the quality of their materials. This would enable Barnet to reduce the levels of materials inventories held.

In addition, she proposes that the workforce is organised as a single team with flexible work practices. This would mean employees helping each other as necessary, with no employee being allocated a particular job. If a job was delayed, the workforce would work overtime without payment in order for the job to be completed on time. In exchange, employees would be guaranteed a fixed weekly wage and time off when production was slack to make up for any overtime incurred.

BPP
LEARNING MEDIA

Cost of quality

Carol has asked to meet you to discuss the implications of her proposals on the existing accounting system. She is particularly concerned to monitor the **cost of quality**. This is defined as the total of all costs incurred in preventing defects plus those costs involved in remedying defects once they have occurred. It is a single figure measuring all the explicit costs of quality – that is, those costs collected within the accounting system.

Task

In preparation for the meeting, produce brief notes. Your notes should:

(a) **Identify FOUR general headings (or classifications) which make up the cost of quality.**

(b) **Give ONE example of a type of cost likely to be found within each category.**

(c) **Assuming Carol Johnson's proposals are accepted, state, with reasons, whether or not:**

    (i) **A standard costing system would still be of help to the managers;**

    (ii) **It would still be meaningful to collect costs by each individual job.**

(d) **Identify ONE cost saving in Carol Johnson's proposals which would not be recorded in the existing costing system.**

....

Task 8.8

(a) You are employed as the assistant management accountant with Local Engineering Ltd, a company which designs and makes a single product, the X4, used in the telecommunications industry. The company has a goods received store which employs staff who carry out random checks to ensure materials are of the correct specification. In addition to the random checks, a standard allowance is made for failures due to faulty materials at the completion stage and the normal practice is to charge the cost of any remedial work required to the cost of production for the month. Once delivered to the customer, any faults discovered in the X4 during its warranty period become an expense of the customer support department.

At the end of each month, management reports are prepared for the Board of Directors. These identify the cost of running the stores and the number of issues, the cost of production and the number of units manufactured, and the cost of customer support.

Jane Greenwood, Local Engineering's management accountant, has just returned from a board meeting to discuss a letter the company recently received from Universal Telecom, Local Engineering's largest customer. In the letter, Universal Telecom explained that it was determined to maintain its position as a world-class provider of telecommunication services and that there was serious concern about the quality of the units delivered by your company. At the meeting, Local Engineering Ltd's board responded by agreeing to establish a company-wide policy of implementing a Total Quality Management (TQM) programme, commencing with a revised model of the X4. Design work on the new model is scheduled to commence in six month's time.

One aspect of this will involve the management accounting department collecting the cost of quality. This is defined as the total of all costs incurred in preventing defects plus those costs involved in remedying defects once they have occurred within the accounting system – attributable to producing output that is not within its specification.

As a first step towards the implementation of TQM, a meeting of the senior staff in the management accounting department has been called to discuss the role the department can play in making TQM a success. **Jane Greenwood has asked you to prepare a brief background paper for the meeting, using the template provided.**

Your paper should do the following.

(i)   **Explain in outline what is meant by Total Quality Management.**

(ii) **Briefly discuss why the current accounting system fails to highlight the cost of quality.**

(iii) **Identify FOUR general categories (or classifications) of Local Engineering's activities where expenditure making up the explicit cost of quality will be found.**

(iv) **Give ONE example of a cost found within each category.**

(v)   **Give ONE example of a cost of quality not normally identified by the accounting system.**

Background paper for meeting

To: Jane Greenwood, Management Accountant

From: Assistant Management Accountant

Subject: Total quality management and the cost of quality

Date: xx/xx/xx

(i)   **The meaning of Total Quality Management**

(ii) **Failure of the current accounting system to highlight the cost of quality**

(iii)/(iv) **Explicit costs of quality**

(v) **Quality costs not identified by the accounting system**

(b) Local Engineering Ltd has capacity to produce no more than 1,000 X4s per month and currently is able to sell all production immediately at a unit selling price of £1,250. A major component of the X4 is a complex circuit board. Spot checks are made on these boards by a team of specialist employees when they are received into stores. In May, 100 units were found to be faulty and returned to the supplier. Good components are then issued to production along with other material.

Upon completion, each X4 is tested. If there is a fault, this involves further remedial work prior to dispatch to customers. For the month of May, 45 units of the X4 had to be reworked because of subsequent faults discovered in the circuit board. This remedial work cost an additional £13,500 in labour charges.

Should a fault occur after delivery to the customer, Local Engineering is able to call upon a team of self-employed engineers to rectify the fault as part of its customer support function. The cost of the remedial work by the self-employed engineers carried out in May – and the number of times they were used – is shown as contractors under customer support.

Extract from the accounting records of Local Engineering Ltd for the month of May

	Units	£		Units	£
Purchases:			**Production:**		
Printed circuits	1,000	120,000	Printed circuits	900	108,000
Less returns	(100)	(12,000)	Other material		121,500
Net costs	900	108,000	Labour		193,500
Other material		121,500	Direct prod'n o/hd		450,000
Total purchases issued to production		229,500	Cost of production		873,000
Other direct stores costs:					
Goods received, labour costs and rent		54,000	**Customer support:**		
Inspection costs		10,000			
Costs of returns	100	4,500	Contractors	54	24,300
Costs of stores		68,500			24,300

As part of the continuing development of Total Quality Management, you are asked by Jane Greenwood to calculate the following:

(i) The explicit cost of quality for Local Engineering Ltd for the month of May.

(ii) A further cost of quality not reported in the above accounting records.

....

Task 8.9

(a) Explain the five stages of the product life cycle and how costs and income will alter in each of the five stages.

(b) How does knowledge of the product life cycle affect forecasting of future sales?

....

Task 8.10

A company is developing a new product. There are currently several other companies manufacturing similar products which sell for a price of £50 each. The company wishes to make a margin of 20%.

The target cost of the new product is £ [ ]

....

Task 8.11

A company can sell 10,000 units in the next year, giving total sales of £250,000. The company wants to make a profit margin of 70%.

The target cost per unit is £ [   ]

....

Answer bank

Answer bank

Chapter 1

Task 1.1

True ☐

False ☑

	16,000 units	22,000 units
Total cost	£54,400	£68,200
Cost per unit	£3.40	£3.10

Therefore this is not a variable cost – if it were a true variable cost then the cost per unit would be the same at each activity level.

Task 1.2

Cost	Behaviour
Cost I	Variable
Cost II	Semi-variable or stepped
Cost III	Fixed
Cost IV	Variable

Task 1.3

Activity level – units	Total production cost £	Cost per unit £
8,000	50,600	6.325
12,000	63,400	5.283
15,000	73,000	4.867

Workings

	8,000 units £	12,000 units £	15,000 units £
Variable costs			
£32,000/10,000 × 8,000	25,600		
£32,000/10,000 × 12,000		38,400	
£32,000/10,000 × 15,000			48,000
Fixed costs	25,000	25,000	25,000
	50,600	63,400	73,000
Cost per unit	£6.325	£5.283	£4.867

Task 1.4

Activity level – units	Total supervisors cost £	Supervisors cost per unit £
500	20,000	40
1,000	40,000	40
1,500	40,000	26.67

Workings

	500 units £	1,000 units £	1,500 units £
Number of supervisors required			
500/750 = 0.67, round up to 1 @ £20,000	20,000		
1,000/750 = 1.33, round up to 2 @ £20,000		40,000	
1,500/750 = 2 @ £20,000			40,000
Cost per unit	£40	£40	£26.67

Task 1.5

		Cost behaviour
(i)	Maintenance department costs which are made up of £25,000 of salaries and an average of £500 cost per call out	Semi-variable
(ii)	Machinery depreciation based upon machine hours used	Variable
(iii)	Salary costs of nursery school teachers where one teacher is required for every six children in the nursery	Stepped fixed
(iv)	Rent for a building that houses the factory, stores and maintenance departments	Fixed

Task 1.6

(i)

Production level – units	Total cost of production £	Cost per unit £
1,000	82,000	82.00
1,500	112,500	75.00
2,000	143,000	71.50

Workings

	1,000 units £	1,500 units £	2,000 units £
Direct materials 6kgs × £4.80 × units	28,800	43,200	57,600
Direct labour 4 hours × £7.00 × units	28,000	42,000	56,000
Building costs – fixed	18,000	18,000	18,000
Leased machines	1,200	1,800	2,400
Stores costs £3,000 + £3.00 × units	6,000	7,500	9,000
	82,000	112,500	143,000
Cost per unit	£82.00	£75.00	£71.50

(ii) The cost per unit is decreasing as production quantities increase. This is due to the fact that not all of the costs are variable. The buildings costs are fixed and part of the stores costs are also fixed. For these elements of total cost, as the production quantity increases, the cost per unit decreases. This in turn reduces the total overall unit cost as the quantity increases.

Task 1.7

The variable cost per machine hour is £15.00

The fixed costs of the maintenance department are £72,000

Workings

Variable costs

	Machine hours	Cost £
June (lowest)	14,200	285,000
August (highest)	15,200	300,000
Increase	1,000	15,000
Variable cost = £15,000/1,000 hours		
= £15 per hour		
Fixed costs:		
June		
Variable element £15 × 14,200 hours		213,000
Fixed element (bal fig)		72,000
Total cost		285,000

··

Task 1.8

(a)   The fixed element of the production cost is £167,000

The variable element of the production cost per unit is £7

Workings

	Activity level	Cost
		£
July (lowest)	63,000	608,000
September (highest)	76,000	699,000
Increase	13,000	91,000
Variable element = £91,000/13,000		
= £7 per unit		
Fixed costs:	£	
July		
Variable element £7 × 63,000 units	441,000	
Fixed element (bal fig)	167,000	
Total cost	608,000	

(b)

Level of production – units	Production cost £
74,000	685,000
90,000	797,000

Workings

(i)   Production level of 74,000 units:

	£
Variable cost £7 × 74,000	518,000
Fixed cost	167,000
Total cost	685,000

(ii) Production level of 90,000 units:

	£
Variable cost £7 × 90,000	630,000
Fixed cost	167,000
Total cost	797,000

(c) The estimate for the 74,000 units of production is likely to be more accurate than the estimate for 90,000 units. Estimating the costs at 74,000 units is an example of interpolation, in that the estimate is being made for a production level that is within the range of production levels used to estimate the variable and fixed costs. 90,000 units of production is significantly higher than the levels of production used in estimating fixed and variable costs and therefore it is possible that the costs would behave differently at this level of production. This is an example of extrapolation.

Task 1.9

(a) The variable element of the production cost per unit is £3

(b)

Level of production – units	Fixed cost – £
40,000	85,000
48,000	135,000

Workings

	Activity level	Cost – £
High	48,000	279,000 – 50,000 = 229,000
Low	40,000	205,000
Increase	8,000	24,000
Variable element = £24,000/8,000		
= £3 per unit		
Fixed element	£	
At 40,000 units:		
Variable element £3 × 40,000 units	120,000	
Fixed element (bal fig)	85,000	
Total cost	205,000	

Fixed element:	£	
At 48,000 units:		
Variable element £3 × 48,000 units	144,000	
Fixed element (bal fig)	135,000	
Total cost	279,000	

Task 1.10

 (a) Cost of 9,000 units = £64,000

 (b) Cost of 11,000 units = £81,000

Workings

Variable cost per unit = $\dfrac{£93,000 - £15,000}{13,000}$ = £6 per unit

Fixed element for activity level up to 9,999 units = £58,000 – (8,000 × £6) = £10,000

Cost at 9,000 units = £10,000 + (9,000 × £6) = £64,000

Cost at 11,000 units = £15,000 + (11,000 × £6) = £81,000

Task 1.11

 (a) £493,000

 (b) £545,000

We have been told that the variable element is £25 per unit so we can find the fixed element from this at each activity level:

Fixed element at 18,000 units = £468,000 – (18,000 × £25) = £18,000

Fixed element at 22,000 units = £570,000 – (22,000 × £25) = £20,000

Therefore:

Cost at 19,000 units = £18,000 + (19,000 × £25) = £493,000

Cost at 21,000 units = £20,000 + (21,000 × £25) = £545,000

Chapter 2

Task 2.1

Absorption rate method	Cutting rate £	Finishing rate £	Most appropriate 1, 2 or 3
Rate per unit	5.86	4.24	2 - most appropriate where all products are of similar size and require a similar input in terms of time and resources of the departments
Rate per direct labour hour	14.65	1.77	3 - most appropriate in labour intensive departments where most of the overhead relates to labour
Rate per machine hour	4.88	21.20	1 - most appropriate in a largely mechanised department where most of the overhead relates to machinery costs

Workings

		Cutting	Finishing
(a)	Rate per unit	$\dfrac{58,600}{10,000}$	$\dfrac{42,400}{10,000}$
		= £5.86 per unit	= £4.24 per unit
(b)	Rate per direct labour hour	$\dfrac{58,600}{4,000}$	$\dfrac{42,400}{24,000}$
		= £14.65 per labour hour	= £1.77 per labour hour
(c)	Rate per machine hour	$\dfrac{58,600}{12,000}$	$\dfrac{42,400}{2,000}$
		= £4.88 per machine hour	£21.20 per machine hour

Task 2.2

(a)

Department	Overhead absorption rate
C	£1.25 per machine hour
D	£2.25 per direct labour hour

Workings

$$C = \frac{£125,000}{100,000}$$

= £1.25 per machine hour

as C is a highly mechanised department most of the overhead will relate to the machinery therefore machine hours have been used to absorb the overhead.

$$D = \frac{£180,000}{80,000}$$

= £2.25 per direct labour hour

as D is a highly labour intensive department then most of the overhead will relate to the hours that are worked by the labour force therefore labour hours are used to absorb the overhead.

(b) The overhead to be included in the cost of product P is £22.00

Working

Product P – department C overhead	£1.25 × 5	= £ 6.25
department D overhead	£2.25 × 7	= £15.75
		£22.00

Task 2.3

Overhead apportioned to packaging department	£11,429
Overhead apportioned to assembly department	£8,571

Workings

Number of employees who use canteen = 20 + 50% × 30 = 35 employees

Cost per employee = £20,000/35 = £571.43 per employee

Therefore cost apportioned to packaging department = 20 × £571.43 = £11,429

Cost apportioned to assembly department = 15 × £571.43 = £8,571

Task 2.4

	Under-absorption £	Over-absorption £	Debit/Credit
Budgeted production was 1,200 units and budgeted overheads were £5,400. Overheads are to be absorbed on a unit basis. The actual production was 1,000 units and the overheads incurred were £5,000.	500		Debit
Budgeted production was 600 units to be produced in 1,800 labour hours. Budgeted overheads of £5,040 are to be absorbed on a direct labour hour basis. The actual production for the period was 700 units in 2,200 labour hours and the actual overheads were £5,100.		1,060	Credit
Budgeted production was 40,000 units and the budgeted machine hours were 2 hours per unit. Budgeted overheads were £320,000 and were to be absorbed on a machine hour basis. The actual overheads incurred were £320,000 and the production was 42,000 units. The total machine hours were 82,000.		8,000	Credit

Workings

(a) Overhead absorption rate = $\dfrac{£5,400}{1,200}$

= £4.50 per unit

Overhead incurred = £5,000

Overhead absorbed

1,000 units × £4.50 = £4,500

Under-absorbed overhead = £500 – a further expense in the statement of profit or loss (income statement)

(b) Overhead absorption rate = $\dfrac{£5,040}{1,800}$

= £2.80 per direct labour hour

Overhead incurred = £5,100

Overhead absorbed

2,200 hours × £2.80   =   £6,160

Over-absorbed overhead   =   £1,060 – a credit to the statement of profit or loss (income statement)

(c)   Overhead absorption rate   = $\dfrac{£320,000}{80,000}$

                                 =   £4.00 per machine hour

Overhead incurred   =   £320,000

Overhead absorbed

82,000 × £4.00   =   £328,000

Over-absorbed overhead   =   £8,000 – a credit to the statement of profit or loss (income statement)

Task 2.5

The unit cost under absorption costing will be £39.50

The unit cost under marginal costing will be £37.50

Workings

(a) **Absorption costing**

	£
Direct materials	12.00
Direct labour – Cutting (2 × £7.40)	14.80
Finishing	6.80
Variable overheads:	
Cutting (2 × £1.40)	2.80
Finishing (1 × £1.10)	1.10
Fixed overheads:	
Cutting (2 × £0.60)	1.20
Finishing (1 × £0.80)	0.80
	39.50

(b) **Marginal costing**

	£
Direct materials	12.00
Direct labour – Cutting (2 × £7.40)	14.80
Finishing	6.80
Variable overheads:	
Cutting (2 × £1.40)	2.80
Finishing (1 × £1.10)	1.10
	37.50

Workings: Hourly absorption rates

	Rate per hour £
Variable overheads:	
Cutting (£336,000/240,000)	1.40
Finishing (£132,000/120,000)	1.10
Fixed overheads:	
Cutting (£144,000/240,000)	0.60
Finishing (£96,000/120,000)	0.80

Task 2.6

(a)   The absorption costing profit for July was £52,800

The absorption costing profit for August was £60,000

The marginal costing profit for July was £49,100

The marginal costing profit for August was £61,850

Workings

Cost per unit – absorption costing

	£
Direct materials	6.80
Direct labour	3.60
Variable costs (£32,400/24,000)	1.35
Fixed costs (£44,400/24,000)	1.85
	13.60

Cost per unit – marginal costing

	£
Direct materials	6.80
Direct labour	3.60
Variable costs (£32,400/24,000)	1.35
	11.75

Absorption costing – statement of profit loss (income statement)

		July £	July £	August £	August £
Sales	(22,000 × £16)		352,000		
	(25,000 × £16)				400,000
Less cost of sales					
Opening inventory	(1,500 × £13.60)	20,400			
	(3,500 × £13.60)			47,600	
Production	(24,000 × £13.60)	326,400		326,400	
		346,800		374,000	
Less closing inventory					
	(3,500 × £13.60)	(47,600)			
	(2,500 × £13.60)			(34,000)	
			299,200		340,000
Profit			52,800		60,000

Marginal costing – statement of profit or loss (income statement)

		July £	£	August £	£
Sales	(22,000 × £16)		352,000		
	(25,000 × £16)				400,000
Less: cost of sales					
Opening inventory	(1,500 × £11.75)	17,625			
	(3,500 × £11.75)			41,125	
Production	(24,000 × £11.75)	282,000		282,000	
		299,625		323,125	
Less: closing inventory					
	(3,500 × £11.75)	(41,125)			
	(2,500 × £11.75)			(29,375)	
			258,500		293,750
Contribution			93,500		106,250
Fixed costs			(44,400)		(44,400)
			49,100		61,850

(b) Reconciliation of profit figures

	July £	August £
Absorption cost profit	52,800	60,000
Increase in inventory (3,500 – 1,500)		
× fixed c.p.u. 2,000 × £1.85	(3,700)	
Decrease in inventory (3,500 – 2,500)		
× fixed c.p.u. 1,000 × £1.85		1,850
Marginal cost profit	49,100	61,850

Task 2.7

(a) The profit for the quarter under absorption costing is £47,560

The profit for the quarter under marginal costing £48,840

Workings

Unit cost – absorption costing

	£
Direct materials	23.60
Direct labour (4 × £5.80)	23.20
Variable overheads (£88,000/8,000)	11.00
Fixed overheads (£51,200/8,000)	6.40
	64.20

Unit cost – marginal costing

	£
Direct materials	23.60
Direct labour (4 × £5.80)	23.20
Variable overheads (£88,000/8,000)	11.00
	57.80

Absorption costing – statement of profit or loss (income statement)

	£	£
Sales (8,200 × £70)		574,000
Less cost of sales		
Opening inventory (840 × £64.20)	53,928	
Production cost (8,000 × £64.20)	513,600	
	567,528	
Less closing inventory (640 × £64.20)	(41,088)	
		526,440
Profit		47,560

Marginal costing – statement of profit or loss (income statement)

	£	£
Sales (8,200 × £70)		574,000
Less cost of sales		
Opening inventory (840 × £57.80)	48,552	
Production cost (8,000 × £57.80)	462,400	
	510,952	
Less closing inventory (640 × £57.80)	(36,992)	
		473,960
Contribution		100,040
Less fixed costs		(51,200)
Profit		48,840

(b)

	£
Absorption costing profit	47,560
Decrease in inventory × fixed cost per unit (200 × £6.40)	1,280
Marginal costing profit	48,840

Task 2.8

(a) The price of job HMG/012 based upon direct costs plus 50% mark-up is £457,500

The price of job CFG/013 based upon direct costs plus 50% mark-up is £279,000

	HMG/012 £	CFG/013 £
Equipment cost	175,000	120,000
Direct labour cost	130,000	66,000
Total direct cost	305,000	186,000
Mark up	50%	50%
Price	£457,500	£279,000

(b) **Calculation of cost per unit of cost driver**

Activity	Budgeted cost pool	Cost driver	Cost driver units pa	Cost per unit of cost driver
	£			£
Design department	675,000	Design hours	25,000	27.00
Site engineers	370,000	Miles travelled	185,000	2.00
Purchasing department	105,000	Items purchased	15,000	7.00
Payroll department	75,000	Direct hours	300,000	0.25
Site management	750,000	Direct hours	300,000	2.50
Post-installation inspection	80,000	Items purchased	20,000	4.00

Cost pool	Working	Total cost HMG/012	Total cost CFG/013
		£	£
Design department	£27 × 1,280/620	34,560	16,740
Site engineers	£2 × (320 × 30)/(90 × 10)	19,200	1,800
Purchasing department	£7 × 650/410	4,550	2,870
Payroll department	£0.25 × 10,000/6,000	2,500	1,500
Site management	£2.50 × 10,000/6,000	25,000	15,000
Post-installation inspection	£4 × 650/410	2,600	1,640
Total cost		88,410	39,550

Task 2.9

	Server allocated overheads £	PC allocated overheads £
Set-up costs	10,000	-
Rent and power (production area)	24,000	96,000
Rent (stores area)	25,000	25,000
Salaries of stores issue staff	8,000	32,000
Total overheads	67,000	153,000

Workings

Reallocation of Little Ltd's budgeted total fixed annual overheads between server and PC production

Step 1. **Calculation of cost per cost driver**

	Budgeted total annual overheads	Cost driver	Number of cost drivers	Cost per cost driver
Set-up costs	10,000	Number of set-ups	5	2,000.00
Rent and power (production area)	120,000	Number of wks' production	50	2,400.00
Rent (stores area)	50,000	Floor area of stores (m^2)	800	62.50
Salaries of store issue staff	40,000	No of issues of inventory	10,000	4.00
	220,000			

Step 2. **Reallocation of overheads based on costs per cost driver**

Server

	(i)	(ii)	(i) × (ii)
	Number of cost drivers	Cost per cost driver £	Allocated overheads £
Set-up costs	5	2,000.00	10,000
Rent and power (production area)	10	2,400.00	24,000
Rent (stores area)	400	62.50	25,000
Salaries of store issue staff	2,000	4.00	8,000
			67,000

PC

	(i)	(ii)	(i) × (ii)
	Number of cost drivers	Cost per cost driver £	Allocated overheads £
Set-up costs	0	2,000.00	–
Rent and power (production area)	40	2,400.00	96,000
Rent (stores area)	400	62.50	25,000
Salaries of store issue staff	8,000	4.00	32,000
			153,000

Task 2.10

	Plastic allocated overheads £	Metal allocated overheads £
Power for machinery	50,000	60,000
Rent of factory	100,000	20,000
Canteen costs	32,000	8,000
Total overheads	182,000	88,000

Workings

Calculation of cost per cost driver

	Budgeted overheads	Cost driver	Number of cost drivers	Cost per cost driver
Power for machinery	110,000	Number of machine hours	5,500	20
Rent of factory	120,000	Floor space	1,200	100
Canteen costs	40,000	Number of employees	250	160

Reallocation of overheads based on costs per cost driver

Plastic	(i)	(ii)	(i) × (ii)
	Number of cost drivers	Cost per cost driver £	Allocated overheads £
Power for machinery	2,500	20	50,000
Rent of factory	1,000	100	100,000
Canteen costs	200	160	32,000
			182,000

Metal	(i)	(ii)	(i) × (ii)
	Number of cost drivers	Cost per cost driver £	Allocated overheads £
Power for machinery	3,000	20	60,000
Rent of factory	200	100	20,000
Canteen costs	50	160	8,000
			88,000

Chapter 3

Task 3.1

The break even point in units is 100,000 units

The margin of safety in units is 15,000 units

The margin of safety as a percentage of budgeted sales is 13%

Workings

Breakeven point $= \dfrac{£1,100,000}{£28 - £17}$

$= 100,000$ units

Margin of safety (units) $=$ Budgeted sales $-$ Breakeven sales

$= (115,000 - 100,000)$ units

$= 15,000$ units

Margin of safety (% budgeted sales) $= \dfrac{115,000 - 100,000}{115,000} \times 100\%$

$= 13\%$

....

Task 3.2

Breakeven point in units $= 5,000$ units

Breakeven point in sales revenue $= £80,000$

Workings

Contribution per unit $= £(16 - 8) = £8$

Contribution required to breakeven $=$ fixed costs $= £40,000$

Breakeven point $= \dfrac{\text{Fixed costs}}{\text{Contribution per unit}}$

$= \dfrac{£40,000}{£8}$

$= 5,000$ units

Sales revenue at breakeven point $= 5,000$ units $\times$ £16 per unit

$= £80,000$

Task 3.3

Units = 500

Sales revenue = £40,000

Workings

Margin of safety = Budgeted sales volume – Breakeven sales volume

$$\text{Breakeven sales volume} = \frac{\text{Fixed costs}}{\text{Contribution per unit}}$$

$$= \frac{£110,000}{£55}$$

$$= 2,000 \text{ units}$$

Therefore, margin of safety (units) = 2,500 units – 2,000 units

$$= 500 \text{ units}$$

Therefore, margin of safety (sales revenue) = Margin of safety (units) × Selling price per unit

$$= 500 \text{ units} \times £80$$

$$= £40,000$$

Task 3.4

The number of units of the product that the business must sell in order to make a target profit of £300,000 is 46,667 units.

Workings

$$\text{Target profit units} = \frac{£540,000 + £300,000}{£83 - 65}$$

$$= 46,667 \text{ units}$$

Task 3.5

The sales revenue required in order to make a target profit of £250,000 is £2,560,000.

Workings

$$\text{Profit volume ratio} = \frac{£40 - 28}{£40} \times 100\% \qquad = 30\%$$

$$\text{Target profit sales revenue} = \frac{£518,000 + £250,000}{0.3} = £2,560,000$$

Task 3.6

Product	Units
B	800
A	1,000
C	50

Workings

Contribution per kg

	A	B	C
Contribution	£12	£16	£16
Kg per unit	2	1	4
Contribution per kg	£6	£16	£4
Ranking	2	1	3

Production plan

	Units	Kg used	Cumulative kg used
B	800	800	800
A	1,000	2,000	2,800
C (balance)	50	200	3,000
		3,000	

Task 3.7

Product	Units
T	8,000
R	20,000
S	12,000

The contribution that will be earned under this production plan is £540,000.

Workings

Identify the limiting factor

Materials – at maximum demand

$(4 \times 20,000) + (5 \times 25,000) + (3 \times 8,000) = 229,000$ kg

Labour hours – at maximum demand

$(2 \times 20,000) + (3 \times 25,000) + (3 \times 8,000) = 139,000$ hours

Machine hours – at maximum demand

$(4 \times 20,000) + (3 \times 25,000) + (2 \times 8,000) = 171,000$ hours

Therefore the only limiting factor is labour hours.

Contribution per labour hour

	R	S	T
Contribution	£11	£14	£19
Labour hours	2	3	3
Contribution per labour hour	£5.50	£4.67	£6.33
Ranking	2	3	1

Production plan

	Units	Labour hours used	Cumulative labour hours used
T	8,000	24,000	24,000
R	20,000	40,000	64,000
S (balance)	12,000	36,000	100,000
		100,000	

Contribution earned

	£
R (20,000 × £11)	220,000
S (12,000 × £14)	168,000
T (8,000 × £19)	152,000
	540,000

Task 3.8

The net present value of the investment is £(5,682)

Workings

Net present value

Year	Cash flow £	Discount factor @ 7%	Present value £
0	(84,000)	1.000	(84,000)
1	26,000	0.935	24,310
2	30,000	0.873	26,190
3	21,000	0.816	17,136
4	14,000	0.763	10,682
Net present value			(5,682)

Task 3.9

The net present value of the potential investment is £41,591.

Workings

Net present value

Year	Cash flow £	Discount factor @ 12%	Present value £
0	(355,000)	1.000	(355,000)
1 (47 + 60)	107,000	0.893	95,551
2 (55 + 60)	115,000	0.797	91,655
3 (68 + 60)	128,000	0.712	91,136
4 (53 + 60)	113,000	0.635	71,755
5 (22 + 60)	82,000	0.567	46,494
Net present value			41,591

Note that depreciation is not a cash flow and having been charged in arriving at the profit figure must be added back to find the cash inflow in each year.

Task 3.10

			Terminal value at time 3 £
Cash inflow at time 1	£90,000 × 1.07 × 1.07	=	103,041
Cash inflow at time 2	£130,000 × 1.07	=	139,100
Cash inflow at time 3		=	70,000
			312,141
Less initial outflow	(£200,000 × 1.07 × 1.07 × 1.07)		(245,009)
Net terminal value			67,132

Task 3.11

(a) **Complete the following table**

	Product X	Product Y
The contribution per unit is	45	57
The contribution per kilogram of materials	7.5	7.13

Workings

Contribution = selling price – variable costs

Contribution for X = £100 – £55 = £45

Contribution for Y = £135 – £78 = £57

Contribution for X per kg of material = £45 ÷ $\dfrac{£30}{5kg}$ = £7.50

Contribution for Y per kg of material = £57 ÷ $\dfrac{£40}{5kg}$ = £7.125 = £7.13 to the nearest penny.

(b) **The optimal production order for products X, and Y is**

Product X then Product Y ▼

(c) **Complete the table below for the optimal production mix**

	Product X	Product Y
Production in units	3,500	3,000

Working

(3,500 × 6kg) + (3,000 × 8kg) = 45,000kg

(d) **Complete the table below for the total contribution for each product.**

	Product X	Product Y
Total contribution	157,500	171,000

Chapter 4

Task 4.1

	Production costs	Three month moving total	Three month moving average
	£	£	£
March	104,500		
April	110,300	327,600	109,200
May	112,800	332,500	110,833
June	109,400	339,800	113,267
July	117,600	343,000	114,333
August	116,000	352,800	117,600
September	119,200	357,500	119,167
October	122,300	362,000	120,667
November	120,500	362,100	120,700
December	119,300		

Task 4.2

		Actual	5-day moving average trend	Seasonal variation (actual – trend)
		£	£	£
Week 1	Day 1	600		
	Day 2	700		
	Day 3	1,000	1,000	–
	Day 4	1,200	1,016	+184
	Day 5	1,500	1,026	+474
Week 2	Day 1	680	1,076	–396
	Day 2	750	1,116	–366
	Day 3	1,250	1,188	+ 62
	Day 4	1,400	1,216	+184
	Day 5	1,860	1,272	+588

		Actual	5-day moving average trend	Seasonal variation (actual − trend)
Week 3	Day 1	820	1,410	−590
	Day 2	1,030	1,550	−520
	Day 3	1,940	1,678	+262
	Day 4	2,100	1,714	+386
	Day 5	2,500	1,772	+728
Week 4	Day 1	1,000	1,696	−696
	Day 2	1,320	1,734	−414
	Day 3	1,560	1,768	−208
	Day 4	2,290		
	Day 5	2,670		

Task 4.3

(i)

		Actual	4-quarter moving average	Centred moving average – trend	Seasonal variations
		£	£	£	£
20X5	Quarter 3	50,600			
	Quarter 4	52,800			
			51,900		
20X6	Quarter 1	55,600		51,975	+3,625
			52,050		
	Quarter 2	48,600		52,188	−3,588
			52,325		
	Quarter 3	51,200		52,625	−1,425
			52,925		
	Quarter 4	53,900		53,075	+825
			53,225		

		Actual	4-quarter moving average	Centred moving average – trend	Seasonal variations
20X7	Quarter 1	58,000		53,450	+4,550
			53,675		
	Quarter 2	49,800		53,763	–3,963
			53,850		
	Quarter 3	53,000		54,113	–1,113
			54,375		
	Quarter 4	54,600		54,488	+112
			54,600		
20X8	Quarter 1	60,100		54,750	+5,350
			54,900		
	Quarter 2	50,700		54,975	–4,275
			55,050		
	Quarter 3	54,200			
	Quarter 4	55,200			

(ii) Seasonal variations

	Quarter 1	Quarter 2	Quarter 3	Quarter 4
	£	£	£	£
20X6	+3,625	–3,588	–1,425	+825
20X7	+4,550	–3,963	–1,113	+112
20X8	+5,350	–4,275		
	+13,525	–11,826	–2,538	+937
Average	+4,508	–3,942	–1,269	+469
Difference *				
234/4	+59	+59	+58	+58
	+4,567	–3,883	–1,211	+527

* Sum of averages = -234, so need to add back 234 to get the total seasonal variation to zero.

Task 4.4

Predicted sales

		£
Quarter 1	£418,500 + £21,500	440,000
Quarter 2	£420,400 + £30,400	450,800
Quarter 3	£422,500 – £16,700	405,800
Quarter 4	£423,800 – £35,200	388,600

Task 4.5

(a)

	Actual costs	RPI	Workings	Costs at January prices
	£			£
January	129,600	171.1	129,600	129,600
February	129,700	172.0	129,700 × 171.1/172.0	129,021
March	130,400	172.2	130,400 × 171.1/172.2	129,567
April	131,600	173.0	131,600 × 171.1/173.0	130,155
May	130,500	174.1	130,500 × 171.1/174.1	128,251
June	131,600	174.3	131,600 × 171.1/174.3	129,184

(b)

	Actual costs	RPI	Workings	Costs at June prices
	£			£
January	129,600	171.1	129,600 × 174.3/171.1	132,024
February	129,700	172.0	129,700 × 174.3/172.0	131,434
March	130,400	172.2	130,400 × 174.3/172.2	131,990
April	131,600	173.0	131,600 × 174.3/173.0	132,589
May	130,500	174.1	130,500 × 174.3/174.1	130,650
June	131,600	174.3	131,600 × 174.3/174.3	131,600

Task 4.6

		Sales		Index
		£		
20X7	Quarter 1	126,500		100.0
	Quarter 2	130,500	130,500/126,500 × 100	103.2
	Quarter 3	131,400	131,400/126,500 × 100	103.9
	Quarter 4	132,500	132,500/126,500 × 100	104.7
20X8	Quarter 1	133,100	133,100/126,500 × 100	105.2
	Quarter 2	135,600	135,600/126,500 × 100	107.2
	Quarter 3	136,500	136,500/126,500 × 100	107.9
	Quarter 4	137,100	137,100/126,500 × 100	108.4

Task 4.7

The updated standard cost for material C is £4.41

Working

£3.50 × 145/115 = £4.41

Task 4.8

Quarter 1 £667,396

Quarter 2 £722,633

Workings

Quarter 1   £657,000 × 128.4/126.4 = £667,396

Quarter 2   £692,500 × 131.9/126.4 = £722,633

Task 4.9

January 20X9	£12.10
February 20X9	£12.20

Workings

In January:

a = 9

b = 0.1

X = 31

Therefore Y = 9 + (0.1 × 31) = £12.10 per kilogram

In February:

a = 9

b = 0.1

X = 32

Therefore Y = 9 + (0.1 × 32) = £12.20 per kilogram

Task 4.10

a is £2,000

b is £5

If production is 750 units, the cost of production is £5,750.

Workings

100 units

£2,500 = a + (100 × b)

1,000 units

£7,000 = a + (1,000 × b)

Subtracting the two equations gives:

£(7,000 – 2,500) = a + (1,000 × b) – a – (100 × b)

£4,500 = 900 × b

b = 5

Substituting b = 5 into the first equation gives:

£2,500 = a + (100 × 5)

£2,500 = a + £500

a = £2,000

Production costs = 2,000 + (5 × 750)

= £5,750

Note that this is similar to the high low technique for finding the variable and fixed elements. of a semi-variable cost, if the activity levels given are assumed to be the highest and lowest.

100 units   £2,500

1,000 units   £7,000

Subtract the highest less the lowest activities to find the variable cost which is b in the equation:

1,000 – 100 = 900 units with additional cost of £(7,000 – 2,500) = £4,500, ie £4,500/900 per unit = £5 per unit

b = £5

Therefore, to find the fixed cost element, consider 100 units:

Fixed costs = Total costs – Variable costs

= £2,500 – 5 × 100

= £2,000

so a = £2,000

Task 4.11

If production is expected to be 105,000 units in the next quarter the anticipated production costs are £810,000

Workings

Production costs = 138,000 + (6.4 × 105,000)

= £810,000

Task 4.12

The anticipated power costs for April are £270,000.

Working

Power costs   80,000 + (380,000 × 0.5) = £270,000

Task 4.13

Month 1	25,600 units
Month 2	26,500 units
Month 3	27,400 units

Workings

Month 1: sales trend $= 3.1 + (0.9 \times 25)$ (month 25)

$\qquad\qquad\qquad = 25,600$ units

Month 2: sales trend $= 3.1 + (0.9 \times 26)$

$\qquad\qquad\qquad = 26,500$ units

Month 3: sales trend $= 3.1 + (0.9 \times 27)$

$\qquad\qquad\qquad = 27,400$ units

Task 4.14

Quarter 1	1,590 units
Quarter 2	2,095 units
Quarter 3	2,125 units
Quarter 4	1,880 units

Workings

	Trend		Seasonal variation		Estimate of actual
Quarter 1	$400 + (105) \times 13$	=	$1,765 - 175$	=	1,590
Quarter 2	$400 + (105) \times 14$	=	$1,870 + 225$	=	2,095
Quarter 3	$400 + (105) \times 15$	=	$1,975 + 150$	=	2,125
Quarter 4	$400 + (105) \times 16$	=	$2,080 - 200$	=	1,880

Task 4.15

(a)

June cost per tonne (£)	177
July cost per tonne (£)	179

Workings

$Y = a + bX$

For June, $X = 26$, therefore $Y = 125 + (2 \times 26) = £177$ per tonne

For July $= X = 27$, therefore $Y = 125 + (2 \times 27) = £179$ per tonne

(b)

June index	101.14
July index	102.29

Workings

As May is the base,   May = 100 when price was £175 per tonne

Therefore,   June = 177/175 × 100 = 101.14

                July = 179/175 × 100 = 102.29

Task 4.16

(a)

	£
a	10,000
b	3

Workings

Substituting the outputs and corresponding distribution costs into the equation gives:

£14,500 = a + 1,500 b

£19,000 = a + 3,000 b

Subtracting the two equations gives:

£4,500 = 1,500 b

b = £3 per unit

Substituting this into the first equation gives:

£14,500 = a + 1,500 × £3

a = £10,000

(b)

Output	£
2,000 units (£10,000 + £3 × 2,000)	16,000
4,000 units (£10,000 + £3 × 4,000)	22,000

(c)   The value of distribution costs for **2,000** units is most accurate.

Tutorial note – this is because this is within the range of the activities (1,500 – 3,000) which were used to determine a and b in the equation (interpolation). 4,000 units is an activity outside the range (and so requires extrapolation).

Chapter 5

Task 5.1

MEMORANDUM

To: New Accounts Assistant

From: Accountant

Date: xx/xx/xx

Subject: **Setting the standard cost of labour**

The standard cost of the direct labour for a product will be made up of:

- The amount of time being spent on each unit of the product

- The hourly wage rate for the employees working on the product

Factors that should be taken into account when setting the standard for the amount of labour time include:

- The level of skill or training of the labour used on the product

- Any anticipated changes in the grade of labour used on the product

- Any anticipated changes in work methods or productivity levels

- The effect on productivity of any bonus scheme to be introduced

The hourly rate for the direct labour used on the product can be found from the payroll records. However consideration should be given to:

- Anticipated pay rises

- Any anticipated changes in the grade of labour to be used

- The effect of any bonus scheme on the labour rate

- Whether any overtime is anticipated and should be built into the hourly rate

Task 5.2

	Variance £	Adverse/Favourable
Total materials cost variance	4,480	Adverse
Materials price variance	2,880	Adverse
Materials usage variance	1,600	Adverse

Workings

(i)   Total materials cost variance

	£
Standard cost of actual production 2,800 units × 5 kg × £4.00	56,000
Actual cost	60,480
Total cost variance	4,480 (A)

(ii)   Materials price variance

	£
14,400 kg should have cost (× £4.00)	57,600
But did cost	60,480
Price variance	2,880 (A)

(iii)   Materials usage variance

2,800 units should have used × 5 kg × £4.00	14,000 kg
But did use	14,400 kg
	400 kg
At standard cost	× £4.00
Usage variance	£1,600 (A)

Task 5.3

	Variance £	Adverse/Favourable
Total materials cost variance	13,680	Adverse
Materials price variance	16,080	Adverse
Materials usage variance	2,400	Favourable

Workings

(i) Total materials cost variance

	£
Standard cost for actual production 11,400 units × 4 kg × £3	136,800
Actual cost	150,480
Total cost variance	13,680 (A)

(ii) Materials price variance

	£
44,800 kg should have cost (× £3)	134,400
But did cost	150,480
Price variance	16,080 (A)

(iii) Materials usage variance

	£
11,400 units should have used (× 4 kg)	45,600
But did use	44,800
	800 (F)
At standard cost	× £3
Usage variance	2,400 (F)

Task 5.4

	Variance £	Adverse/Favourable
Total labour cost variance	12,715	Adverse
Labour rate variance	9,430	Adverse
Labour efficiency variance	3,285	Adverse

Workings

(i) Total labour cost variance

	£
Standard cost for actual production 12,100 units × 4.5 hours × £7.30	397,485
Actual cost	410,200
Total cost variance	12,715 (A)

BPP
LEARNING MEDIA

(ii)   Labour rate variance

		£
54,900 hours should have cost (× £7.30)		400,770
But did cost		410,200
Rate variance		9,430 (A)

(iii) Labour efficiency variance

12,100 units should have taken (× 4.5 hours)	54,450 hrs
But did take	54,900 hrs
	450 hrs (A)
At standard rate	× £7.30
Efficiency variance	£3,285 (A)

Task 5.5

	Variance £	Adverse/Favourable
Total labour cost variance	2,200	Favourable
Labour rate variance	4,200	Favourable
Labour efficiency variance	2,000	Adverse

Workings

(i)   Total labour cost variance

		£
Standard cost for actual production 10,680 units × 5 hours × £10		534,000
Actual cost		531,800
Total cost variance		2,200 (F)

(ii) Labour rate variance

		£
53,600 hours should have cost (× £10)		536,000
But did cost		531,800
Rate variance		4,200 (F)

(iii) Labour efficiency variance

10,680 units should have taken (× 5 hours)	53,400 hrs
But did take	53,600 hrs
	200 hrs (A)
At standard rate	× £10
Efficiency variance	£2,000 (A)

Task 5.6

	Variance £	Adverse/Favourable
Total labour cost variance	8,600	Adverse
Labour rate variance	4,100	Adverse
Labour efficiency variance	4,500	Adverse

Workings

(i) Total labour cost variance

	£
Standard cost for actual production 11,400 × 3 hours × £9	307,800
Actual cost	316,400
Total variance	8,600 (A)

(ii) Labour rate variance

	£
34,700 hours should have cost (× £9)	312,300
But did cost	316,400
Rate variance	4,100 (A)

(iii) Labour efficiency variance

11,400 units should have taken (× 3 hours)	34,200 hrs
But did take	34,700 hrs
	500 hrs (A)
At standard rate × £9	× £9
Efficiency variance	£4,500 (A)

....

Task 5.7

The fixed overhead expenditure variance is £5,000 Adverse

The fixed overhead volume variance is £10,500 Favourable

Workings

(i) Fixed overhead expenditure variance

	£
Budgeted overhead £7 × 10,000 units	70,000
Actual overhead	75,000
Expenditure variance	5,000 (A)

(ii) Fixed overhead volume variance

	£
Actual production @ standard OAR 11,500 × £7	80,500
Budgeted production @ standard OAR 10,000 × £7	70,000
Volume variance	10,500 (F)

....

Task 5.8

	Variance £	Adverse/Favourable
Fixed overhead expenditure variance	80,000	Favourable
Fixed overhead volume variance	91,200	Favourable
Fixed overhead efficiency variance	15,200	Favourable
Fixed overhead capacity variance	76,000	Favourable

Workings

Fixed overhead expenditure variance

	£
Budgeted fixed overhead 50,000 units × 6 hours × £7.60	2,280,000
Actual fixed overhead	2,200,000
Expenditure variance	80,000 (F)

Fixed overhead volume variance

	£
Standard hours for actual production @ standard OAR 52,000 units × 6 hours × £7.60	2,371,200
Standard hours for budgeted production @ standard OAR 50,000 units × 6 hours × £7.60	2,280,000
Volume variance	91,200 (F)

Fixed overhead efficiency variance

	£
Standard hours for actual production @ standard OAR 52,000 × 6 hours × £7.60	2,371,200
Actual hours @ standard OAR 310,000 × £7.60	2,356,000
Efficiency variance	15,200 (F)

Fixed overhead capacity variance

	£
Actual hours @ standard OAR 310,000 × £7.60	2,356,000
Budgeted hours @ standard OAR 50,000 × 6 × £7.60	2,280,000
Capacity variance	76,000 (F)

Task 5.9

(i)   The budgeted fixed overhead for the month was £201,600
(ii) The fixed overhead expenditure variance was £1,400 Adverse
(iii) The fixed overhead volume variance was £11,520 Adverse
(iv) The fixed overhead efficiency variance was £10,080 Favourable
(v)   The fixed overhead capacity variance was £21,600 Adverse

Workings

(i)

	£
Budgeted fixed overhead	
14,000 units × 4 hours × £3.60	201,600

(ii) Fixed overhead expenditure variance

	£
Budgeted fixed overhead	201,600
Actual fixed overhead	203,000
Expenditure variance	1,400 (A)

(iii) Fixed overhead volume variance

	£
Standard hours for actual production @ standard OAR	
13,200 units × 4 hours × £3.60	190,080
Standard hours for budgeted production @ standard OAR	
14,000 units × 4 hours × £3.60	201,600
Volume variance	11,520 (A)

(iv) Fixed overhead efficiency variance

	£
Standard hours for actual production @ standard OAR	
13,200 × 4 hours × £3.60	190,080
Actual hours @ standard OAR 50,000 × £3.60	180,000
Efficiency variance	10,080 (F)

(v)   Fixed overhead capacity variance

	£
Actual hours @ standard OAR 50,000 × £3.60	180,000
Budgeted hours @ standard OAR 14,000 × 4 × £3.60	201,600
Capacity variance	21,600 (A)

Task 5.10

	Favourable £	Adverse £	Total £
Budgeted cost of actual production 1,240 × £38.69			47,976
Variances			
Materials price		860	
Materials usage	426		
Labour rate	820		
Labour efficiency		1,530	
Fixed overhead expenditure		250	
Fixed overhead efficiency		288	
Fixed overhead capacity	848		
Total variances	2094	2928	834
Actual cost of actual production (17,100 + 27,060 + 4,650)			48,810

Task 5.11

The correct answer is £98.40

	£	£
Materials		
A 1.2 kg × £11 =	13.20	
B 4.7 kg × £6 =	28.20	
		41.40
Labour		
1.5 hours × £8		12.00
Prime cost		53.40
Overheads		
1.5 hours × £30		45.00
Standard cost per unit		98.40

Task 5.12

The correct answer is £1,113 Adverse

Budgeted fixed overhead absorption rate = £22,260 ÷ 8,400 hours = £2.65 per labour hour

Budgeted hours of work	8,400 hrs
Actual hours of work	7,980 hrs
	420 hrs (A)
× standard rate per hour	× £2.65
Fixed production overhead capacity variance	£1,113 (A)

Task 5.13

(i)

Budgeted fixed overhead expenditure (4,100 × 40 × £12.50)	2,050,000
Actual fixed overhead expenditure	2,195,000
Fixed overhead **expenditure variance**	145,000 (A)

(ii)

	£
Actual production at standard rate (3,850 × 40 × £12.50)	1,925,000
Budgeted production at standard rate (4,100 × 40 × £12.50)	2,050,000
Fixed overhead **volume variance**	125,000 (A)

(iii)

Budgeted hours (4,100 × 40)	164,000 hrs
Actual hours	159,000 hrs
Fixed overhead capacity variance in hours	5,000 hrs (A)
× standard rate per hour	× £12.50
Fixed overhead **capacity variance**	£62,500 (A)

(iv)

3,850 units should have taken (× 40 hrs)	154,000 hrs
but did take	159,000 hrs
Fixed overhead efficiency variance in hours	5,000 hrs (A)
× standard rate per hour	× £12.50
Fixed overhead **efficiency variance**	£62,500 (A)

Task 5.14

The correct answer is the work in progress control account.

Task 5.15

	Variance £	Adverse/Favourable
Total variable production overhead variance	30	Adverse
Variable production overhead efficiency variance	60	Favourable
Variable production overhead expenditure variance	90	Adverse

Workings

Tutorial note: Since this question relates to variable production costs, the total variance is based on actual units of production. (If the overhead had been a variable selling cost, the variance would be based on sales volumes.)

Total variable production overhead variance

	£
400 units of product X should cost (× £3)	1,200
but did cost	1,230
Variable production overhead total variance	30 (A)

Variable overhead expenditure variance

	£
760 hours of variable production overhead should cost (× £1.50)	1,140
but did cost	1,230
Variable production overhead expenditure variance	90 (A)

Variable overhead efficiency variance

400 units of product X should take (× 2hrs)	800 hrs
but did take (active hours)	760 hrs
Variable production overhead efficiency variance in hours	40 hrs (F)
× standard rate per hour	× £1.50
Variable production overhead efficiency variance in £	£60 (F)

Task 5.16

(a) The variable production cost variance is £208,000 Adverse

Workings

This is simply a 'total' variance.

	£
1,000 units should have cost (× £600)	600,000
but did cost (£720,000 + £63,000 + £25,000)	808,000
Variable production cost variance	208,000 (A)

(b) (i)   The direct labour rate variance is £2,600 Favourable

Workings

	£
8,200 hours should cost (× £8)	65,600
but did cost	63,000
Direct labour rate variance	2,600 (F)

(ii)   The direct labour efficiency variance is £14,400 Favourable

Workings

1,000 units should take (× 10 hours)	10,000 hrs
but did take	8,200 hrs
Direct labour efficiency variance in hrs	1,800 hrs (F)
× standard rate per hour	× £8
Direct labour efficiency variance in £	£14,400 (F)

(c) (i)   The direct material price variance is £270,000 Adverse

Workings

	£
90,000 kg should cost (× £5)	450,000
but did cost	720,000
Direct material price variance	270,000 (A)

(ii)   The direct material usage variance is £50,000 Favourable

Workings

1,000 units should use (× 100 kg)	100,000 kg
but did use	90,000 kg
Direct material usage variance in kgs	10,000 kg (F)
× standard cost per kg	× £5
Direct material usage variance in £	£50,000 (F)

(d) (i) The variable production overhead expenditure variance is £8,600 Adverse

Workings

	£
8,200 hours incurring o/hd should cost (× £2)	16,400
but did cost	25,000
Variable production overhead expenditure variance	8,600 (A)

(ii) The variable production overhead efficiency variance is £3,600 Favourable

Workings

Efficiency variance in hrs (from (b)(ii))	1,800 hrs (F)
× standard rate per hour	× £2
Variable production overhead efficiency variance	£3,600 (F)

....

Task 5.17

(a) (1) Standard price of fuel = £497,664/1,244,160 litres = £0.40 per litre

(2) Standard litres of fuel per crossing = 1,244,160/6,480 = 192 litres

Standard litres of fuel for 5,760 crossings = 192 × 5,760 = 1,105,920 litres

(3) Standard labour rate per hr = £699,840/93,312 hrs = £7.50 per hour

(4) Standard labour hours per crossing = 93,312/6,480 = 14.4 hours

Standard labour hours for 5,760 crossings = 14.4 × 5,760 = 82,944 hours

(5) Standard fixed overhead cost per budgeted operating hour = £466,560/7,776 = £60 per hour

(6) Standard operating hours per crossing = 7,776/6,480 = 1.2 hours

Standard operating hours for 5,760 crossings = 1.2 × 5,760 = 6,912 hours

(7) Standard fixed overhead cost absorbed by 5,760 crossings = 6,912 hours (6) × £60 per hour (from (5)) = £414,720

(b) (1)

	£
1,232,800 litres should cost (× £0.40 (a)(i)(1))	493,120
but did cost	567,088
Material price variance for fuel	73,968 (A)

(2)

	£
5,760 crossings should have used ((a)(i)(2))	1,105,920 litres
but did use	1,232,800 litres
Usage variance in litres	126,880 litres (A)
× standard price per litre ((a)(i)(1))	× £0.40
Material usage variance for fuel	£50,752 (A)

(3)

	£
69,858 hours should have cost (× £7.50 (a)(i)(3))	673,920
but did cost	696,384
Labour rate variance	22,464 (A)

(4)

5,760 crossing should have used ((a)(i)(4))	82,944 hours
but did take	89,856 hours
Efficiency variance in hours	6,912 hours (A)
× standard rate per hours ((a)(i)(3))	× £7.50
Labour efficiency variance	£51,840 (A)

(5)

	£
Budgeted fixed overhead expenditure	466,560
Actual fixed overhead expenditure	472,440
Fixed overhead expenditure variance	5,880 (A)

(6)

	£
Actual number of crossings (5,760) at standard rate ((a)(i)(7))	414,720
Budgeted number of crossings at standard rate	466,560
Fixed overhead volume variance	51,840 (A)

(7)

Budgeted operating hours	7,776
Actual operating hours	7,488
Capacity variance in hours	288 (A)
× std fixed o/hd cost per operating hours ((a)(i)(5))	× £60
Fixed overhead capacity variance	£17,280 (A)

(8)

5,760 crossing should take ((a)(i)(6))	6,912 operating hours
But did take	7,488 operating hours
Efficiency variance in operating hours	576 operating hours (A)
× std fixed o/hd cost per op hr ((a)(i)(5))	× £60
Fixed overhead efficiency variance	£34,560 (A)

(c) **Statement reconciling the actual cost of operations to the standard cost of operations for year ended 30 November 20X8**

Number of ferry crossings		5,760
	£	£
Actual cost of operations		1,735,912
Cost variances	*Adverse*	
Material price for fuel	73,968	
Material usage for fuel	50,752	
Labour rate	22,464	
Labour efficiency	51,840	
Fixed overhead expenditure	5,880	
Fixed overhead capacity	17,280	
Fixed overhead efficiency	34,560	
		256,744 (A)
Standard cost of operations		1,479,168*

* Check. 5,760/6,480 × £1,664,064 = £1,479,168

··

Task 5.18

(a)

Standard cost of materials for actual production			£114,000
Variances	Favourable	Adverse	
Direct material price variance		£45,600	
Direct material usage variance	£22,800		
Total variance			£22,800
Actual cost of materials for actual production			£136,800

Workings

Standard cost for actual units produced = 11,400 units × 5kg × £2 = £114,000

	£
Materials price variance	
45,600 kg should have cost (× £2)	91,200
But did cost	136,800
Price variance	45,600 (A)

Materials usage variance	
11,400 units should have used (× 5 kg)	57,000 kg
But did use	45,600
	11,400 (F)
At standard price per kg	× £2
Usage variance	22,800 (F)

(b)

Standard cost of labour for actual production			£182,400
Variances	Favourable	Adverse	
Direct labour rate variance	£11,400		
Direct labour efficiency variance	£91,200		
Total variance			£(102,600)
Actual cost of labour for actual production			£79,800

Workings

Standard cost for actual units produced = 11,400 units × 2hrs × £8 = £182,400

	£
Labour rate variance	
11,400 hrs should have cost (× £8)	91,200
But did cost	79,800
Rate variance	11,400 (F)

Labour efficiency variance	
11,400 units should have taken (× 2 hours)	22,800 hrs
But did take	11,400 hrs
	11,400 (F)
At standard cost	× £8
Usage variance	91,200 (F)

(c)

Standard cost of fixed overhead for actual production			91,200
Variances	Favourable	Adverse	
Fixed overhead expenditure variance	1,000		
Fixed overhead volume variance		4,800	
Total variance			3,800
Actual cost of fixed overhead for actual production			95,000

Workings

Standard cost for actual units produced = 11,400 units × 2hrs × £4 = £91,200

	£
Budgeted fixed overhead expenditure (12,000 × 2 × £4)	96,000
Actual fixed overhead expenditure	95,000
Fixed overhead **expenditure variance**	1,000 (F)

	£
Standard hours for actual production @ standard OAR	
11,400 units × 2 hours × £4	91,200
Standard hours for budgeted production @ standard OAR	
12,000 units × 2 hours × £4	96,000
Volume variance	4,800 (A)

Task 5.19

Capacity variance:

OAR = Budgeted overheads £810,000 ÷ budgeted hours 108,000 = £7.50 per hour

	Hours
Budgeted hours of work	108,000
Actual hours of work	118,000
Fixed overhead capacity variance	10,000 (F)
× standard fixed overhead absorption rate per hour	× £7.50
Fixed overhead capacity variance in £	£75,000 (F)

Efficiency variance:

Actual production 29,000 units × 4 (expected number of hours per unit) = 116,000 hours

	Hours
Actual units should take	116,000
But did take	118,000
Fixed overhead efficiency variance in hours	2,000 (A)
× standard fixed overhead absorption rate per hour	× £7.50
Fixed overhead efficiency variance in £	£15,000 (A)

Chapter 6

Task 6.1

Variance	Possible causes
Favourable materials price variance	• Negotiation of a better price from a supplier • Negotiation of a trade or bulk purchase discount from a supplier • Purchase of a lower grade of materials
Favourable materials usage variance	• Use of a higher grade of material which led to less wastage • Use of more skilled labour leading to less wastage than normal • New machinery which provides greater efficiency
Adverse labour rate variance	• Unexpected increase in labour costs • Use of a higher grade of labour than anticipated • Unexpectedly high levels of overtime
Adverse labour efficiency variance	• Use of a less skilled grade of labour • Use of a lower grade of material which takes longer to work on • More idle time than budgeted for • Poor supervision of the workforce • Problems with machinery

Task 6.2

Scenario	Possible effects
A business has had to use a less-skilled grade of labour in its production process	• Favourable labour rate variance • Adverse labour efficiency variance • Adverse materials usage variance

Scenario	Possible effects
A factory had a machine breakdown which resulted in three days of production delays last month	• Adverse labour efficiency variance • Adverse fixed overhead expenditure variance (due to additional costs of mending the machine) • Adverse fixed overhead volume variance • Adverse fixed overhead efficiency variance • Adverse fixed overhead capacity variance

Task 6.3

The total materials price variance is £36,600 Adverse

The non-controllable element of the materials price variance that has been caused by the price increase is £22,550 Adverse

The controllable element of the materials price variance caused by other factors is £14,050 Adverse

Workings

Total materials price variance

	£
Standard cost for actual quantity 45,100 × £8	360,800
Actual cost	397,400
	36,600 (A)

Non-controllable variance caused by price increase

	£
Standard cost for actual quantity 45,100 × £8	360,800
Adjusted cost for actual quantity 45,100 × £8.50	383,350
	22,550 (A)

Controllable variance caused by other factors

	£
Adjusted cost for actual quantity 45,100 × £8.50	383,350
Actual cost	397,400
	14,050 (A)

Task 6.4

The total materials price variance is £4,240 Adverse

The non-controllable variance due to price increase is £5,300 Adverse

The controllable variance due to other factors is £1,060 Favourable

Workings

Total materials price variance

	£
Standard cost of actual quantity 10,600 × £6.50	68,900
Actual cost	73,140
	4,240 (A)

Non-controllable variance due to price increase

	£
Standard cost of actual quantity 10,600 × £6.50	68,900
Price adjusted cost of actual quantity 10,600 × £7.00	74,200
	5,300 (A)

Controllable variance due to other factors

	£
Price adjusted cost of actual quantity 10,600 × £7.00	74,200
Actual cost	73,140
	1,060 (F)

Task 6.5

The total materials price variance is £12,800 Favourable

The non-controllable variance due to the season is £38,640 Favourable

The controllable variance due to other factors is £25,840 Adverse

Workings

Total materials price variance

	£
Standard cost of actual quantity 92,000 × £7.00	644,000
Actual cost	631,200
	12,800 (F)

Non-controllable variance due to season

	£
Standard cost of actual quantity 92,000 × £7.00	644,000
Seasonally adjusted price 92,000 × (£7.00 – £0.42)	605,360
	38,640 (F)

Controllable variance due to other factors

	£
Seasonally adjusted price 92,000 × (£7.00 − £0.42)	605,360
Actual cost	631,200
	25,840 (A)

Task 6.6

The total materials price variance is £25,380 Adverse

The non-controllable variance caused by the seasonal price change is £30,456 Adverse

The controllable variance caused by other factors is £5,076 Favourable

Workings

Total materials cost variance

	£
Standard cost of actual quantity 42,300 × £4.00	169,200
Actual cost	194,580
	25,380 (A)

Non-controllable variance due to season

	£
Standard cost of actual quantity 42,300 × £4.00	169,200
Seasonally adjusted cost 42,300 × (£4.00 + £0.72)	199,656
	30,456 (A)

Controllable variance due to other factors

	£
Seasonally adjusted cost 42,300 × (£4.00 + £0.72)	199,656
Actual cost	194,580
	5,076 (F)

Task 6.7

The total materials price variance is £26,000 Adverse

The non-controllable variance caused by the index change is £76,667 Adverse

The controllable variance caused by other factors is £50,667 Favourable

Workings

Total materials cost variance

	£
Standard cost of actual quantity 46,000 × £20	920,000
Actual cost	946,000
	26,000 (A)

Non-controllable variance due to index change

	£
Standard cost of actual quantity 46,000 × £20	920,000
Index adjusted cost 46,000 × £20 × 130/120	996,667
	76,667 (A)

Controllable variance due to other factors

	£
Index adjusted cost 46,000 × £20 × 130/120	996,667
Actual cost	946,000
	50,667 (F)

Task 6.8

(a) **MEMO**

To:	Managing Director
From:	Assistant Management Accountant
Date:	xx/xx/xx
Subject:	The use of standard marginal costing at Finchley Ltd

As discussed at our earlier meetings, because all companies within the Hampstead Group use standard marginal costing, Finchley Ltd will need to adopt the system from 1 August 20X8. This report is intended to demonstrate and describe the use of standard marginal costing in your company.

(i) (1) **Standard marginal cost of a unit of Alpha**

	£
Material (36,000m ÷ 12,000) 3m × (£432,000 ÷ 36,000) £12 per m	36.00
Labour (72,000 hrs ÷ 12,000) 6 hrs × (£450,000 ÷ 72,000) £6.25 per hr	37.50
	73.50

(2) **Standard cost of producing 10,000 units of Alpha**

	£
Material (£36 × 10,000)	360,000
Labour (£37.50 × 10,000)	375,000
Standard marginal cost	735,000
Fixed overheads	396,000
Total cost	1,131,000

(ii) (1)

	£
32,000 m should have cost (× £12)	384,000
but did cost	377,600
Material price variance	6,400 (F)

(2)

10,000 units should have used (× 3 m)	30,000 m
but did use	32,000 m
Material usage variance in metres	2,000 m (A)
× standard cost per metre	× £12
Material usage variance in £	£24,000 (A)

(3)

	£
70,000 hrs should have cost (× £6.25)	437,500
but did cost	422,800
Labour rate variance	14,700 (F)

(4)

10,000 units should have taken (× 6 hrs)	60,000 hrs
but did take	70,000 hrs
Efficiency variance in hours	10,000 hrs (A)
× standard rate per hour	× £6.25
Labour efficiency variance in £	£62,500 (A)

(5)

	£
Budgeted fixed overhead expenditure	396,000
Actual fixed overhead expenditure (£330,000 + £75,000)	405,000
Fixed overhead expenditure variance	9,000 (A)

(iii) Set out below is a statement reconciling the standard cost of production for the three months ended 31 May 2008 with the actual cost of production for that period.

	Fav £	Adv £	£
Standard cost of output ((see (a)(i)(2))			1,131,000
Variances			
Material price	6,400		
Material usage		24,000	
Labour rate	14,700		
Labour efficiency		62,500	
Fixed overhead expenditure		9,000	
	21,100	95,500	74,400 (A)
Actual cost of output			1,205,400

(iv) The total labour variance in the statement above (£47,800 (A)) differs from that in your absorption costing management report for the three months ended 31 May 20X8 because the original report compares the actual cost of producing 10,000 units and the budgeted cost of producing 12,000 units. It therefore fails to compare like with like. The report above, however, compares actual costs of producing 10,000 units and what costs should have been given the actual output of 10,000 units. The total material variances in the two reports also differ for this reason. There is very little point comparing a budgeted cost with an actual cost if the production level upon which the budgeted cost was based is not achieved.

The fixed overhead expenditure variance in the statement above also differs from the fixed overhead variance reported in the absorption costing statement. This is because the absorption costing statement compares overhead absorbed whereas the marginal costing statement compares overhead expenditure.

(v) There are other reasons why the reconciliation statement provides improved management information. (**Note**. Only ONE is actually required)

(1) It separates total variances into their components and so you will be able to determine whether, for example, the total material variance is the responsibility of the purchasing manager (price variance) or the production manager (usage variance).

(2) It avoids the use of under-or over-absorbed overhead, which is simply a bookkeeping exercise and does not reflect higher or lower cash spending.

(3) It allows management by exception.

(4) The original statement conveys the wrong message (that the overall variance was favourable).

I hope this information has proved useful. If I can be of further assistance or you have any questions, please do not hesitate to contact me.

(b)

	(F) £	(A) £	£
Standard cost of output			1,131,000
Variances			
Labour rate due to machine breakdown (W1)	2,520		
Labour rate due to normal working (W1)	12,180		
Labour efficiency due to machine breakdown (W2)		75,000	
Labour efficiency due to normal working (W2)	12,500		
Material price due to change in price index (W3)	38,400		
Material price due to other reasons (W3)		32,000	
Material usage		24,000	
Fixed overhead expenditure		9,000	
	65,600	140,000	74,400 (A)
Actual cost of output			1,205,400

Workings

(1)

	£
Total labour rate variance	14,700 (F)
Labour rate variance due to machine breakdown	
(12,000/70,000 × £14,700)	2,520 (F)
Labour rate variance due to normal working (balance)	12,180 (F)

Or:

	£
Actual amount paid during breakdown	72,480
(12,000 × £422,800/70,000)	
Should have paid	
(12,000 × £6.25)	75,000
Labour rate variance due to breakdown	2,520 (F)
Labour rate variance due to normal working (balance)	12,180 (F)

(2)

	£
Total labour efficiency variance	62,500 (A)
Labour efficiency variance due to machine breakdown	
(12,000 hrs × £6.25)	75,000 (A)
Labour efficiency variance due to normal production	12,500 (F)

(3)

	£	£
Total material price variance		6,400 (F)
Variance due to price index change 32,000 m		
should have cost (× £12 × 420.03/466.70)	345,600	
but should originally have cost (× £12)	384,000	
		38,400 (F)
Variance due to other reasons		32,000 (A)

···

Task 6.9

(a) (i) **Actual litres of material used** = actual total cost of materials/actual cost per litre
= £23,985/£58.50 = 410 litres

(ii) **Standard litres of material required for 40 barrels of X14** = standard litres per barrel × 40 = 10 litres × 40 = 400 litres

(iii) **Average actual labour rate per hour** = actual total cost of labour/actual number of hours = £2,788/328 hours = £8.50

(iv) **Standard labour hours required for 40 barrels of X14** = standard labour hours per barrel × 40 = 8 hours × 40 = 320 hours

(v) **Budgeted number of machine hours** = budgeted production × budgeted number of hours per barrel = 45 barrels × 16 = 720 hours

(vi) **Budgeted fixed overheads** = standard fixed overhead per barrel × budgeted production = £320 × 45 = £14,400

or = budgeted number of machine hours for processing department × standard rate per machine hour = 720 hours × £20 = £14,400

or = (budgeted machine hours for processing department/factory budgeted machine hours) × factory budgeted fixed overheads = (720 hours/1,152 hours) × £23,040 = £14,400)

(vii) **Actual fixed overheads** (for the processing department) = (budgeted machine hours for processing department/factory budgeted machine hours) × factory actual fixed overheads = (720 hours/1,152 hours) × £26,000 = £16,250

(viii) **Standard machine hours for actual production** = actual production output × standard machine hours per barrel = 40 barrels × 16 machine hours = 640 standard machine hours

(ix) **Standard absorption cost of actual production** = standard absorption cost per barrel × actual production = £984 × 40 barrels = £39,360

(x) **Actual absorption cost of actual production** = actual cost of material + labour + fixed overheads = £(23,985 + 2,788 + 16,250(a)(vii)) = £43,023

(b) (i) **Material price variance**

	£	
410 litres (from (a)(i)) should have cost (× £60)	24,600	
but did cost	23,985	
	615	(F)

(ii) **Material usage variance**

40 barrels should have used (× 10 litres) (from (a)(ii))	400	litres
but did use (from (a)(i))	410	litres
Variance in litres	10	litres (A)
× standard cost per litre	× £60	
	£600	(A)

(iii) **Labour rate variance**

	£	
328 hours should have cost (× £8)	2,624	
but did cost	2,788	
	164	(A)

(iv) **Labour efficiency variance**

40 barrels should have taken (× 8 hours) (from (a)(iv))	320	hours
but did take	328	hours
Variance in hours	8	hours (A)
× standard cost per hour	× £8	
	£64	(A)

(v) **Fixed overhead expenditure variance**

	£	
Budgeted fixed overhead expenditure (from (a)(vi))	14,400	
Actual fixed overhead expenditure (from (a)(vii))	16,250	
	1,850	(A)

(vi) **Fixed overhead volume variance**

	£	
Actual production at standard rate (40 barrels × £320)	12,800	
Budgeted production at standard rate (45 barrels × £320)	14,400	
	1,600	(A)

(vii) **Fixed overhead efficiency variance**

40 barrels should take (× 16 hours) (from (a)(viii))	640	hours
but did take	656	hours
Variance in hours	16	hours (A)
× standard rate per hour	× £20	
	£320	(A)

(viii) **Fixed overhead capacity variance**

Budgeted machine hours (from (a)(v))	720	
Actual machine hours	656	
Variance in hours	64	(A)
× standard absorption rate per hour	× £20	
	£1,280	(A)

(c) **Reconciliation statement – five weeks ended 31 May 20X8**

	£ (F)	£ (A)	£	
Standard absorption cost of actual production (from (a)(ix))			39,360	
Variances				
Material price	615			
Material usage		600		
Labour rate		164		
Labour efficiency		64		
Fixed overhead expenditure		1,850		
Fixed overhead efficiency		320		
Fixed overhead capacity		1,280		
	615	4,278	3,663	(A)
Actual absorption cost of actual production (from (a)(x))			43,023	

(d) **MEMO**

To: Judith Green, production manager

From: Accounting technician

Date: 7 August 20X5

Subject: **Croxton Ltd – analysis of variances for 5 weeks ended 31 May 20X8**

Following our recent meeting, I set out below some issues to consider in relation to our discussions.

(i) **Revised standard material price per litre** = £60 × 133/140 = £57

(ii) **Subdivision of material price variance**

	£	£
410 litres were expected to have cost (at the original standard of £60 per litre)	24,600	
but should then have been expected to have cost (at the revised standard of £57 per litre)	23,370	
Variance due to the change in the price index		1,230 (F)
410 litres should have cost, if the revised standard of £57 had been used	23,370	
but did cost	23,985	
Variance due to other reasons		615 (A)
Total material price variance		615 (F)

(iii) **Reasons for the occurrence of the material price variance**

A favourable material price variance of £615 was reported for the five weeks ended 31 May 20X8. The standard price used as the basis for this calculation was out of date, however, and was too high. If a more realistic standard had been used, the actual cost was in fact greater than the standard cost, not less than the standard cost. The purchasing department had therefore purchased material at a price greater than the realistic standard (although at a price lower than the out of date standard).

The purchasing department have therefore been inefficient, not efficient.

(iv) **Implications of one scrapped barrel**

(1) **Material usage variance**

The material usage variance shows that 10 litres more than standard were used. As the standard usage per barrel is 10 litres it is possible that the scrapped barrel is the reason for this adverse variance.

(2) **Labour efficiency variance**

The labour efficiency variance shows that eight hours more than standard were worked. As a standard eight hours should be worked per barrel it is possible that the scrapped barrel is the reason for this adverse variance.

(3) **Labour rate variance**

328 hours were actually worked during the five weeks. Overtime is paid on hours in excess of 320 hours, and hence an overtime premium of eight hours × £8 = £64 was paid in the period. Suppose the eight hours of overtime were worked because one barrel was scrapped (see (2) above). The total labour rate variance is £164 and so there is still £164 – £64 = £100 of the variance not explained by the scrapping of the barrel. This £100 would be due to other, unexplained reasons.

(v) **Why the fixed overheads might not be controllable by the processing department**

(1) The apportionment of both budgeted and fixed overheads to the department is done on the arbitrary basis of budgeted machine hours. Budgeted machine hours are determined by budgeted production volume, which is outside the control of the processing department.

(2) The actual overheads apportioned to the processing department are a share of total fixed overheads. The processing department is unable to control the fixed overheads incurred in other parts of Croxton Ltd, however.

Note. Only one reason was required for (v).

···

Task 6.10

(a) (i) (1) Actual number of meals served   = 4 meals × 7 days × 648 guests

= 18,144 meals

(2) Standard number of meals
for actual number of guests   = 3 meals × 7 days × 648 guests

= 13,608 meals

(3) Actual hourly rate of pay   = £5,280 ÷ 1,200 hours

= £4.40 per hour

(4) Standard hours allowed for
actual number of guests   = (648 guests × 3 meals × 7 days) ÷ 12 meals per hour

= 1,134 hours

(5) Standard fixed overhead per guest = budgeted overheads ÷ budgeted number of guests

= £38,340 ÷ 540 = £71 per guest

(6) Total standard cost for actual number of guests

	£
Meal costs (13,608 meals × £3 per meal)	40,824
Catering staff costs (1,134 hours × £4 per hour)	4,536
Fixed overhead costs (648 × £71 per guest)	46,008
Total standard cost	91,368

(ii) (1)

	£
18,144 meals should cost (× £3)	54,432
but did cost	49,896
Material price variance for meals served	4,536 (F)

(2)

	£
648 guests should have used ((a)(i)(2))	13,608 meals
but did use ((a)(i)(1))	18,144 meals
Usage variance in meals	4,536 meals (A)
× standard cost per meal	× £3
Material usage variance for meals served	£13,608 (A)

(3)

	£
1,200 hrs worked should have cost ($\times$ £4/hr)	4,800
but did cost	5,280
Labour rate variance for catering staff	480 (A)

(4)

Meals for 648 guests should have taken ((a)(i)(4))	1,134 hours
but did take	1,200 hours
Labour efficiency variance in hours	66 hours (A)
$\times$ standard rate per hour	$\times$ £4
Labour efficiency variance for catering staff	£264 (A)

(5)

	£
Budgeted fixed overhead expenditure	38,340
Actual fixed overhead expenditure	37,800
Fixed overhead expenditure variance	540 (F)

(6)

Actual number of guests	648
Budgeted number of guests	540
Volume variance – number of guests	108
$\times$ standard fixed overhead per guest ((a)(i)(5))	$\times$ £71
Fixed overhead volume variance	£7,668 (F)

(iii) **Bare Foot Hotel complex**

Standard cost reconciliation for seven days ended 27 November 20X8

Budgeted number of guests   540

Actual number of guests   648

	£		£	
Standard cost for 648 guests ((a)(i)(6))			91,368	
Cost variances				
Material price variance ((a)(ii)(1))	4,536	(F)		
Material usage variance ((a)(ii)(2))	13,608	(A)		
			9,072	(A)
Catering labour rate variance ((a)(ii)(3))	480	(A)		
Catering labour efficiency variance ((a)(ii)(4))	264	(A)		
			744	(A)
Fixed overhead expenditure variance ((a)(ii)(5))	540	(F)		
Fixed overhead volume variance ((a)(ii)(6))	7,668	(F)		
			8,208	(F)
Actual cost for 648 guests			92,976	

Note. (A) denotes adverse variance, (F) denotes favourable variance.

(b) **MEMO**

To: Alice Groves, general manager
From: Assistant management accountant
Date: xx.xx.xx
Subject: **Performance report for seven days ended 27 November 20X8**

This memorandum deals with a number of issues arising from the standard cost reconciliation statement prepared for the seven days ended 27 November 20X8.

(i) **Subdivision of the catering labour efficiency variance**

The adverse catering labour efficiency variance of £264 can be divided into that part due to guests taking more meals than planned and that part due to other efficiency reasons.

Standard hours allowed for 648 guests taking 3 meals ((a)(i)(4))	1,134 hours
Standard hours allowed for 648 guests taking 4 meals = (648 guests × 4 meals × 7 days) ÷ 12 meals per hour	1,512 hours
Excess hours due to guests taking more meals than planned	378 hours (A)
× standard rate per hour	× £4
Efficiency variance due to guests taking more meals than planned	£1,512 (A)
Standard hours allowed for 648 guests taking 4 meals (from above)	1,512 hours
Actual hours worked	1,200 hours
Efficiency variance due to other reasons (in hours)	312 hours (F)
× standard rate per hour	× £4
Catering labour efficiency variance due to other reasons	£1,248 (F)

(ii) **The meaning of the fixed overhead capacity and efficiency variances**

The fixed overhead absorption rate for our hotel is based on the budgeted overhead expenditure for the period, divided by the budgeted number of guests.

$$\text{Fixed overhead absorption rate} = \frac{\text{budgeted fixed overhead}}{\text{budgeted number of guests}}$$

If the actual overhead, or the actual number of guests, or both, are different from budget then over or under absorption of overhead may occur, so that there may be a fixed overhead variance.

A **volume variance** arises when the activity level is different from that budgeted, in our case if the actual number of guests is different from the budgeted number. In some organisations it may be possible to sub-divide the volume variance into two parts: the capacity variance and the efficiency variance.

The **capacity variance** arises when the utilisation of the available capacity is higher or lower than budgeted. It is usually calculated as the difference between budgeted and actual hours worked, multiplied by the fixed overhead absorption rate. Under or over utilisation of capacity can potentially lead to under– or over-absorbed overhead.

The **efficiency variance** arises when employees are working at a more or less efficient rate than standard to produce a given output. Producing output at a faster or slower rate could also potentially lead to under– or over-absorbed overhead.

(iii) **Calculating the fixed overhead capacity and efficiency variances for the Bare Foot Hotel complex**

The above descriptions of the fixed overhead capacity and efficiency variances highlight the need to be able to measure hours of work so that the volume variance can be subdivided.

It is not feasible to do this for the Bare Foot Hotel complex. We do have a measure of hours worked within the catering activity, but a large proportion of overheads are incurred on entertainment, for which we have no record of hours worked.

The absence of an activity measure based on hours worked therefore makes it difficult and meaningless to subdivide the fixed overhead volume variance into its capacity and efficiency elements.

Chapter 7

Task 7.1

Organisation	Possible productivity measures
Taxi firm	• Number of fares per shift • Number of miles per shift
Hospital	• Out-patients seen per day
Motorbike courier service	• Miles per week • Number of packages per day
Firm of accountants	• Chargeable hours as a percentage of total hours
Retail store	• Sales per employee • Sales per square foot of shop floor
Maker of hand-made pottery	• Number of pots thrown per day • Number of pots painted per day

Task 7.2

The total value added is £394,200

The value added per employee is £26,280

Workings

	£
Sales	1,447,600
Less: cost of materials	(736,500)
cost of services	(316,900)
Total value added	394,200
Value added per employee	£394,200/15
	£26,280

Task 7.3

(a)

	Calculation	Explanation
Efficiency ratio	92.61%	As the efficiency ratio is less than 100% this indicates that the workforce have not worked as efficiently as was anticipated. The actual hours worked are more than the standard hours for that level of production.
Capacity ratio	102.22%	The capacity ratio indicates whether as many hours have been worked as were budgeted for. In this instance the capacity ratio is greater than 100% meaning that the number of hours worked was more than those budgeted for.
Production volume ratio	94.67%	The production volume ratio is an indicator of how the volume of actual production compares to the budgeted level of output. In this instance as the production volume ratio is below 100% this indicates that the actual level of output was below the budgeted level.

Workings

Efficiency ratio $= \dfrac{\text{Standard hours for actual production}}{\text{Actual hours worked}} \times 100$

$= \dfrac{14{,}200 \times 3}{46{,}000} \times 100$

$= 92.61\%$

Capacity ratio $= \dfrac{\text{Actual hours worked}}{\text{Budgeted hours}} \times 100$

$= \dfrac{46{,}000}{15{,}000 \times 3} \times 100$

$= 102.22\%$

Production volume ratio $= \dfrac{\text{Actual output}}{\text{Budgeted output}} \times 100$

$= \dfrac{14{,}200}{15{,}000} \times 100$

$= 94.67\%$

(b) Hours worked @ 95% efficiency = $\dfrac{14{,}200 \times 3}{0.95}$

$\qquad\qquad\qquad\qquad\qquad\qquad\qquad$ = 44,842

$\qquad$ Hours saved (46,000 – 44,842) = 1,158 hours

....

Task 7.4

Gross profit margin	38%
Operating profit margin	12.7%
Return on capital employed	14.4%
Asset turnover	1.13
Non-current asset turnover	1.38
Current ratio	3.19
Quick ratio	2.19
Receivables' collection period	55 days
Inventory holding period in days	41 days
Payables' payment period	42 days
Interest cover	9.35 times
Gearing ratio	34.5%

Workings

(a) (i) Gross profit margin $\qquad$ = $\dfrac{\text{Gross profit}}{\text{Revenue}} \times 100$

$\qquad\qquad\qquad\qquad\qquad\qquad\quad$ = $\dfrac{1{,}007{,}200}{2{,}650{,}400} \times 100$

$\qquad\qquad\qquad\qquad\qquad\qquad\quad$ = 38%

$\qquad$ (ii) Operating profit margin $\quad$ = $\dfrac{\text{Operating profit}}{\text{Revenue}} \times 100$

$\qquad\qquad\qquad\qquad\qquad\qquad\quad$ = $\dfrac{336{,}600}{2{,}650{,}400} \times 100$

$\qquad\qquad\qquad\qquad\qquad\qquad\quad$ = 12.7%

(iii) Return on capital employed $= \dfrac{\text{Operating profit}}{\text{Non-current assets + Net current assets}} \times 100$

$= \dfrac{336,600}{2,337,500} \times 100$

$= 14.4\%$

(iv) Asset turnover $= \dfrac{\text{Revenue}}{\text{Capital employed}}$

$= \dfrac{2,650,400}{2,337,500}$

$= 1.13$

(v) Non-current asset turnover $= \dfrac{\text{Revenue}}{\text{Non-current assets}}$

$= \dfrac{2,650,400}{1,920,400}$

$= 1.38$

(vi) Current ratio $= \dfrac{\text{Current assets}}{\text{Current liabilities}}$

$= \dfrac{607,400}{190,300}$

$= 3.19$

(vii) Quick ratio $= \dfrac{\text{Current assets} - \text{Inventory}}{\text{Current liabilities}}$

$= \dfrac{607,400 - 191,200}{190,300}$

$= 2.19$

(viii) Receivables' collection period $= \dfrac{\text{Receivables}}{\text{Revenue}} \times 365$

$= \dfrac{399,400}{2,650,400} \times 365$

$= 55 \text{ days}$

(ix) Inventory days $= \dfrac{\text{Average inventory}}{\text{Cost of sales}} \times 365$

$= \dfrac{(180,000 + 191,200)/2}{1,643,200} \times 365$

$= 41$ days

(x) Payables' payment period $= \dfrac{\text{Payables}}{\text{Purchases}} \times 365$

$= \dfrac{190,300}{1,654,400} \times 365$

$= 42$ days

(xi) Interest cover $= \dfrac{\text{Profit before interest}}{\text{Interest charge}}$

$= \dfrac{336,600}{36,000}$

$= 9.35$

(xii) Gearing ratio $= \dfrac{\text{Total debt}}{\text{Share capital + Reserves}}$

$= \dfrac{600,000}{1,737,500}$

$= 34.5\%$

(b) Increase in cash balance $= \dfrac{£1,654,400}{365} \times (60 - 42)$

$= £81,587$

Task 7.5

(a)

	July	Aug	Sept	Oct	Nov	Dec
Gross profit margin	34%	34%	34%	32%	31%	31%
Operating profit margin	12%	12%	12%	11%	10%	9%
Expenses to sales %	22%	22%	22%	21%	21%	22%
Return on capital employed (W1)	15.2%	14.6%	13.1%	11.6%	10.9%	10.0%
Asset turnover (W2)	1.27	1.21	1.09	1.06	1.09	1.11

(b) Sales revenue decreased from July to September and then increased significantly until the end of the year. However the increase in sales has been at the cost of the gross profit margin which has decreased from 34% to 31%. Although the expenses to sales percentage has remained reasonably constant over the period, the operating profit margin has fallen due to the decrease in gross profit margin.

Return on capital employed fell dramatically in the first four months of the period although this was due to a significant decrease in asset turnover in that period more than a decline in profitability. The fall in return on capital employed continues in the last three months of the year due to the fall in operating profit margin; however the drop in return is not as bad as it might have been, as the asset turnover is again improving.

Workings

(1) Here, return on capital employed is calculated as

$$\text{ROCE} = \frac{\text{Profit before interest}}{\substack{\text{Capital employed} \\ \text{(shareholders funds + loan)}}} = \frac{(550 - 374 - 116)}{468 + 50} = 11.6\% \text{ for October, etc}$$

Alternatively, it may be computed as a return on net assets:

$$\text{RONA} = \frac{\text{Profit after interest}}{\text{Shareholders' funds}} = \frac{(550 - 374 - 116 - 3)}{468} = 12.2\% \text{ for October, etc}$$

(2) To be consistent with the ROCE definition used, asset turnover has been calculated as

$$\text{Asset turnover} = \frac{\text{Revenue}}{\substack{\text{Total capital employed} \\ \text{(shareholders' funds + loan)}}} = \frac{550}{468+50} = 1.06 \text{ for October, etc}$$

Task 7.6

(a)

	North	South	Central
Gross profit margin	32.0%	30.0%	35.0%
Operating profit margin	18.0%	11.1%	13.4%
Return on capital employed	16.0%	9.0%	14.0%
Asset turnover	0.89	0.81	1.04
Inventory holding in months	0.7 months	1.1 months	1.0 months
Receivables' collection period in months	1.4 months	2.3 months	1.6 months
Payables' payment period in months	2.1 months	1.3 months	1.9 months
Units per square metre	34.0 units	25.5 units	29.3 units
Units per employee	944 units	850 units	820 units
Units per hour	2 units	1.8 units	1.8 units

(b) In terms of profitability North is clearly the most profitable with the highest operating profit margin and return on capital employed. However Central has a higher gross profit margin which may be due to production of a different product to North or due to higher local selling prices or lower purchasing prices for Central. Although Central's operating profit margin is significantly lower than North's its return on capital employed is not so different due to a higher asset turnover in Central. South seems to have profitability problems with gross and operating profit margins, asset turnover and return on capital employed significantly lower than those of the other two divisions.

North again appears to have the best working capital control with the lowest inventory holding and receivables' collection period and the longest payables' payment period. Central's working capital control appears to be adequate but again there are questions to be asked at South with a relatively long receivables' collection period and a month shorter payables' payment period.

Finally, whichever way productivity is measured, the productivity at North is significantly greater than at either of the other two divisions. Central makes the same number of units per hour as South but less per employee, indicating that there could be room for improvement in employee productivity at Central.

BPP
LEARNING MEDIA

Workings

	North £	South £	Central £
Statement of profit or loss (Income statement)			
Revenue	870,000	560,000	640,000
COS: Opening inventory	34,000	41,000	34,000
Purchases	590,000	380,000	420,000
Closing inventory	(32,000)	(29,000)	(38,000)
	592,000	392,000	416,000
Gross profit	278,000	168,000	224,000
Expenses	(121,000)	(106,000)	(138,000)
Operating profit	157,000	62,000	86,000
Statement of financial position			
Receivables	100,100	107,300	87,600
Payables	(103,400)	(42,600)	(66,700)
Other net assets	983,300	625,300	594,100
Capital	980,000	690,000	615,000

	North	South	Central
Gross profit margin	278/870	168/560	224/640
Operating profit margin	157/870	62/560	86/640
Return on capital employed	157/980	62/690	86/615
Asset turnover	870/980	560/690	640/615
Inventory holding in months (using average inventory)	33/592 × 12	35/392 × 12	36/416 × 12
Receivables' collection period in months	100.1/870 × 12	107.3/560 × 12	87.6/640 × 12
Payables' payment period in months	103.4/592 × 12	42.6/392 × 12	66.7/416 × 12
Units per square metre	17,000/500	10,200/400	12,300/420
Units per employee	17,000/18	10,200/12	12,300/15
Units per hour	17,000/8,500	10,200/5,800	12,300/7,000

Task 7.7

(i)	Gross profit	=	380,000 × 0.48
		=	£182,400
(ii)	Sales	=	£425,000/0.34
		=	£1,250,000
(iii)	Gross profit	=	£85,000 × 0.40
		=	£34,000
	Operating profit	=	£85,000 × 0.115
		=	£9,775
	Expenses	=	£34,000 – £9,775
		=	£24,225
(iv)	Capital employed	=	£100,000/0.116
		=	£862,069
(v)	Asset turnover	=	0.10/0.08
		=	1.25
(vi)	Average inventory	=	(£158,000 + £182,000)/2
		=	£170,000
	Cost of sales	=	£158,000 + £560,000 – £182,000
		=	£536,000
	Inventory turnover	=	£536,000/£170,000
		=	3.2 times
(vii)	Sales	=	£96,000/48 × 365
		=	£730,000

Task 7.8

(a)

	Y/e 31 Dec 20X8	Y/e 31 Dec 20X7
Gross profit margin	45.3%	42.4%
Operating profit margin (Operating profit/Revenue)	18.3%	17.0%
Return on capital employed (Operating profit/ Share capital + Retained earnings + Loan)	14.7%	13.9%
Asset turnover	0.80	0.82
Non-current asset turnover	0.85	0.89
Current ratio	1.75	2.3
Quick ratio	1.2	1.6
Receivables' collection period	40 days	44 days
Inventory holding	31 days	36 days
Payables' payment period	61 days	51 days
Interest cover	11.0	9.6
Gearing ratio (Total debt/Share capital + Retained earnings)	25%	27.8%

(b) Return on capital employed has increased over the two-year period and this is solely due to increased profitability as both the asset turnover and non-current asset turnover have decreased over the period. There has been a significant increase in gross profit margin in 20X8 and, although operating profit margin has also increased, it has not done so at the rate of the gross profit margin, indicating that expenses are in fact increasing at a faster rate than sales. This may be due to a large advertising campaign which has increased costs but allowed the gross profit margin to increase or some similar reason.

As well as an increase in sales and profitability there also appears to be general improvement in the working capital management. Both the current and quick ratios have fallen but are still at acceptable levels. The receivables' collection period and inventory holding period have both been reduced by a few days and in combination with the increase in the payables' payment period by 10 days this will have a significant positive effect on the cash flows of the business.

The level of gearing does not appear to be a problem, as the gearing ratios are quite low and the interest cover is quite high.

Task 7.9

(a) To: Angela Wade

From: A Technician

Date: xx.xx.xx

Subject: **West Ltd and East Ltd – Performance Report**

(i) **Return on net assets (RONA)**

The ROCE is a key financial ratio which shows the amount of profit which has been made in relation to the amount of resources invested. It also gives some idea of how efficiently the company has been operating.

$$RONA = \frac{\text{Operating profit}}{\text{Net assets}}$$

$$RONA \text{ (West Ltd)} = \frac{3,068}{15,340} = 0.2 \times 100\% = 20\%$$

$$RONA \text{ (East Ltd)} = \frac{2,795}{6,500} = 0.43 \times 100\% = 43\%$$

(ii) **Net asset turnover**

The net asset turnover is one of the main ratios for the statement of financial position, and is a measure of how well the assets of a business are being used to generate sales.

$$\text{Asset turnover} = \frac{\text{Net revenue}}{\text{Net assets}}$$

$$\text{Asset turnover (West Ltd)} = \frac{17,910}{15,340} = 1.17 \text{ times}$$

$$\text{Asset turnover (East Ltd)} = \frac{17,424}{6,500} = 2.68 \text{ times}$$

(iii) **Operating profit margin**

The operating profit margin ratio is a measure of overall profitability and it provides a measure of performance for management. Unsatisfactory operating profit margins are investigated by management, and are generally followed by control action. Increasing selling prices and reducing costs will have a direct effect on this ratio.

$$\text{Operating profit margin} = \frac{\text{Operating profit}}{\text{Net revenue}}$$

$$\text{Operating profit margin (West Ltd)} = \frac{3,068}{17,910} = 0.171 \times 100\% = 17.1\%$$

$$\text{Operating profit margin (East Ltd)} = \frac{2,795}{17,424} = 0.16 \times 100\% = 16\%$$

(b) **Measure of customer service: faulty sales**

The percentage of faulty sales as a measure of the level of customer service is calculated as:

$$\frac{\text{Returns}}{\text{Gross sales}}$$

West Ltd $= \dfrac{100}{20,000} = 0.005 \times 100\% = 0.5\%$

East Ltd $= \dfrac{220}{22,000} = 0.01 \times 100\% = 1\%$

(c) **Further measure of customer service**

Another possible measure of the level of customer service which could be derived from the accounting data is the number of days between order and delivery of goods.

This can be calculated as follows.

$$\frac{\text{Time between}}{\text{order and delivery}} = \frac{\text{Orders received in year-net sales ('000 litres)}}{\text{Net sales ('000 litres)}} \times 365 \text{ days}$$

West Ltd $= \dfrac{20,173-19,900}{19,900} \times 365$ days = 5 days

East Ltd $= \dfrac{22,854-21,780}{21,780} \times 365$ days = 18 days

The amount of money which the subsidiaries invest in research and development, and training could also provide a measure of customer service.

(d) **Limitations of financial ratios**

Financial ratios as a measure of performance are only concerned with the data recorded in the accounts. For example, East Ltd appears to be a much more efficient company than West Ltd based on its RONA and net asset turnover ratios. However, when calculations are made to measure customer service, West Ltd has far fewer days between order and delivery of goods, and half as many faulty sales (as a percentage of gross sales).

The financial ratios also treat research and development, and training costs as expenses which are written off to the statement of profit or loss (income statement). These expenses are likely to have an impact on the future profitability of the company, and are more of an investment than expense.

Both West Ltd and East Ltd use plant of similar size and technology. There is however, a large difference in the net book values of the plant, and hence a large difference in the net assets of each company.

East Ltd purchased its plant before West Ltd, and has a lower cost, and a higher depreciation to date than West Ltd. These differences arise mainly due to the fact that the accounts are prepared using historic cost accounting. The fact that East Ltd's net assets are so much lower than those of West Ltd, means that the RONA of East Ltd will be much higher than that of West Ltd.

Task 7.10

(a)

Performance indicator	Workings	
Return on net assets	(Operating profit ÷ Net assets) × 100% (975,000/4,875,000) × 100%	20%
Net asset turnover	Revenue/Net assets 3,900,000/4,875,000	0.8
Operating profit margin	(Operating profit/Revenue) × 100% (975,000/3,900,000) × 100%	25%
Average age of receivables in months	(Receivables/Revenue) × 12 (325,000/3,900,000) × 12	1 month
Average age of finished inventory in months	(Average finished goods inventory/Cost of sales) × 12 (½ × (140,000 + 50,000)/840,000) × 12	1.4 months

(b) **Briefing notes on the usefulness of performance indicators**

Prepared for Angela Frear

Prepared by Financial Analyst

Dated: xx.xx.xx

(i) **Return on net assets**

The return on net assets can be misleading.

(1) Profits should be related to average capital employed but we compute the ratio using year-end assets. Using year-end figures can distort trends and comparisons. If a new investment is undertaken near to a year end and financed, for example, by an issue of shares, the capital employed will rise by the finance raised but profits will only have a month or two of the new investment's contribution.

(2) The RONA would be higher if costs such as marketing, research and development and training were not treated as revenue expenditure but were viewed as investment for the future and were capitalised.

(ii) **Operating profit margin**

The operating profit margin can be manipulated in a number of ways. The following activities would result in short-term improvements in the margin, but probably at the expense of the organisation's long-term viability:

(1) Reducing expenditure on discretionary cost items such as research and development.

(2) Depreciating assets over a longer period of time, so that the depreciation charge is less.

(3) Choosing an alternative inventory valuation method to increase the value of closing inventory.

(iii) **Average delay in fulfilling orders**

	£
Orders during the year	4,550,000
Revenue during the year	3,900,000
Unfulfilled orders	650,000

Average delay = (£650,000/£3,900,000) × 12 months = 2 months

(iv) **Measures of customer satisfaction**

As well as the delay in fulfilling orders, other measures of customer satisfaction include the following.

- Repeat business ((£3,120,000/£3,900,000) × 100% = 80%)

- Cost of customer support per £ of revenue (£400,000/£3,900,000 = 10p)

- Cost of customer support per customer (information not available)

(v) **Measuring performance from an internal perspective**

A number of indicators may help to measure performance from an internal perspective.

- Training costs as a percentage of production costs ((£140,000/£930,000) × 100% = 15.05%)

- Reworked faulty production as a percentage of total production ((£37,200/ £930,000) × 100% = 4%)

- Returns as a percentage of sales ((£100,000/£4m) × 100% = 2.5%)

The first indicator should be relatively high, the second and third as low as possible.

(vi) **Measuring the innovation and learning perspective**

The innovation and learning perspective could be measured with one of the following indicators.

- Revenue from new products as a percentage of total revenue ((£1.56m/£3.9m) × 100% = 40%)

- Research and development expenditure as a percentage of cost of production ((£750,000/£930,000) × 100% = 81%)

- Research and development expenditure as a percentage of revenue ((£750,000/£3.9m) × 100% = 19.2%)

Note. A fuller answer has been given here than was required in the task for assessment purposes, where in most cases only ONE point was required.

Task 7.11

(a) (i) Gross profit margin $= \dfrac{£221,760}{£633,600} \times 100\%$ $= 35\%$

(ii) Operating profit margin $= \dfrac{£76,032}{£633,600} \times 100\%$ $= 12\%$

(iii) Return on capital employed $= \dfrac{£76,032}{£95,040} \times 100\%$ $= 80\%$

(iv) Asset turnover $= \dfrac{£633,600}{£95,040}$ $= 6.7$ times

(v) No. of passengers in the year $= \dfrac{\text{Revenue (turnover)}}{\text{Fare per passenger}} = \dfrac{£633,600}{£1}$

$= 633,600$ passengers

(vi) Total cost per mile $= \dfrac{£633,600 - £76,032}{356,400}$ $= £1.56$

(vii) No. of journeys in the year $= \dfrac{356,400 \text{ miles}}{18 \text{ miles per journey}}$ $= 19,800$ journeys

No. of journeys per day $= \dfrac{19,800}{360}$ $= 55$ journeys

(viii) Maintenance cost per mile $= \dfrac{£28,512}{356,400}$ $= £0.08$

(ix) Passengers per day $= \dfrac{633,600 \text{ (from v))}}{360}$ $= 1,760$ passengers

(x) Passengers per journey $= \dfrac{1,760 \text{ (from(ix))}}{55 \text{ (from(vii))}}$ $= 32$ passengers

(xi) Number of drivers $= \dfrac{\text{Wages paid}}{\text{Wages per driver}} = \dfrac{£142,000}{£14,200}$

$= 10$ drivers

(b) **MEMO**

To: Chief executive

From: Management accountant

Date: xx.xx.xx

Subject: **Performance of Travel Bus Ltd for the year to 30 November 20X8**

This memo addresses a number of issues concerning the productivity and profitability of Travel Bus Ltd.

(i) **Productivity and profitability**

Productivity is the quantity of service produced (output) in relation to the resources put in (input). It measures how efficiently resources are being used.

An increase in productivity does not always lead to increased profitability. For example the number of passengers carried per driver, a measure of productivity, could increase. The extra passengers may have been attracted by offering substantial fare reductions, however, and this could lead to reduced profitability.

Another example might be an increase in productivity in terms of the number of journeys per bus. This increase in 'output' arising from the increase in productivity may not be saleable: the buses may be running empty. The revenue gained might be less than the additional costs incurred, leading to reduced profitability.

(ii) **Driver productivity**

A possible measure of driver productivity is the number of miles per driver.

	20X7	20X8
Miles per driver	$\dfrac{324{,}000}{8} = 40{,}500$	$\dfrac{356{,}400}{10} = 35{,}640$

The number of miles per driver has decreased between 20X7 and 20X8 and so, in terms of this measure of productivity, the drivers' claim that their productivity has increased is incorrect.

Even if the productivity had increased, the drivers might still be unable to claim that this had resulted in improved profitability. As discussed above, the extra miles might have been travelled with too few fare-paying passengers, so profitability would not necessarily have improved.

(iii) **Reason for improved profitability**

A major reason for the improved profitability was the Council's decision not to charge for parking. This reduced the overall cost of using the service for passengers, and demand therefore increased considerably. Since many of the costs incurred by Travel Bus Ltd are fixed, costs did not increase at the same rate as revenue, and profitability improved.

(iv) **Performance indicators to measure the satisfaction of passenger needs**

(1) The satisfaction of passenger needs could be monitored by the number of passengers per journey.

	20X7	20X8
Number of passengers per journey	30	32

Depending on the size of the buses, passenger needs may have been less satisfied during 20X8 because of more crowding or the need to stand because no seats were available.

Another measure of the satisfaction of passenger needs is the number of journeys per day.

	20X7	20X8
Number of journeys per day	50	55

This increase probably led to reduced waiting times and so passenger needs may have been better satisfied in 20X8.

(2) A measure of the satisfaction of customer needs that cannot be derived from the existing data is cleanliness of the buses.

Monitoring the cleaning cost per day or per bus might give some indication of the effort put into keeping the buses clean.

Another measure of the satisfaction of customer needs is punctuality of the buses and their adherence to published timetables.

Monitoring the percentage of buses arriving and departing within five minutes of their published time would give an indication of performance in this area.

Note. Only one measure required by the task

(v) **Monitoring the safety aspect of Travel Bus's operations**

(1) The safety aspect of Travel Bus's operations could be monitored by the maintenance cost per mile.

	20X7	20X8
Maintenance cost per mile	£0.10	£0.08

This has reduced, which may indicate a reduction in attention to safety, especially as maintenance costs are likely to increase as buses become older. No new buses have been added to the fleet (cost value of buses has remained at £240,000); the buses are older and likely to require more maintenance.

On the other hand, some of this reduction in the cost per mile may have been caused by the spreading of the fixed element of maintenance costs over a higher number of miles in the year 20X8.

Another indicator of attention to the safety aspect might be the average age of the buses. The depreciation charge for the year 20X8 was £12,000 (£180,000 – £168,000). On a cost value of £240,000, assuming straight line

depreciation and no residual value, this suggests a useful life of 20 years. Accumulated depreciation of £180,000 means that the buses were on average 15 years old by the end of 20X6, and thus nearing the end of their useful lives.

(2) A measure of the safety aspect that cannot be derived from the existing data is the number of accidents per year.

Another measure could be the percentage of maintenance cost that is incurred to prevent faults compared with the percentage incurred to correct faults. This would indicate whether faults were being prevented before they occurred, or whether maintenance was being carried out 'after the event', which could compromise safety.

Note. Only one measure required by the task.

Task 7.12

(a) **Budgeted statements of profit or loss (income statements)**

	Pickmaster	Pickmaster 2
	£	£
Revenue	1,125,000	1,125,000
Cost of sales		
Tea pickers	150,000	150,000
Tea processor operators (W)	48,000	4,800
Depreciation (W)	16,000	72,000
Seed and fertiliser costs	75,000	75,000
Total cost of sales	289,000	301,800
Gross profit	836,000	823,200
Administration costs	150,000	135,000
Distribution costs	350,000	350,000
Operating profit	336,000	338,200

Net assets at year end

	Pickmaster	Pickmaster 2
	£	£
Budgeted net assets	935,500	935,500
Operating profit	336,000	338,200
	1,271,500	1,273,700

Workings

	Pickmaster	Pickmaster 2
	£	£
Tea processor operators (10 × £6 × 100 × 8)	48,000	
(1 × £6 × 100 × 8)		4,800
Depreciation of tea machines (8 × £2,000)	16,000	
(8 × £9,000)		72,000

Tutorial note. The value of the new machines has not been included in the net asset figure as their purchase would have to be funded in some way ie bank loan, leasing, leading to an increase in liabilities which would cancel out the increase in asset values. This will not be an exact cancellation but we have no information about the method of funding.

(b)

	Pickmaster	Pickmaster 2
Gross profit margin	74.31%	73.17%
Operating profit margin	29.87%	30.06%
Return on net assets	26.43%	26.55%

Workings

	Pickmaster	Pickmaster 2
	%	%
(i) Gross profit margin		
$\dfrac{836,000}{1,125,000} \times 100$	74.31	
$\dfrac{823,200}{1,125,000} \times 100$		73.17
(ii) Operating profit margin		
$\dfrac{336,000}{1,125,000} \times 100$	29.87	
$\dfrac{338,200}{1,125,000} \times 100$		30.06

BPP
LEARNING MEDIA

		Pickmaster	Pickmaster 2
(iii)	**Return on net assets**		
	$\dfrac{336,000}{1,271,500} \times 100$	26.43	
	$\dfrac{338,200}{1,273,700} \times 100$		26.55

(c)

REPORT

To:	Managing Director
From:	Accounting technician
Date:	December 20X7
Subject:	Purchase of new machinery

I have been asked to write this report with regard to the decision as to whether to replace our current tea machines with eight new Pickmaster machines or Pickmaster 2 machines.

Performance indicators

(i) In terms of our profitability and return on net assets, there is little to be chosen between the two options. The Pickmaster machines give a slightly higher gross profit margin due to the much smaller depreciation charge, although costing more in terms of tea processor operators. However due to a reduction in administration costs if the Pickmaster 2 machines are purchased, then the gross profit and operating profit margins hardly differ under the two options. Equally the return on net assets under each of the two options is very similar.

Other considerations

(ii) Firstly we need to consider the funding of the purchase of these machines. If the Pickmaster machines are purchased then they will cost £160,000 (8 × £20,000) but if the Pickmaster 2 machines are purchased then these will cost £720,000 (8 × £90,000). These purchases will have to be funded in some way such as a bank loan or by purchasing them under lease finance. In either event if the Pickmaster 2 machines are purchased then this will significantly increase the gearing of the organisation and incur high service costs in the form of interest payments on a loan or finance charges on a lease.

The second consideration is the relative benefits and costs of the two machines. The advantage of the Pickmaster 2 is that only 1 operator per day is required rather than 10. However these operators are employed as and when needed on temporary contracts, therefore if the harvest was low less operatives could be employed. However the depreciation charges on the machines at £72,000 (8 × £9,000) for the Pickmaster 2 machines compared to £16,000 (8 × £2,000) for the Pickmaster machines are fixed costs that will be incurred whatever the level of revenue and harvest. Therefore if there is a low harvest investment in the Pickmaster 2 machines will depress profit.

(**Tutorial note.** A third consideration might be the expected residual value of each type of machine at the end of the 10-year period but only two further considerations were required for the task).

Conclusion

(iii) As the choice of machines has little effect on profit at the budgeted level but the Pickmaster 2 machines increase the risk of the operation, due to increased gearing and depreciation charges, then on balance purchase of the Pickmaster machines for £160,000 would be recommended.

Task 7.13

(a) **Performance indicators**

	September	October	November
Profit margin	$\frac{£148,687}{£690,000}\times100$	$\frac{£154,125}{£697,200}\times100$	$\frac{£125,480}{£672,000}\times100$
	= 21.55%	= 22.11%	= 18.67%

Direct material cost as a percentage of revenue

	September	October	November
	$\frac{£185,000}{£690,000}\times100$	$\frac{£185,100}{£697,200}\times100$	$\frac{£185,220}{£672,000}\times100$
	= 26.81%	= 26.55%	= 27.56%

Direct labour cost as a percentage of revenue

	September	October	November
	$\frac{£274,313}{£690,000}\times100$	$\frac{£275,975}{£697,200}\times100$	$\frac{£279,300}{£672,000}\times100$
	= 39.76%	= 39.58%	= 41.56%

Return on capital employed (ROCE)

	September	October	November
	$\frac{£148,687}{£1,211,000}\times100$	$\frac{£154,125}{£1,218,700}\times100$	$\frac{£125,480}{£1,204,700}\times100$
	= 12.28%	= 12.65%	= 10.42%

Alternatively:

	September	October	November
	$\frac{£148,687}{£2,011,000}\times100$	$\frac{£154,125}{£2,018,700}\times100$	$\frac{£125,480}{£2,004,700}\times100$
	= 7.39%	= 7.63%	= 6.26%

Meals produced as a percentage of orders

$\dfrac{115{,}500}{115{,}000}$	$\dfrac{116{,}200}{117{,}000}$	$\dfrac{117{,}600}{112{,}000}$
= 100.43%	= 99.32%	= 105.00%

Meals produced as a percentage of capacity

$\dfrac{115{,}500}{125{,}000}$	$\dfrac{116{,}200}{125{,}000}$	$\dfrac{117{,}600}{125{,}000}$
= 92.4%	= 92.96%	= 94.08%

(b)

REPORT

To:	Managing Director
From:	Accounting Technician
Subject:	Performance of the Catering Division
Date:	7 December 20X6

This report examines key areas of the performance of the catering division in November 20X6.

(1) Overall, the division performed significantly worse in November compared with the previous two months. Profit margin fell by 13% from 21.55% in October to 18.67%, and ROCE fell by 15% from 12.28% to 10.42% in the same period.

(2) The problem in the division arises from the difference between meals ordered and meals produced in November. 117,600 meals were produced, which was 5% greater than the number ordered of 112,000. As the meals are perishable, excess production one day cannot be used the next day, and so leads to wastage.

(3) The excess production in November meant that materials and labour costs were increased without the costs being recovered in increased sales.

(4) The division worked at 94.08% of capacity in the month. We would not expect full capacity at all times as work should only be done to fulfil orders placed.

(c)

	Renting	Purchasing
(i)	£	£
Revenue (120,000 × £6)	720,000	720,000
Cost of sales		
Materials (120,000 × £2)	240,000	240,000
Labour (120,000 × £1.50)	180,000	180,000
Fixed overheads	82,000	82,000
Rent	50,000	
Depreciation (£3m – £900,000)/(12 × 10 months)		17,500
Total cost of sales	552,000	519,500
Profit	168,000	200,500
Net assets		
(£1,204,700 + £168,000)	1,372,700	
(£1,204,700 + £1m + £200,500)		2,405,200

(ii)

	Renting	Purchasing
Profit margin =	$\dfrac{£168,000}{£720,000}\times100$	$\dfrac{£200,500}{£720,000}\times100$
	= 23.33%	= 27.85%
ROCE =	$\dfrac{£168,000}{£1,372,700}\times100$	$\dfrac{£200,500}{£2,405,200}\times100$
	= 12.24%	= 8.34%

(iii) Renting the machine gives a higher ROCE than buying the machine because the higher profit earned with a bought machine is outweighed by the large increase in net assets. Therefore the machine should be rented rather than bought. However, the ROCE is not necessarily improved when compared with the figures for October to November 20X6, and further consideration should be given to whether the machine is obtained at all.

Task 7.14

(a) **Sales price and sales volume:**

The sales price is higher for S1 which will improve the gross profit margin for S1. However, the sales volume is higher for S2, which will improve the gross profit margin for this product as there are fixed production costs that remain constant. This is because these costs will be spread over more units therefore increasing the gross profit per unit.

(b) **Material cost:**

The material cost per unit is constant which therefore has no effect on the gross profit margin.

(c) **Fixed production cost:**

The fixed production cost is constant which means that the increased volume will reduce the fixed cost per unit. This is because the fixed costs are being spread over more units. A lower fixed cost per unit will increase the gross profit margin for S2.

Chapter 8

Task 8.1

		Type of cost
(i)	Lost contribution on defective products sold as seconds	Internal failure
(ii)	Cost of replacing faulty products	External failure
(iii)	Claims from customers relating to defective products	External failure
(iv)	Products scrapped due to faulty raw materials	Internal failure
(v)	Training for quality control staff	Prevention
(vi)	Maintenance of quality control equipment	Prevention
(vii)	Performance testing of finished goods	Appraisal
(viii)	Costs of customer after sales service department	External failure
(ix)	Costs of inspection of raw materials	Appraisal
(x)	Costs of production delays due to re-working defective products discovered in quality inspection	Internal failure

Task 8.2

		Prevention	Appraisal	Internal failure	External failure
(i)	Zippers	Increase due to costs of design	No effect	Reduced as product is more reliable	Reduced as zipper has longer lifespan
(ii)	Jumpers	No effect	Increase as machines need to be checked regularly	Increase due to investigation, repairs to machines and re-inspection costs	Damages claims from customers and loss of future sales.
(iii)	Men's suits	Finding a new supplier	Increase due to inspection procedures	Lost contribution but reduction of costs as benefits from inspection controls are felt	Reduce as fewer defective products sold

Task 8.3

Explicit costs of quality

- Costs of repairing defective products
- Costs of quality control inspections
- Costs of repair of returned goods from customers

Implicit costs of quality

- The opportunity cost of lost sales to customers who are dissatisfied due to faulty goods and will not purchase from the organisation again.

- Loss of goodwill or reputation due to factors such as the widespread recall of one of an organisation's products.

- Costs of production disruption due to reworking of faulty products – these costs will be included in the production costs but cannot be separately identified.

Task 8.4

Prevention costs	None
Appraisal costs	£35,000
Internal failure costs	£16,000
External failure costs	£210,000

Workings

Number of estimated defective goods 10 million/1,000 × 3 = 30,000 units

	£
Appraisal costs – quality inspections	35,000
Internal failure costs – lost contribution on sales of seconds 4,000 × (£15 – £11)	16,000
External failure costs – replacement cost 30,000 × £10 × 70%	210,000
	261,000

Task 8.5

Quality inspection costs	£340,000	– appraisal cost – explicit
Lost contribution from seconds		
5,200 units × (£200 – £108)	£478,400	– internal failure cost – explicit
Replacement of defective units		
1,000,000/2,000 × 60% × £120	£36,000	– external failure cost – explicit
Lost customers		
1,000,000/2,000 × 40% × (£200 – £120)	£16,000	– external failure cost – implicit

Task 8.6

Under traditional costing methods the costs of a product are only recorded and analysed once production of the product has begun. However, it is recognised that a large proportion of the costs of a product are incurred before production has started in the early stages of the product life cycle. Life cycle costing recognises all of these pre-production costs of the product such as:

• Design costs
• Prototyping
• Programming
• Process design
• Equipment acquisition

The aim of life cycle costing is to ensure that all the costs of the product are accumulated over the whole of its life cycle in order to ensure that all costs are covered by revenue from the product.

Task 8.7

(a) The four general headings making up the cost of quality are as follows.

(i)   Prevention costs
(ii) Appraisal costs
(iii) Internal failure costs
(iv) External failure costs

(b) Examples of types of cost likely to be found in each category are as follows.

   (i)   Prevention costs. Maintenance of quality control equipment, training in quality control.

   (ii) Appraisal costs. Inspection of goods inwards, inspection costs of in-house processing.

   (iii) Internal failure costs. Losses from failure of purchased items, losses due to lower selling prices for sub-quality goods.

   (iv) External failure costs. Costs of customer complaints section, cost of repairing products returned from customers.

(c) Implications for the existing costing system

   (i)   If there are fixed price contracts with guaranteed levels of quality there are likely to be few, if any, material price variances or material usage variances due to poor quality.

   (ii) The cost of labour will effectively become a fixed cost, the actual unit cost of labour simply depending on the volume produced. Labour efficiency variances could therefore be calculated but they will not reflect costs saved or excess wages paid. Labour rate variances are likely to be minimal if there is a guaranteed weekly wage.

   (iii) Predetermined standards conflict with the TQM philosophy of continual improvement.

   (iv) Continual improvements should alter prices, quantities of inputs and so on, whereas standard costing systems are best used in stable, standardised, repetitive environments.

   (v)   Standard costing systems often incorporate a planned level of scrap in material standards. This is at odds with the TQM aim of 'zero defects'.

   Results of these implications

   (i)   There is less need for a standard costing system: variances are likely to be small or non-existent and, if incurred, non-controllable; the use of standards is inappropriate in a TQM environment.

   (ii) With the flexible work practices, capture of actual labour costs by individual jobs would be very difficult. Only material costs could be collected in the normal way. It is therefore unlikely that the full marginal cost of individual jobs could be collected.

(d) A cost saving not recorded in the existing costing system

   With the introduction of a TQM system, the cost of having money tied up in high levels of inventory will be saved. This cost would not normally be captured by Barnet Ltd's existing costing system.

   Note. A fuller answer has been given here than was required for assessment purposes.

Task 8.8

(a) **Background paper for meeting**

To: Jane Greenwood, Management Accountant

From: Assistant Management Accountant

Subject: Total quality management and the cost of quality

Date: xx/xx/xx

(i) **The meaning of Total Quality Management**

Total Quality Management (TQM) is a philosophy that guides every activity within a business. It is concerned with developing and sustaining a culture of continuous improvement which focuses on meeting customers' expectations.

One of the basic principles of TQM is therefore a dissatisfaction with the status quo: the belief that it is always possible to improve and so the aim should be to 'get it more right next time'. This involves the development of a commitment to quality by all staff and a programme of continuous learning throughout the entire organisation, possibly by empowering employees and making them responsible for the quality of production or by introducing quality circles. Customer-centred approach of TQM hinges upon identifying the 'customers', focusing attention on them and then meeting their needs in terms of price, quality and timing. Organisations must therefore be customer-oriented rather than, as is traditionally the case, production-oriented.

One of the goals of TQM is to get it right first time. By continuously improving towards zero defects, the quality of the product delivered to the customer is improved. The quality of output depends on the quality of materials input, however, and so either extensive quality control procedures are needed at the point where goods are accepted and inspected or quality assurance schemes, whereby the supplier guarantees the quality of the goods supplied, must be in place.

A small proportion of mistakes are inevitable in any organisation but more often than not those mistakes have been 'designed' into the production process. Because TQM aims to get it right first time, however, quality and not faults must be designed into an organisation's products and operations from the outset. Quality control must therefore happen at the production design and production engineering stages of a product's life, as well as actually during production.

In summary, TQM involves getting it right first time and improving continuously.

(ii) **Failure of the current accounting system to highlight the cost of quality**

Traditionally, the costs of scrapped units, wasted materials and reworking have been subsumed within the costs of production by assigning the costs of an expected level of loss (a normal loss) to the costs of good production, while accounting for other costs of poor quality within production or marketing overheads. Such costs are therefore not only considered as inevitable but are not highlighted for management attention. Moreover, traditional accounting reports tend to ignore the hidden but real costs of excessive inventory levels (held to enable faulty material to be replaced without hindering production) and the facilities necessary for storing that inventory.

(iii)/(iv) **Explicit costs of quality**

There are four recognised categories of cost identifiable within an accounting system which make up the cost of quality.

(1) Prevention costs are the costs of any action taken to investigate, prevent or reduce the production of faulty output. Included within this category are the costs of training in quality control and the cost of the design/development and maintenance of quality control equipment.

(2) Appraisal costs are the costs of assessing the actual quality achieved. Examples include the cost of the inspection of goods delivered and the cost of inspecting production during the manufacturing process.

(3) Internal failure costs are the costs incurred by the organisation when production fails to meet the level of quality required. Such costs include losses due to lower selling prices for sub-quality goods, the costs of reviewing product specifications after failures and losses arising from the failure of purchased items.

(4) External failure costs are the costs which arise outside the organisation (after the customer has received the product) due to failure to achieve the required level of quality. Included within this category are the costs of repairing products returned from customers, the cost of providing replacement items due to sub-standard products or marketing errors and the costs of a customer service department.

(v) **Quality costs not identified by the accounting system**

Quality costs which are not identified by the accounting system tend to be of two forms.

(1) Opportunity costs such as the loss of future sales to a customer dissatisfied with faulty goods.

(2) Costs which tend to be subsumed within other account headings such as those costs which result from the disruption caused by running out of inventory due to faulty purchases.

(b) (i) **Explicit cost of quality**

	£
Reworking (labour cost)	13,500
Customer support (contractors)	24,300
Store inspection costs	10,000
Cost of returns	4,500
	52,300

(ii) **Cost of quality not reported in the accounting records**

Opportunity cost (lost contribution from 100 X4s due to faulty circuit board) = £795 (W1) × 100 = £79,500.

Workings

(1)		£
Labour (W2)		200
Printed circuit board (£120,000 ÷ 1,000)		120
Other material (£121,500 ÷ 900)		135
Marginal cost		455
Selling price		(1,250)
Contribution		795

(2)		£
Total labour cost		193,500
Less cost of reworking		(13,500)
		180,000

Unit cost per good unit = £180,000 ÷ 900 = £200

* * *

Task 8.9

(a) The product life cycle is generally thought to split naturally into five separate stages:

- Development
- Launch
- Growth
- Maturity
- Decline

During the development and launch stage of the product's life there are large outgoings in terms of development expenditure, non-current assets necessary for production, the building up of inventory levels and advertising and promotion expenses. It is likely that even after the launch sales will be quite low and the product will be making a loss at this stage.

If the launch of the product is successful then during the growth stage there will be fairly rapid increases in sales and a move to profitability as the costs of the earlier stages are covered. However, these sales increases are not likely to continue indefinitely.

In the maturity stage of the product demand for the product will probably start to slow down and become more constant. In many cases this is the stage where the product is modified or improved in order to sustain demand and this may then see a small surge in sales.

At some point in a product's life, unless it is a consumable item such as chocolate bars, the product will reach the end of its sales life, this is known as the decline stage. The market will have bought enough of the product and sales will decline. This is the point where the business should consider no longer producing the product.

(b) If the future demand for a product is to be forecast using time series analysis it is obviously important that the stage in the product life cycle that has been reached is taken into account. For example, if the trend is based upon the growth stage whereas in fact the product is moving into the maturity stage then the trend would show an overly optimistic forecast for sales.

Task 8.10

Target cost = Market price – Desired profit margin

= £50 – (£50 × 20%)

= £50 – £10

= £40

Task 8.11

Target cost = Price – Desired profit margin

= £25 – (£25 × 70%)

= £7.50 per unit

Sales price per unit = £250,000/10,000 = £25

AAT AQ2013 SAMPLE ASSESSMENT 1
FINANCIAL PERFORMANCE

Time allowed: 2.5 hours

Task 1 (12 marks)

The budgeted and actual results for the month of June 20X1 are as follows.

		Budget		Actual
Production (units of X07)		14,000		13,500
Direct materials	17,500 litres	£28,875	16,800 litres	£106,000
Direct labour	3,500 hours	£59,500	3,650 hours	£65,700
Fixed overheads (absorbed on a unit basis)		£77,000		£79,500
Total		£165,375		£251,200

Complete the following sentences:

(a) The standard quantity of labour per unit is [   ] minutes.

(b) The budgeted quantity of materials needed to produce 13,500 units of X07 is [   ] litres.

(c) The budgeted labour hours to produce 12,000 units of X07 is [   ] hours.

(d) The budgeted labour cost to produce 13,500 units of X07 is £ [   ].

(e) The budgeted overhead absorption rate per unit is £ [   ].

A company budgeted to produce 25,000 units with fixed production costs of £436,250. The actual volume of production was 27,000 units and the actual fixed costs were £475,230.

(f) The fixed production overheads were [▼] by £ [   ].

Drop-down list:

Under absorbed
Over absorbed

Task 2 (16 marks)

A company purchases 3,700 kilograms of material at a cost of £10,915. The total material price variance is £1,665 adverse.

(a) **Complete the following statement.**

The standard cost per kilogram is £ ☐

A company purchases and uses 200,000 litres of material at a cost of £0.55 per litre. The budgeted production was 22,000 units which requires 220,000 litres of material at a total standard cost of £132,000. The actual production was 19,000 units.

(b) **Complete the following statement.**

The material usage variance is £ ☐ ☐▼

Drop-down list:

Adverse
Favourable

A company expects to produce 10,000 units of X using 6,000 hours of labour. The standard cost of labour is £15 per hour. The actual output was 12,000 units. 6,900 hours of labour were worked and 7,300 hours were paid at a total cost of £105,850.

(c) **Complete the following statement.**

The total labour efficiency variance is £ ☐ ☐▼

Drop-down list:

Adverse
Favourable

The idle time variance is £ ☐ ☐▼

Drop-down list:

Adverse
Favourable

Task 3 (16 marks)

Bert manufactures product RPB. Bert operates a standard cost system in which production overheads are fixed and absorbed on a unit basis.

The budgeted activity is for the production of 28,000 units at a total fixed production cost of £350,000. The actual volume of production was 30,000 units and the fixed overhead expenditure variance was £35,000 favourable.

Complete the following sentences.

(a) The fixed overhead volume variance is £ [_____] [_____ ▼]

Drop-down list:

Adverse
Favourable

(b) The actual fixed production overheads incurred were £ [_____] .

Ernie manufactures product RTF. The budgeted activity and actual results for the month are as follows.

	Budget	Actual
Production units (RTF)	64,000	67,000
Direct labour costs	£5,760,000	£5,896,000
Fixed overheads	£3,840,000	£3,950,000

Overheads are absorbed on a labour hour basis and the budget uses 480,000 labour hours. The actual labour hours used to produce 67,000 units totalled 536,000 labour hours.

(c) **Calculate the following variances.**

Variance	Amount £	Sign
Fixed overhead capacity		[_____ ▼]
Fixed overhead efficiency		[_____ ▼]

Drop-down list:

Adverse
Favourable

Task 4 (12 marks)

The following budgetary control report has been provided together with the variances calculated below.

	Budget		Actual	
Production (units)		12,400		13,600
Direct materials	37,200 kg	£130,200	37,400 kg	£112,200
Direct labour	24,800 hours	£223,200	28,560 hours	£285,600
Fixed overheads		£234,000		£221,000
Total cost		£587,400		£618,800

Variance	Amount
Direct material price	£18,700 F
Direct materials usage	£11,900 F
Direct labour rate	£28,560 A
Direct labour efficiency	£12,240
Fixed overhead expenditure	£13,000

The company normally prepares an operating statement under standard absorption costing principles but the financial director has asked you to prepare one under standard marginal costing principles.

(a) **Place each variance into the correct column (Favourable or Adverse) and complete the table.**

Budgeted variable cost for actual production			£
Budgeted fixed cost			£
Total budgeted cost for actual production			£
Variance	**Favourable**	**Adverse**	
Direct materials price			
Direct materials usage			
Direct labour rate			
Direct labour efficiency			
Fixed overhead expenditure			
Fixed overhead volume	▼	▼	
Total variance	£	£	£
Actual cost of actual production			£

Variances:

£18,700

£11,900

£28,560

£12,240

£13,000

Drop-down list:

22,645.16
N/A

A company has a budgeted overhead absorption rate of £95 per unit and budgeted production of 27,000 units. The actual production was 25,000 units and the actual overheads incurred were £2,423,600.

(b) **Complete the following statement.**

The [▼] of overheads is £ [ ]

Drop-down list:

Over absorption
Under absorption

Task 5 (12 marks)

Keta operates a standard costing system and uses raw material C2X which is a global commodity. The standard price was set based upon a market price of £450 per litre when the material price index for C2X was 120.50. The following information has been gathered:

- The price index increased to 126.525 in June X3.
- The raw material price variance for June was £375,000 adverse.
- 12,500 litres of material C2X were purchased in June.

Complete the statements below. In order to calculate your answers, you should split the raw material price variance into two components by calculating the part of the variance explained by the change in the price index and the part of the variance not explained by the changes in the price index.

(a) The part of the variance explained by the increase in the price index is
£ [   ]

(b) The part of the variance not explained by the increase in the price index is
£ [   ]

(c) The percentage increase in the index is [   ] %

Hamma uses product Z4QX and has collected data from the last few months in order to forecast the cost per kilogram of Z4QX in the next period.

	April X3	May X3	June X3
Cost per kilogram of Z4QX (£)	1,457.92	1,593.66	1,729.40

(d) **Complete the table below to forecast the expected price of product Z4QX in September and December X3.**

	September X3	December X3
Cost per kilogram of Z4QX(£)		

A colleague has calculated the least squares regression line (the line of best fit) as
y = 24.69 + 2.14x, where y is the cost per kilogram and x is the period. June X3 is period 41.

(e) **Complete the statement below.**

The forecast cost per kilogram, using the regression line, for September X3 is
£ [   ]

Task 6 (22 marks)

You have been provided with the following information for an organisation, which manufactures a product called Becks, for the month just ended.

	Budget		Actual	
Production (units)		20,000		21,000
Direct materials	80,000 kg	£880,000	83,000 kg	£954,500

The finance director has asked you to write a note to help in the training of a junior accounting technician. The notes are to explain the calculation of the total direct material variance and how this variance can be split into a price variance and a usage variance.

Prepare a note explaining the total direct material variance and how it can be split into a price variance and usage variance. Calculations should be used to illustrate the explanation.

....

Task 7 (20 marks)

You have been provided with the following information for two scenarios involving a company which operates an absorption costing system.

	Scenario 1	Scenario 2
Sales volume (units)	120,000	150,000
	£	£
Revenue	1,680,000	1,800,000
Gross profit	600,000	450,000
Profit from operations	275,000	200,000
Net assets	2,298,400	2,100,340
Inventory	147,950	167,500

(a) **Calculate the following performance indicators for Scenario 1 and 2. Give your answers to TWO decimal places.**

	Scenario 1	Scenario 2
Return on net assets		
Inventory holding period in days		
Sales price per unit		
Full production cost per unit		

(b) **Complete the table below for Scenario 3.**

	Scenario 3
Net assets (£)	£175,000
Return on net assets (%)	13
Profit margin (%)	14
Gearing (%)	32.75
Profit (to the nearest £)	
Sales revenue (to the nearest £)	

(c) **Fill in the boxes with the appropriate options to show how to calculate the gearing. If there is more than one correct answer either answer will achieve full marks.**

$$\frac{\boxed{}}{\boxed{}} \times \boxed{}$$

Options:

Total Debt	Profit	365
Net Assets	Total Equity	100
Total Debt plus Total Equity	Total Debt less Total Equity	%

Task 8 (12 marks)

Alpha makes two products, Tig and Tag. The following information is available for the next month.

	Product Tig	Product Tag
	£ per unit	£ per unit
Selling price	4,000	4,950
Variable costs		
Material cost (£400 per kilogram)	2,400	3,000
Labour cost	400	600
Total variable cost	2,800	3,600
Fixed costs		
Production cost	450	450
Administration cost	300	300
Total fixed costs	750	750
Profit per unit	450	600
Monthly demand	200 units	300 units

The materials are in short supply in the coming month and only 3,000 kilograms of material will be available from the existing supplier.

(a) **Complete the table below.**

	Product Tig	Product Tag
The contribution per unit is		
The contribution per kilogram of materials is		

(b) **Complete the following statement.**

The optimal production order for products Tig and Tag is ⬛⬛⬛⬛⬛ ▼

Drop-down list:

Tig then Tag
Tag then Tig

(c) **Complete the table below for the optimal production mix.**

	Product Tig	Product Tag
Production in units		

(d) **Complete the table below for the total contribution for each product.**

	Product Tig £	Product Tag £
Total contribution		

Alpha has been approached by another materials supplier who can supply up to 500 kilograms of material at a cost per kilogram of £500. This is a premium of £100 above the normal cost per kilogram.

(e) **Complete the table below.**

Should Alpha purchase the additional material?	Give a reason
▼	▼

Drop-down list:

Yes
No

Drop-down list:

The additional cost per kilogram is greater than the contribution per kilogram
The additional cost per kilogram is greater than the contribution per unit
The additional cost per kilogram is less than the contribution per kilogram
The additional cost per kilogram is less than the contribution per unit

Task 9 (12 marks)

Alpha Limited is considering designing a new product, product BPT, and will use target costing to arrive at the target cost of the product. You have been given the following information.

- The price at which the product will be sold has not yet been decided.

- It has been estimated that if the price is set at £40 the demand will be 500,000 units, and if the price is set at £50 the demand will be 430,000 units.

- The costs of production include fixed production costs of £8,500,000 which will give a production capacity of 500,000 units.

- In order to produce above this level the fixed costs will step up by £1,500,000.

- The required profit margin is 30%.

- The variable cost per unit is £13 for the production volume of 430,000 units.

- For production volume of 500,000 units the variable cost will be £12 per unit.

(a) **Complete the table for both levels of demand.**

	Sales price £40	Sales price £50
The target total production cost per unit		
The target fixed production cost per unit		
The target fixed production cost		

(b) **Complete the following sentence.**

Alpha should set the price at [▼] in order to achieve the target profit margin.

Drop-down list:

£40
£50

....

Task 10 (22 marks)

You have been provided with the following information for Alpha Limited.

Current position

The price is currently £22 per unit. At this price demand is 150,000 units each year. The advertising costs are currently £500,000 per year. The current factory can produce a maximum of 400,000 units per annum. The labour and material costs are the only variable costs.

Proposed position

The price will reduce to £18 per unit. Advertising costs will increase to £750,000 per year and it is expected that this will increase demand to 300,000 units per year. The factory will still be limited to 400,000 units per year. The labour and material costs are the only variable costs.

The forecast information for each scenario is shown below.

Income statement	Current position (Actual)	Proposed position (Forecast)
Sales price per unit	£22	£18
Sales volume	150,000	300,000
	£	£
Revenue	3,300,000	5,400,000
Direct materials	750,000	1,200,000
Direct labour	900,000	1,800,000
Fixed production costs	600,000	600,000
Total cost of sales	2,250,000	3,600,000
Gross profit	1,050,000	1,800,000
Fixed advertising costs	500,000	750,000
Administration costs	300,000	400,000
Profit	250,000	650,000

Income statement	Current position (Actual)	Proposed position (Forecast)
Material cost per unit	£5.00	£4.00
Labour cost per unit	£6.00	£6.00
Fixed production cost per unit	£4.00	£2.00
Fixed advertising cost per unit	£3.33	£2.50
Gross profit margin	31.82%	33.33%
Profit margin	7.58%	12.04%
Inventory of finished goods	£350,000	
Trade receivables	£500,000	

Draft a report for the finance director covering the following:

(a) An explanation of why the gross profit margin for the proposed position is higher than the current position, referring to the following:

- Sales volume
- Materials cost
- Labour cost
- Fixed production costs

(b) An explanation of what is likely to happen to the current asset position of the business by considering the following:

- Inventory levels (include a prediction of inventory level based upon the current inventory holding period)

- Trade receivable levels (include a prediction of the level based upon current trade receivables collection period)

To: Finance Director

From: Accounting Technician

Subject: Variances

Date: Today

(a) **Sales volume**

Materials

Labour

Fixed production costs

(b) **Inventory levels**

Trade receivables levels

AAT AQ2013 SAMPLE ASSESSMENT 1 FINANCIAL PERFORMANCE

ANSWERS

Task 1 (12 marks)

(a) The standard quantity of labour per unit is [15] minutes.

(b) The budgeted quantity of materials needed to produce 13,500 units of X07 is [16,875] litres.

(c) The budgeted labour hours to produce 12,000 units of X07 is [3,000] hours.

(d) The budgeted labour cost to produce 13,500 units of X07 is £ [57,375] .

(e) The budgeted overhead absorption rate per unit is £ [5.50] .

(f) The fixed production overheads were [under absorbed ▼] by £ [4,080] .

Workings

(a) 3,500 direct labour hours / 14,000 units = 0.25 hours (15 minutes).

(b) Budgeted quantity per unit = 17,500 litres / 14,000 units = 1.25 litres

13,500 units × 1.25 litres = 16,875 litres

(c) Budgeted labour hours per unit = 0.25 hours (see part (a))

12,000 units × 0.25 hours = 3,000 hours

(d) Budgeted labour cost per unit = £59,500 / 14,000 units = £4.25

13,500 units × £4.25 hours = £57,375

(e) Budgeted OAR = £77,000 / 14,000 units = £5.50 per unit

(f) Budgeted OAR = £436,250 / 25,000 units = £17.45 per unit

Overheads absorbed = 27,000 units × £17.45 = £471,150

Actual fixed costs	£475,230
Under absorbed	£4,080

....

Task 2 (16 marks)

(a) The standard cost per kilogram is £ [2.50] .

£10,915 – £1,665 = £9,250 standard cost

Standard cost per kilogram = £9,250 / 3,700 kilograms = £2.50

(b) The material usage variance is £ [6,000] [Adverse. ▼]

19,000 units should use (× 10 litres per unit)	190,000 litres
but did use	200,000 litres
Material usage variance in litres	10,000 litres (A)
× standard cost per litre (£132,000/220,000 litres)	× £0.60
Material usage variance in £	£6,000 (A)

(c) The total labour efficiency variance is £ | 4,500 | | Favourable. | ▼ |

The idle time variance is £ | 6,000 | | Adverse. | ▼ |

Workings

Labour efficiency variance

12,000 units should have taken (× 0.6 hours)	7,200 hrs
But did take	6,900 hrs
	300 hrs (F)
At standard rate	× £15.00
Efficiency variance	£4,500 (F)

Idle time variance

7,300 hours – 6,900 hours = 400 hours idle time

400 hours × £15.00 = £6,000 (A)

· ·

Task 3 (16 marks)

(a) The fixed overhead volume variance is £ | 25,000 | | Favourable. | ▼ |

	£
Actual production @ standard OAR 30,000 × £12.50	375,000
Budgeted production @ standard OAR 28,000 × £12.50	350,000
Volume variance	25,000 (F)

(b) The actual fixed production overheads incurred were £ | 315,000 |.

	£
Budgeted overhead	350,000
Actual overhead (Balancing figure)	315,000
Expenditure variance	35,000 (F)

(c)

Variance	Amount £	Sign
Fixed overhead capacity	448,000	Favourable. ▼
Fixed overhead efficiency	268,000	Adverse. ▼

Workings

Fixed overhead capacity variance

	£
Actual hours @ standard OAR 536,000 × £8.00	4,288,000
Budgeted hours @ standard OAR 480,000 × £8.00	3,840,000
Capacity variance	448,000 (F)

Fixed overhead efficiency variance

	£
Standard hours for actual production @ standard OAR 67,000 × 7.5 hours × £8.00	4,020,000
Actual hours @ standard OAR 536.000 × £8.00	4,288,000
Efficiency variance	268,000 (A)

Task 4 (12 marks)

(a)

	Favourable	Adverse	
Budgeted variable cost for actual production			£387,600
Budgeted fixed cost			£234,000
Total budgeted cost for actual production			£621,600
Variance	**Favourable**	**Adverse**	
Direct materials price	£18,700		
Direct materials usage	£11,900		
Direct labour rate		£28,560	
Direct labour efficiency		£12,240	
Fixed overhead expenditure	£13,000		
Fixed overhead volume	N/A ▼	N/A ▼	
Total variance	£43,600	£40,800	£–2,800
Actual cost of actual production			£618,800

Workings

Budgeted variable cost per unit = (£130,200 + £223,200)/12,400 units = £28.50

Budgeted variable cost for actual production = £13,600 units × £28.50 = £387,600

Total budgeted cost for actual production = £387,600 + £234,000 (fixed costs)

= £621,600

Direct labour efficiency variance

13,600 units should have taken (× 2 hours)	27,200 hrs
But did take	28,560 hrs
	1,360 hrs (A)
At standard rate	× £9.00
Efficiency variance	£12,240 (A)

Fixed overhead expenditure variance = Actual £13,000 lower than budgeted, so favourable.

(b)

The [under absorption ▼] of overheads is £ [48,600]

	£
Overheads absorbed 25,000 × £95	2,375,000
Actual overheads	2,423,600
Under absorbed	48,600

Task 5 (12 marks)

(a) The part of the variance explained by the increase in the price index is
£ [281,250]

	£
12,500 litres × £450 (original standard rate)	5,625,000
12,500 litres × £472.50 (£450 × 126.525/120.50)	5,906,250
	281,250 (A)

(b) The part of the variance not explained by the increase in the price index is
£ [93,750]

£375,000 – £281,250 = £93,750

(c) The percentage increase in the index is [5] %

(126.525 – 120.50) / 120.50 = 0.05 (5%)

(d)

	September X3	December X3
Cost per kilogram of Z4QX(£)	2,136.62	2,543.84

Difference between April X3 and May X3 = £135.74

Difference between May X3 and June X3 = £135.74

September X3 cost = £1,729.40 (June X3) + (£135.74 × 3) = £2,136.62

December X3 cost = £2,136.62 (September X3) + (£135.74 × 3) = £2,543.84

(e) The forecast cost per kilogram, using the regression line, for September X3 is

£ | 118.85 |

June X3 is period 41. Therefore September X3 = period 44

$y = 24.69 + 2.14x$ where y = cost per kilogram   x = the period

$y = 24.69 + (2.14 \times 44)$

$y = 118.85$

Task 6 (22 marks)

Total direct material variance

The total direct material variance simply compares the **flexed budget** for materials with the actual cost incurred. The flexed budget is the total budgeted cost of materials for the actual production; 21,000 units in this example. It is incorrect to calculate the variance as £74,500 adverse by comparing the actual cost of £954,500 with the budgeted cost of £880,000.

The flexing of the budget calculates the **quantity of materials** which are expected to be used to produce the **actual production**. Therefore, the expected usage of materials to produce 21,000 units is £924,000 (if 80,000 units costing £880,000 is required to make 20,000 units then it follows, assuming that the material cost and quantity is perfectly variable, that to make 21,000 units requires 84,000 kilograms at a cost of £11 per kilogram (£880,000/80,000)).

This flexed budget can now be **compared with the actual** costs to produce the total material variance of £30,500. This variance is adverse because the **actual cost was greater than the flexed budgeted cost**.

This total variance can now be split into two elements:

- The variance due to the price being different to that which was expected. The material price variance.

- The variance due to the quantity of material used per unit of production being different to that which was expected. The material usage variance.

The expected (standard or budgeted or planned) price is £11 per kilogram (£880,000/80,000) and therefore the expected cost of 83,000 kilograms must be 83,000 kilograms at £11 per kilogram. This is £913,000.

The price variance can now be calculated by taking the actual cost (price paid) for the 83,000 kilograms and comparing this to the expected cost. This results in £913,000, compared to £954,500: a variance of £41,500. This variance is adverse because the **actual cost is greater than the expected cost**.

The material usage variance is calculated by taking the quantity of materials which would be expected to be used to produce the actual volume of production. In this case 21,000 units were produced and the expected quantity of materials for each unit is 4 kilograms (80,000 kilograms/20,000 units). Therefore, to produce 21,000 units requires 84,000 kilograms of material. Compare this to the actual quantity used of 83,000 kilograms produces a variance of 1,000 kilograms. This is favourable and needs to be **valued at the expected cost** of £11 per kilogram.

The usage variance is always **valued at the standard cost** (expected/planned or budgeted) because the price variance has already been isolated. If both variances have been calculated correctly they should reconcile back to the total materials variance. In this example, the price of £41,500 adverse less £11,000 favourable is reconciled to the total variance of £30,500.

Task 7 (20 marks)

(a)

	Scenario 1	Scenario 2
Return on net assets	11.96%	9.52%
Inventory holding period in days	50.00	45.29
Sales price per unit	£14.00	£12.00
Full production cost per unit	£9.00	£9.00

Workings

Return on net assets
Scenario 1 = £275,000/£2,298,400 × 100% = 11.96%
Scenario 2 = £200,000/£2,100,340 × 100% = 9.52%

Inventory holding period
Scenario 1 = £147,950/(£1,680,000 – £600,000) × 365 = 50.00 days
Scenario 2 = £167,500/(£1,800,000 – £450,000) × 365 = 45.29 days

Sales price per unit
Scenario 1 = £1,680,000/120,000 = £14.00
Scenario 2 = £1,800,000/150,000 = £12.00

Full production cost per unit
Scenario 1 = (£1,680,000 – £600,000)/120,000 = £9.00
Scenario 2 = (£1,800,000 – £450,000)/150,000 = £9.00

(b)

	Scenario 3
Net assets (£)	175,000
Return on net assets (%)	13
Profit margin (%)	14
Gearing (%)	32.75
Profit (to the nearest £)	22,750
Sales revenue (to the nearest £)	162,500

Workings

Profit (to the nearest £) = £175,000 × (13/100) = £22,750

Sales revenue (to the nearest £) = £22,750 ÷ (14/100) = £162,500

(c)

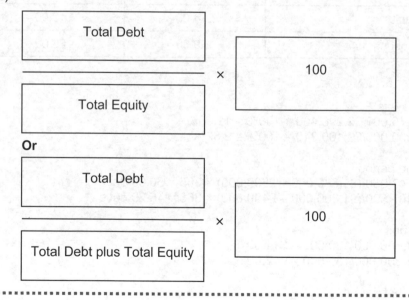

Total Debt
——————————— × [100]
Total Equity

Or

Total Debt
——————————— × [100]
Total Debt plus Total Equity

Task 8 (12 marks)

(a)

	Product Tig	Product Tag
The contribution per unit is	1,200	1,350
The contribution per kilogram of materials is	200	180

Workings

Contribution per unit

Product Tig = £4,000 – £2,800 = £1,200
Product Tag = £4,950 – £3,600 = £1,350

Contribution per kilogram of material
Product Tig = £1,200/6kg = £200
Product Tag = £1,350/7.5kg = £180

(b) The optimal production order for products Tig and Tag is Tig then Tag. ▼

(based on the contribution per kilogram of material calculated in part (a)).

(c)

	Product Tig	Product Tag
Production in units	200	240

Supply is limited to 3,000 kilograms of material

Product Tig then Tag (based on part (b)).

200 units of Tig × 6kg per unit = 1,200kg (so 1,800kg remaining to produce Tag)

1,800kg/7.5kg per unit = 240 units of Tag

(d)

	Product Tig £	Product Tag £
Total contribution	240,000	324,000

Product Tig = 200 units × £1,200 = £240,000

Product Tag = 240 units × £1,350 = £324,000

(e)

Should Alpha purchase the additional material?	Give a reason
Yes ▼	The additional cost per kilogram is less than the contribution per kilogram. ▼

Task 9 (12 marks)

(a)

	Sales price £40	Sales price £50
The target total production cost per unit	£28	£35
The target fixed production cost per unit	£16	£22
The target fixed production cost	£8,000,000	£9,460,000

Workings

Target total production cost per unit
Sales price £40 = £40 × 70/100 = £28
Sales price £50 = £50 × 70/100 = £35

Target fixed production cost per unit
Sales price £40 = £28 – £12 = £16
Sales price £50 = £35 – £13 = £22

Target fixed production cost
Sales price £40 = £16 per unit × 500,000 = £8,000,000
Sales price £50 = £22 per unit × 430,000 = £9,460,000

(b) Alpha should set the price at £50 ▼ in order to achieve the target profit margin.

Task 10 (22 marks)

To: Finance Director   **Subject:** Variances

From: Accounting Technician   **Date:** Today

(a) **Sales volume**

The sales volume is expected to increase by 2x (200%).

The volume increase will increase the profit margin if the fixed costs remain constant.

In this case the fixed production costs are remain unchanged and therefore the increased volume will improve the gross profit margin (GPM).

Materials cost

The material cost per unit reduces by 20% to £4 per unit which will also improve the margin for the proposed position. The doubling of the volume is likely to allow the company to purchase in greater quantities and access additional discounts.

Labour cost

The labour cost per unit is unchanged and therefore has no effect on the margin.

There have been no economies of scale or learning effect.

Fixed production costs

The fixed production costs are constant in total but the important point is that they are spread over more units. The proposed position increases the volume by 2x (200%) which reduces the fixed cost per unit. Fixed costs reduce by 50%. This will improve the margin for the proposed position.

(b) **Inventory levels**

Inventory levels are likely to increase significantly because the volume of demand is expected to be higher and therefore higher inventory levels will be needed to fulfil orders. Based upon the current inventory levels in relation to turn-over the forecast position will be that inventory levels may increase to around £560,000 (current inventory days = 350,000/2,250,000 × 365 = 56.78 days, therefore cost of sales of (£3.6 million/365) × 56.78 days = £560k).

Trade receivable levels

Trade receivables' levels are likely to increase significantly because the turnover increases. The current position is that trade receivable days are 55.3 days (500/3,300) × 365. Therefore assuming similar profile trade receivables will increase to around £820k (5,400.000/365) × 55.3 = £818k.

AAT AQ2013 SAMPLE ASSESSMENT 2
FINANCIAL PERFORMANCE

Time allowed: 2.5 hours

Task 1 (12 marks)

The budgeted and actual results for the month of June 20X1 are as follows.

		Budget		Actual
Production (units of XX6)		14,000		13,500
Direct materials	17,500 L	£28,875	16,800 L	£106,000
Direct labour	3,500 hours	£59,500	3,650 hours	£65,700
Fixed overheads (absorbed on a unit basis)		£77,000		£79,500
Total		£165,375		£251,200

(a) **Complete the standard cost card for the production of 1 unit of XX6.**

1 units of XX6	Quantity	Cost per unit £	Total £
Materials			
Labour			
Fixed overheads			
Total			

A company budgeted to produce 55,000 units with fixed production costs of £233,750. The actual volume of production was 57,000 units and the actual fixed costs were £241,000.

(b) **Complete the following sentence.**

The fixed production overheads were [▼] by [   ].

Drop-down list:

Under absorbed
Over absorbed

Task 2 (16 marks)

The budgeted activity and actual results for the month of August 20X1 are as follows:

	Budget		Actual	
Production (KK1)		18,000		15,000
Direct materials	9,000 kg	£60,750	7,800 kg	£55,770
Direct labour	5,400 hours	£47,250	4,230 hours	£38,070
Fixed overheads		£76,500		£71,300
Total cost		£184,500		£165,140

(a) **Complete the following table.**

Variance	Amount £	Adverse/Favourable
Direct material usage variance		▼
Direct material price variance		▼
Total direct labour variance		▼

Drop-down list:

Adverse
Favourable

Delta manufactures 5,400 units of product QR1 using 11,880 labour hours. The budgeted production was 5,000 units using 11,250 labour hours at a cost of £163,125. The labour rate variance is £14,850 favourable.

(b) **Complete the following sentence.**

The actual labour rate per hour is £ [   ] .

Task 3 (16 marks)

Albert manufactures product BRP. Albert operates a standard cost system in which production overheads are fixed and absorbed on a unit basis.

The budgeted activity and actual results for the month are as follows:

	Budget	Actual
Production units (BRP)	25,000	27,000
Fixed overheads	£1,043,750	£947,500

(a) **Calculate the following variances.**

Variance	Amount £	Sign
Fixed overhead expenditure		▼
Fixed overhead volume		▼

Drop-down list:

Adverse
Favourable

Gordon manufactures product PHT. The budgeted activity and actual results for the month are as follows:

	Budget	Actual
Production units (PHT)	54,000	50,000
Fixed overheads	£1,350,000	£947,500

Overheads are absorbed on a labour hour basis and the budgeted production was 54,000 using 270,000 labour hours. The actual labour hours used to produce 50,000 units totalled 265,000 labour hours.

(b) **Calculate the following variance.**

Variance	Amount £	Sign
Fixed overhead capacity		▼
Fixed overhead efficiency		▼

Drop-down list:

Adverse
Favourable

Task 4 (12 marks)

A budgetary control report has been provided for the manufacture of product PD98 and variances have been calculated.

	Budget		Actual	
Production (units)		450		520
Direct materials	337.5 kg	£20,250	338 kg	£25,350
Direct labour	1,080 hours	£12,960	988 hours	£14,820
Fixed overheads		£28,080		£31,300
Total cost		£61,290		£71,470

Variance	Amount
Direct materials price	£5,070 A
Direct materials usage	£3,120
Fixed overhead expenditure	£3,220
Fixed overhead capacity	£2,392 A
Fixed overhead efficiency	£6,760 F
Direct labour rate	£2,964
Direct labour efficiency	£3,120 F

Complete the operating statement for the manufacture of PD98. Do not use brackets or minus signs for the variances.

Operating Statement – PD98			£
Budgeted/Standard cost for actual production			
Variances	**Adverse**	**Favourable**	
Direct material price			
Direct materials usage			
Direct labour rate			
Direct labour efficiency			
Fixed overhead expenditure			
Fixed overhead capacity			
Fixed overhead efficiency			
Total variance	0	0	
Actual cost of actual production			

Task 5 (12 marks)

The cost per kilogram for a raw material used in the production of product TNG for the last three months is shown below:

Month	Actual price £	Seasonally adjusted price £
1	985	1,040
2	1,223	1,015
3	1,150	990

(a) **Complete the sentences below.**

The trend in prices is [   ] of £ [   ] per month.

The seasonal variation for month 1 is [   ] of £ [   ].

Drop-down list:

A decrease
An increase

Production costs for product MIN2 are semi-variable. The company uses the regression equation y = a + bx to forecast costs where:

y = total costs

x = units

a = fixed element

b = variable element

Data has been gathered on previous costs:

Units (x)	Total cost (y) £
8,000	52,000
12,000	72,000
13,500	79,500

(b) **Using the data provided and the regression equation, calculate the values of a and b.**

a = £	
b = £	

A labour rate index is used to forecast labour costs. The index base was set when the hourly rate was £12.

(c) **Complete the table below to forecast the hourly labour rate for each month to the nearest penny.**

Month	Index number	Forecast hourly rate £
March	103.9	
April	105.2	
May	105.7	

(d) **Based on your calculations in part (c), forecast the total labour cost for April assuming that 1,920 hours are worked.**

The forecast total labour cost for April is £ [   ]

Task 6 (22 marks)

Dickenson plc manufactures a range of products for use in the motor racing industry. The company uses a standard absorption costing system with variances calculated quarterly.

It is midway through quarter 3 of the current financial year and a number of events have occurred which may impact on the quarter-end variances for a particular product, MTRF1.

The production director has asked for a report indicating the possible effects of the various events.

Production notes for MTRF1

- MTRF1 uses a specialist industry material – POL89.

- Recent advances in the production of POL89 have increased its availability which has led to a reduction in the price per litre by 18% in the last month. It is expected that the reduction in price will remain until at least the end of quarter 3.

- The standard price was set before the decrease in price occurred.

- The quality control officer has tested the latest batch of POL89 and reported that it is of a higher quality than expected.

- The company implemented a strict material usage policy at the beginning of quarter 3 to monitor levels of wastage. This was overseen by the quality control department with no additional payroll costs being incurred.

- Employees usually receive an annual pay rise at the beginning of quarter 3 and this was included in the standard cost. Due to the current economic climate this pay rise has been suspended indefinitely.

- The budgeted production for the quarter is 12,000 units.

- An order for 3,000 units was cancelled shortly after the beginning of quarter 3. The company has been unable to replace this order and the actual production for the quarter is now expected to be 9,000 units. The production machinery needed to be recalibrated to deal with the higher quality POL89. In addition, one of the machines was found to be defective and required a complete overhaul. These costs are to be included in fixed overheads at the end of the quarter.

Complete the report for the Production Director on the possible impact of the above events on the POL89 price and usage variances, direct labour rate and efficiency variances and the fixed overhead expenditure and volume variances. The report should:

- **Identify whether each variance is likely to be adverse or favourable at the end of the quarter**

- **Explain what each variance means**

- **Provide one possible reason why each variance is likely to be adverse or favourable at the end of the quarter**

- **Identify possible links between the variances**

You are NOT required to make any calculations.

To:	Production Director	Subject:	Analysis of variances
From:	Accounts Technician	Date:	XX/XX/20XX

POL89 price variance

POL89 usage variance

Direct labour efficiency variance

Fixed overhead expenditure variance

Fixed overhead volume variance

Task 7 (20 marks)

The following information, shown in the Income Statement below, has been supplied for two different companies. The sales volume of Company A is 900,000 units and for Company B is 1,400,000 units.

Income statement	Company A	Company B
	£000	£000
Total sales revenue	37,800	49,000
Production costs		
Material cost	6,300	8,400
Labour cost	16,200	16,800
Fixed production cost	3,150	4,200
Total cost of sales	25,650	29,400
Gross profit	**12,150**	**19,600**
Selling and distribution costs	900	1,680
Administration costs	1,980	2,940
Advertising costs	1,260	3,220
Profit	**8,010**	**11,760**
Additional information		
Net assets	89,000	60,000

(a) **Complete the table below by calculating the performance indicators for Company A and Company B. If rounding is required, show your answer to two decimal places.**

	Company A	Company B
Selling price per unit		
Labour cost per unit		
Fixed production cost per unit		
Selling and distribution costs as a % of revenue		
Gross profit margin %		
Profit margin %		
Return on net assets %		

You have been requested to calculate control ratios for a company. The following has been provided to assist you in making the calculations.

Labour efficiency ratio

Standard hours for actual production/actual hours worked expressed as a percentage

Capacity ratio

Actual hours worked/Budgeted hours expressed as a percentage

Activity ratio

Actual output/Budgeted output expressed as a percentage

Data is available for two years:

	Year 1	Year 2
Budgeted production (units)	42,000	48,000
Standard hours per unit	0.8 hours	0.8 hours
Actual hours worked	30,920	38,720
Actual production (units)	37,200	51,000

(b) **Calculate the labour efficiency ratio for each year. Round your answers to two decimal places.**

Ratio	Year 1 %	Year 2 %
Labour efficiency ratio		

Task 8 (12 marks)

A company manufactures and sells an electronic product and is preparing information for the next period.

The marketing department has estimated that if the price is set at £70 the demand will be 10,000 units and if the price is set at £90 the demand will be 6,000 units.

The cost information below has been provided by the finance department.

	Option 1	Option 2
Sales price	£70	£90
Sales volume	10,000	6,000
Costs		
Variable materials cost	£20	£20
Variable labour cost	£10	£10
Fixed production cost per unit	£24	£40
Total cost	£54	£70

The production manager says that the capacity of the factory is 8,000 units.

(a) **Calculate the profit achieved if the price is set at £90 and the demand is 6,000 units.**

The profit achieved is £ [   ] .

(b) **Calculate the profit achieved if the price is set at £70 and the demand is 10,000 units but the factory can only produce 8,000 units.**

The profit achieved is £ [   ] .

An overseas supplier has offered to manufacture 4,000 units at a price of £45.

(c) **Calculate the profit achieved if the price is set at £70 with demand of 10,000 units, manufacturing 6,000 units and purchasing 4,000 units from the overseas supplier.**

The profit achieved is £ [   ] .

Company Alpha is developing a new product and expects the target cost to be £50 and will set the sales price to achieve a profit margin of 20%.

(d) **Complete the following sentence.**

The sales price per unit will need to be £ [   ] to achieve a profit margin of 20%.

Company Beta sells a product with a mark up of 30% on cost. The cost of the product is £80.

(e) **Complete the following sentence.**

The sales price to achieve a mark up of 30% is £ [   ] .

··

Task 9 (12 marks)

Beta Limited will be replacing some machines in the next year and needs to decide whether to purchase or lease the machines.

(a) **Calculate the discounted lifecycle cost of purchasing the machines based upon the following:**

- **Purchase price of £400,000**

- **Annual running costs of £50,000 in year 1 increasing by 5% for year 2 and another 5% for year 3 and then remaining constant for the next two years**

- **The running costs are paid annually in arrears**

- **A residual value of £35,000 at the end of the five years**

If there are nil cashflows for any years you MUST enter 0 in the appropriate box. Net cash outflows must be shown as positive figures and net cash inflows as negative figures (use minus signs).

Round to the nearest whole £.

Year	0	1	2	3	4	5
Cash flow (£)						
Discounted factor	1	0.952	0.907	0.864	0.823	0.784
Present value (£)						
Net present cost (£)						

(b) **Calculate the discounted lifecycle cost of leasing the machines for five years based upon annual costs of £140,000 paid annually in advance.**

If there are nil cashflows for any years you **MUST** enter 0 in the appropriate box. Net cash outflows must be shown as positive figures and net cash inflows as negative figures (use minus signs).

Round to the nearest whole £.

Year	0	1	2	3	4	5
Cash flow (£)			140,000	140,000		
Discounted factor	1	0.952	0.907	0.864	0.823	0.784
Present value (£)						
Net present cost (£)						

(c) **Complete the following sentence.**

Based on the calculations it is best to [▼] as this saves £[ ] .

Drop-down list:

Purchase
Lease

Task 10 (22 marks)

Wash4all manufactures washing powder for sale to supermarkets. Wash4all has several brands including Diz and Boold. The Finance department has produced the following information for each product.

Quarterly information	Diz	Boold
Unit information		
Sales price	£2	£2.50
Weight of materials in grams	1,000	1,100
Material cost per unit	£1.20	£1.43
Fixed production overheads	£0.40	£0.21
Full production cost per unit	£1.60	£1.64
Gross profit per unit	£0.40	£0.86
Gross profit percentage	20.00%	34.40%
Volume of sales	**400,000**	**750,000**
	£	£
Sales revenue	**800,000**	**1,875,000**
Variable production costs	480,000	1,072,500
Fixed production costs	160,000	157,500
Gross profit	**160,000**	**645,000**
Marketing costs	50,000	200,000
Profit	**110,000**	**445,000**
Profit margin	**13.75%**	**23.73%**

A new manager has asked for your help in understanding the figures for Diz and Boold. He has reviewed the information and has the following questions:

(a) Why is the gross profit margin of Boold less than double that of Diz when the gross profit per unit is more than double? Should the gross profit margin also be more than double that of Diz?

(b) I was told that the material cost is £1.20 per kilogram for Diz and £1.30 per kilogram for Boold. Therefore, I do not understand why the material cost per unit for Boold is £1.43. Is this correct?

(c) If the fixed production costs are constant does that mean they have no effect on the profit margin?

(d) Can you explain why Boold is more profitable than Diz?

Draft an email to the new manager answering his questions

To:	Manager	Subject:	Diz and Boold
From:	Accounting Technician	Date:	Today

(a) **Why is the gross profit margin of Boold less than double that of Diz when the gross profit per unit is more than double? Should the gross profit margin also be more than double that of Diz?**

(b) **I was told that the material cost is £1.20 per kilogram for Diz and £1.30 per kilogram for Boold. Therefore, I do not understand why the material cost per unit for Boold is £1.43. Is this correct?**

(c) **If the fixed production costs are constant does that mean they have no effect on the profit margin?**

(d) **Can you explain why Boold is more profitable than Diz?**

AAT AQ2013 SAMPLE ASSESSMENT 2
FINANCIAL PERFORMANCE

ANSWERS

Task 1 (12 marks)

(a)

1 unit of XX6	Quantity	Cost per unit £	Total £
Materials	1.25	1.65	2.06
Labour	0.25	17.00	4.25
Fixed overheads	1	5.50	5.50
Total			11.81

Workings

Standard materials quantity per unit of XX6: $\dfrac{17,500}{14,000}$ = 1.25 litres

Standard labour quantity per unit of XX6: $\dfrac{3,500}{14,000}$ = 0.25 hours

Standard fixed overhead units: Fixed overheads absorbed on a unit basis = 1

Standard materials cost per litre: $\dfrac{£28,875}{17,500}$ = £1.65

Standard labour rate per hour: $\dfrac{£59,500}{3,500}$ = £17.00

Fixed overheads cost per unit: $\dfrac{£77,000}{14,000}$ = £5.50

Materials total cost per unit of XX6: $\dfrac{£28,875}{14,000}$ = £2.06

Labour total cost per unit of XX6: $\dfrac{£59,500}{14,000}$ = £4.25

Fixed overheads total cost per unit of XX6: $\dfrac{£77,000}{14,000}$ = £5.50

(b)   The fixed production overheads were | over absorbed | by | 1250 | .

Workings

Budgeted overhead absorption rate per unit: $\dfrac{£233,750}{55,000} = £4.25$

Overhead absorbed = actual production at the standard rate: 57,000 × £4.25 = £242,250.

Actual fixed costs incurred: £241,000.

£242,250 – £241,000 = £1,250.

....

Task 2 (16 marks)

(a)

Variance	Amount £	Adverse / Favourable
Direct material usage variance	2,025	Adverse
Direct material price variance	3,120	Adverse
Total direct labour variance	1,305	Favourable

Workings

Direct material usage variance

Budgeted direct material per unit of KK1: $\dfrac{9,000\,kg}{18,000\,units} = 0.5kg$

Budgeted direct material price per kg: $\dfrac{£60,750}{9,000} = £6.75$

15,000 units should have used (× 0.5kg)	7,500 kg
But did use	7,800 kg
Variance in kg	300 kg Adverse
× standard cost per kg	× £6.75
Variance in £	£2,025 Adverse

Direct material price variance

	£
7,800 kg should have cost (× £6.75)	52,650
But did cost	55,770
Direct material price variance	3,120 Adverse

Total direct labour variance

Standard hours per unit $\dfrac{5,400\,hrs}{18,000\,units}$ = 0.3 hours per unit

Standard labour cost per hour $\dfrac{47,250}{5,400\,hrs}$ = £8.75 per hr

Therefore one unit should cost 0.3 hours × £8.75 = £2.625

	£
Actual production should have cost 15,000 units × £2.625	39,375
But did cost	38,070
Variance	1,305 Favourable

Delta manufactures 5,400 units of product QR1 using 11,880 labour hours. The budgeted production was 5,000 units using 11,250 labour hours at a cost of £163,125. The labour rate variance is £14,850 favourable.

(b)   The actual labour rate per hour is £ [13.25] .

Workings

Standard labour rate per hour: $\dfrac{£163,125}{11,250}$ = £14.50 hr

Actual production at standard labour rate: 11,880 × £14.50 = £172,260

Adjust for the variance: £172,260 – £14,850 = £157,410

Calculate actual rate based on actual hours: $\dfrac{£157,410}{11,880}$ = £13.25 hr

Task 3 (16 marks)

(a)

Variance	Amount £	Sign
Fixed overhead expenditure	96,250	Favourable
Fixed overhead volume	83,500	Favourable

Workings

Fixed overhead expenditure variance: (£1,043,750 – £947,500) = £96,250 Favourable

Fixed overhead expenditure budgeted absorption rate: $\dfrac{£1,043,750}{25,000}$ = £41.75 per unit

Fixed overhead volume variance: (27,000 units – 25,000 units) × £41.75 = £83,500 Favourable

(b)

Variance	Amount £	Sign
Fixed overhead capacity	25,000	Adverse
Fixed overhead efficiency	75,000	Adverse

Workings

Budgeted labour hours per unit: $\dfrac{270,000 \text{ hrs}}{54,000 \text{ units}}$ = 5 hours per unit

Fixed overhead budgeted overhead absorption rate: $\dfrac{£1,350,000}{270,000}$ = £5 per hr

Fixed overhead capacity variance

Budgeted hours of work	270,000 hours
Actual hours of work	265,000 hours
Fixed overhead capacity variance in hours	5,000 hours Adverse
× standard fixed o/h absorption rate	× £5
Fixed overhead capacity variance in £	£25,000 Adverse

Fixed overhead efficiency variance

Actual units should take (50,000 × 5 hrs)	250,000 hrs
But did take	265,000 hrs
Variance in hours	15,000 hrs Adverse
× standard fixed o/h absorption rate	× £5
Fixed overhead efficiency variance	£75,000 Adverse

··

Task 4 (12 marks)

Operating statement – PD98			£
Budgeted/Standard cost for actual production			70,824
Variances	**Adverse**	**Favourable**	
Direct materials price	5,070		
Direct materials usage		3,120	
Direct labour rate	2,964		
Direct labour efficiency		3,120	
Fixed overhead expenditure	3,220		
Fixed overhead capacity	2,392		
Fixed overhead efficiency		6,760	
Total variance	13,646	13,000	646
Actual cost of actual production			71,470

Workings

Budgeted/Standard cost for actual production, $\left(\dfrac{£61,290}{450}\right) \times 520 = £70,824$

Direct materials price variance: given in the question.

Direct materials usage variance:

520 units should use $\left(\dfrac{337.5\,kg}{450} = 0.75\,kg\right) = 390\,kg$

But did use   338 kg

Variance in kg   52 kg Favourable

Therefore the variance in the question is favourable.

Direct labour rate variance:

$$\frac{£12,960}{1,080} = £12 \text{ hr}$$

Actual hours should cost (£12 × 988) £11,856

But did cost   £14,820

                                                     £2,964 Adverse

Therefore the £2,964 variance, as provided in the question is Adverse.

Direct labour efficiency variance: given in the question.

Fixed overhead expenditure variance: £3,220 figure given in question. Variance is Adverse as the £31,300 Actual figure is higher than the £28,080 Budget figure.

Fixed overhead capacity variance: given in the question.

Fixed overhead efficiency variance: given in the question.

Task 5 (12 marks)

(a) The trend in prices is | a decrease | of £ | 25 | per month.

The seasonal variation for month 1 is | a decrease | of £ | 55 |.

Workings

£1,040 – **£25** = £1,015   £1,015 – **£25** = £990

£1,040 – £985 = £55

(b)

a = £	12,000
b = £	5

Workings

1: 52,000 = a + (b × 8,000)

2: 72,000 = a + (b × 12,000)

3: 79,500 = a + (b × 13,500)

Equation 2 less Equation 1 gives:

20,000 = (b × 4,000)

b = £5

Substitute b in equation 3

79,500 = a + (5 × 13,500)

79,500 = a + 67,500

a = £12,000

Alternatively you could have used the high-low method to calculate a and b.

(c)

Month	Index number	Forecast hourly rate £
March	103.9	12.47
April	105.2	12.62
May	105.7	12.68

Workings

Index base 100 = £12

$$\left(\frac{103.9}{100}\right) \times £12 = £12.47$$

$$\left(\frac{105.2}{100}\right) \times £12 = £12.62$$

$$\left(\frac{105.7}{100}\right) \times £12 = £12.68$$

(d)   The forecast total hour cost for April is £ | 24,230.40 |

Workings

1,920 × £12.62 = £24,230.40

Task 6 (22 marks)

POL89 price variance

The POL89 price variance is likely to be favourable.

This is due to a reduction in price of 18% during the quarter, resulting in the actual price being lower than the standard price.

The quality of the latest batch of POL89 is higher than expected even though the price is lower, which may lead to a favourable POL89 usage variance.

POL89 usage variance

The POL89 usage variance is likely to be favourable.

The purchase of a higher quality product would usually be expected to result in less wastage, and therefore the actual quantity used would be lower than the standard usage.

The usage and price variances are often linked when a higher priced and therefore higher quality product may reduce wastage costs, however in this case the higher quality is probably due to the advances in production of POL89 and so is unlikely to be linked with the POL89 price variance.

Employees may be demotivated from the lack of pay rise but the new material usage control policy recently implemented should keep material usage favourable.

Direct labour efficiency variance

The direct labour efficiency variance is likely to be adverse, with each unit taking more hours to manufacture than expected.

Efficiency will be affected by the demotivational effects of the suspension of the pay rise.

In addition the cancelled order means that production will be lower by 25% during the quarter and there is likely to be idle time for employees which will have an adverse effect on the labour efficiency.

Fixed overhead expenditure variance

The fixed overhead expenditure variance is likely to be adverse, due to costs of recalibrating the machines and the repair of the defective machine. Therefore the actual fixed overheads will be higher than expected.

Fixed overhead volume variance

The fixed overhead volume variance is likely to be adverse because the actual volume produced is likely to be 25% lower than the forecast volume due to the cancellation of the order for 3,000 units. Therefore overheads are likely to be under-absorbed.

Task 7 (20 marks)

(a)

	Company A	Company B
Selling price per unit	42	35
Labour cost per unit	18	12
Fixed production cost per unit	3.50	3.00
Selling and distribution costs as a % of revenue	2.38	3.43
Gross profit margin %	32.14	40
Profit margin %	21.19	24
Return on net assets %	9	19.60

Workings

Selling price per unit Company A $\dfrac{37,800,000}{900,000} = £42$

Selling price per unit Company B $\dfrac{49,000,000}{1,400,000} = £35$

Labour cost per unit Company A $\dfrac{16,200,000}{900,000} = £18$

Labour cost per unit Company B $\dfrac{16,800,000}{1,400,000} = £12$

Fixed production cost per unit Company A $\dfrac{3,150,000}{900,000} = £3.50$

Fixed production cost per unit Company B $\dfrac{4,200,000}{1,400,000} = £3$

Selling and distribution costs as a % of revenue Company A $\left(\dfrac{900,000}{37,800,000}\right) \times 100 = 2.38\%$

Selling and distribution costs as a % of revenue Company B $\left(\dfrac{1,680,000}{49,000,000}\right) \times 100 = 3.43\%$

Gross profit margin % Company A $\left(\dfrac{12,150,000}{37,800,000}\right) \times 100 = 32.14\%$

Gross profit margin % Company B $\left(\dfrac{19,600,000}{49,000,000}\right) \times 100 = 40\%$

Profit margin % Company A $\left(\dfrac{8,010,000}{37,800,000}\right)$ × 100 = 21.19%

Profit margin % Company B $\left(\dfrac{11,760,000}{49,000,000}\right)$ × 100 = 24%

Return on net assets % Company A $\left(\dfrac{8,010,000}{89,000,000}\right)$ × 100 = 9%

Return on net assets % Company B $\left(\dfrac{11,760,000}{60,000,000}\right)$ × 100 = 19.6%

(b)

Ratio	Year 1 %	Year 2 %
Labour efficiency ratio	96.25	105.37

Workings

Year 1 $\left(\dfrac{(37,200\times0.8)}{30,920}\right)$ × 100 = 96.25%

Year 2 $\left(\dfrac{(51,000\times0.8)}{38,720}\right)$ × 100 = 105.37%

Task 8 (12 marks)

(a) The profit achieved is £ 120,000 .

(b) The profit achieved is £ 80,000 .

(c) The profit achieved is £ 100,000 .

(d) The sales price per unit will need to be £ 62.50 to achieve a profit margin of 20%.

(e) The sales price to achieve a mark up of 30% is £ 104 .

Workings

(a)   6,000 × £90 = £540,000. Less: 6,000 × £70 = £420,000. Profit £120,000

(b)   8,000 × £70 = £560,000. Less: 8,000 × £60 = £480,000. Profit £80,000

   Note. The £60 cost per unit includes £30 fixed costs (£240,000/8,000).

(c)   Breakeven on the 6,000 units manufactured and sold at £70

   Profit of £25 per unit on the units from overseas, 4,000 × £25 = £100,000

(d) $\dfrac{£50}{(1-0.2)}$ = £62.50. Proof: £62.50 less £50 = £12.50

   Profit margin: $\left(\dfrac{12.50}{62.50}\right)$ × 100 = 20%

(e)   £80/100 × 130 = £104

Task 9 (12 marks)

(a)

Year	0	1	2	3	4	5
Cash flow (£)	400,000	50,000	52,500	55,125	55,125	20,125
Discounted factor	1	0.952	0.907	0.864	0.823	0.784
Present value (£)	400,000	47,600	47,618*	47,628	45,368*	15,778
Net present cost (£)	603,992					

Workings

*Note that the question states that you should 'round to the nearest whole pound'.

The figures are clearly signposted in the question.

Note that Year 5 cash flow figure includes the cash inflow for the residual value, so is calculated as £55,125 – £35,000 = £20,125.

(b)

Year	0	1	2	3	4	5
Cash flow (£)	140,000	140,000	140,000	140,000	140,000	0
Discounted factor	1	0.952	0.907	0.864	0.823	0.784
Present value (£)	140,000	133,280	126,980	120,960	115,220	0
Net present cost (£)	636,440					

Workings

Ensure you enter the annual lease payments in the correct years. The lease fee is paid in advance (so the year 1 fee is paid in year 0). The lease is for five years, so the final year fee will be paid in advance in year 4.

(c) Based on the calculations it is best to | purchase | as this saves

£ | 32,448 | .

Workings

£636,440 – £603,992 = £32,448

- -

Task 10 (22 marks)

(a) **Why is the gross profit margin of Boold less than double that of Diz when the gross profit per unit is more than double? Should the gross profit margin also be more than double that of Diz?**

You are correct that the gross profit margin has not doubled. The increase is only 71%. The gross profit per unit is more than double at 115%. The reason for this apparent anomaly is due to the sales price per unit of Boold being 25% higher than Diz

Therefore the calculation of the gross profit margin for Boold results in a larger denominator, and therefore 86p per unit as a percentage of £2.50 is not double the calculation of gross profit margin for Diz.

(b) **I was told that the material cost is £1.20 per kilogram for Diz and £1.30 per kilogram for Boold. Therefore, I do not understand why the material cost per unit for Boold is £1.43. Is this correct?**

The cost per kilogram is correct at £1.30 for Boold. However, Boold requires 1.1 kilograms of material per unit, which is why the cost per unit is £1.43 (1.1 × £1.30).

(c) **If the fixed production costs are constant does that mean they have no effect on the profit margin?**

No, even though the fixed costs are constant in total the production volume of Boold is 350,000 units greater than Diz, resulting in the fixed production cost per unit being lower. This is because the fixed costs are spread over more units, which reduces the cost per unit of Boold and therefore the profit margin will be improved.

(d) **Can you explain why Boold is more profitable than Diz?**

The reasons that Boold is more profitable than Diz are as follows:

- Sales price per unit of Boold is higher than Boold by 25% which will improve the margin.

- The sales volume is much higher for Boold which means that fixed costs per unit are lower than Diz again improving the margin.

- The variable cost per unit is higher for Boold which will have a negative effect and decrease the margin for Boold.

- The fixed production costs per unit is lower for Boold due to the volume being greater than Diz which improves the margin for Boold.

- The marketing costs for Boold are 4 × higher than Diz which will result in a much higher marketing cost per unit (£0.27 v £0.13). This will reduce the profit margin for Boold.

- The main reasons that Boold is more profitable is the greater sales price and the greater sales volume which combined outweigh the increased marketing costs and increased material costs.

BPP PRACTICE ASSESSMENT 1
FINANCIAL PERFORMANCE

Time allowed: 2.5 hours

PRACTICE ASSESSMENT 1

Task 1

RD Ltd manufactures rubberised asphalt and operates a standard costing system.

The standard cost card for the coming month is being prepared and you have been given the following information.

- 50 tonnes of CR materials will be transferred from the CR Division of the company at a cost of £474 per tonne.
- 200 tonnes of asphalt material will be purchased at a cost of £150 per tonne.
- Labour required to produce 250 tonnes of output is 800 hours.
- Labour cost is £10 per hour.
- Fixed running costs of the machines are £150,000 per month.
- Budgeted production is 250 tonnes per month.
- Fixed production overheads are absorbed on the basis of tonnes.

Complete the standard cost card for the production of 250 tonnes of rubberised asphalt.

		Quantity	Unit price	Total cost
			£	£
CR materials	tonnes			
Asphalt	tonnes			
Direct labour	hours			
Fixed production overheads	tonnes			————
Standard cost				————

Task 2

The budgeted activity and actual results for a business for the month of May 20X8 are as follows:

		Budget		Actual
Production (tonnes)		200		210
Direct labour	600 hours	£4,800	600 hours	£5,100

Complete the following sentences.

The standard labour rate per hour is £ [   ] per hour.

The standard labour hours for actual production is [   ] hours.

The direct labour rate variance is £ [   ] (Adverse/Favourable).

The direct labour efficiency variance is £ [   ] (Adverse/Favourable).

Task 3

A business has a single product into which fixed overheads are absorbed on the basis of labour hours. The standard cost card shows that fixed overheads are to be absorbed on the basis of 8 labour hours per unit at a rate of £10.00 per hour. The budgeted level of production is 100,000 units.

The actual results for the period were that fixed overheads were £7,800,000 and that the actual hours worked were 820,000 and the actual units produced were 98,000.

Calculate the following variances.

	Variance £	Adverse/Favourable
Fixed overhead expenditure variance		
Fixed overhead volume variance		
Fixed overhead efficiency variance		
Fixed overhead capacity variance		

Task 4

ABC Ltd manufactures one product, the ZZ. The company operates a standard costing system and analysis of variances is made every month. The standard cost card for the ZZ is as follows:

	£
Direct materials 0.5 kg at £4.00 per kg	2.00
Direct wages 2 hours at £8.00 per hour	16.00
Variable overheads 2 hours at £0.30 per hour	0.60
	18.60

The budgeted production was for 5,100 units in the month of June. The actual costs during the month of June for the production of 4,850 units were as follows:

	£
Direct materials 2,300 kg	9,800
Direct labour 8,500 hours paid	£67,800
Actual operating hours amounted to 8,000 hours	
Variable overheads	2,600

The following variances have been calculated.

Materials price	£600 Adv
Materials usage	£500 Fav
Labour rate	£200 Fav
Labour efficiency	£13,600 Fav
Idle time variance	£4,000 Adv
Variable overhead expenditure	£200 Adv
Variable overhead efficiency	£510 Fav

Calculate the standard cost of 4,850 units of production and insert the variances in the correct place in the following operating statement. Total the variances and reconcile the standard cost of actual production to the actual cost of actual production.

	Favourable £	Adverse £	Total £
Standard cost of actual production			
Variances			
Materials price			
Materials usage			
Labour rate			
Labour efficiency			
Labour idle time			
Variable overhead expenditure			
Variable overhead efficiency			
Total variances			
Actual cost of actual production			

Task 5

A company imports tea from India and the historical cost per kilogram is shown below.

	June X7 £	July X7 £	Aug X7 £	Sept X7 £	Oct X7 £	Nov X7 £
Cost per kg of tea	4.95	4.97	4.99	5.05	5.08	5.10

(a) The price per kilogram at January 20X7 was £4.80.

Convert the costs per kilogram for June and November to index numbers using January 20X7 as the base year.

June cost	
November cost	

(b) It is expected that the index number for tea for January 20X8 will be 108.25.

What is the expected cost per kilogram for January 20X8?

£5.52

£5.36

£5.20

£5.40

(c) **The percentage increase in the price of tea from January 20X7 to January 20X8 is:**

8.33%

7.69%

5.80%

5.58%

Task 6

You are employed as part of the management accounting team in a large industrial company. The production director, who has only recently been appointed, is unfamiliar with fixed overhead variances. Because of this, the group management accountant has asked you to prepare a report to the production director.

Your report should do the following.

(a) Outline the similarities and differences between fixed overhead variances and other cost variances such as the material and labour variances.

(b) Explain what is meant by the fixed overhead expenditure, volume, capacity and efficiency variances, and show, by way of examples, how these can be of help to the production director in the planning and controlling of the division.

REPORT

To: Production Director

From: Assistant Management Accountant

Date: xx/xx/xx

Subject: **Fixed overhead variances**

Similarities between fixed overhead variances and other variances

The meaning of fixed overhead variances

Fixed overhead variances and planning and control

Task 7

Given below is a summary of the performance of a business for the last two years:

	20X6	20X7
	£'000	£'000
Sales	1,420	1,560
Cost of sales	850	950
Expenses	370	407
Interest	–	7
Share capital and reserves	1,500	1,600
Long term loan	–	100
Non-current assets	1,100	1,300
Receivables	155	198
Inventory	105	140
Payables	140	162
Bank balance	280	224

For each of the two years complete the table to calculate the performance measures.

	20X6	20X7
Gross profit margin		
Operating profit margin		
Return on capital employed		
Asset turnover		
Non-current asset turnover		
Current ratio		
Quick ratio		
Receivables' collection period		
Inventory holding in days		
Payables' payment period		

Task 8

A business sells a single product and has budgeted sales of 130,000 units for the next period. The selling price per unit is £56 and the variable costs of production are £36. The fixed costs of the business are £2,000,000.

Complete the following sentences.

The breakeven point in units is [   ] units.

The margin of safety in units is [   ] units.

The margin of safety as a percentage of budgeted sales is [   ] %.

Task 9

HM Ltd is considering purchasing a new machine to reduce the labour time taken to produce one of its products. The machine would cost £300,000. The labour time would be reduced from five hours to two hours without compromising quality and the failure rates will remain at zero.

The discount factors you will need are shown below.

Year	Discount factor 5%
0	1.000
1	0.952
2	0.907
3	0.864
4	0.823
5	0.784

(a) **Calculate the discounted lifecycle cost of the machine based upon the following:**

    (i)   Purchase price of £300,000

    (ii) Annual running costs of £30,000 for the next 5 years

    (iii) A residual value of £50,000 at the end of the 5 years

Year	0	1	2	3	4	5
	£'000	£'000	£'000	£'000	£'000	£'000
Purchase price						
Running cost						
Residual value	_____	_____	_____	_____	_____	_____
Net cost						
Discount factor						
Present cost						

Net Present Cost = £ [   ]

The discounted lifecycle cost of the machine is £ [   ]

(b) **Calculate the discounted labour savings based upon annual production of 5,000 units, a three hour saving per unit and a labour rate of £7 per hour.**

Year	0	1	2	3	4	5
	£'000	£'000	£'000	£'000	£'000	£'000
Labour cost Saving						
Discount factor						
Present value						

Net Present Labour Cost Saving = £ [   ]

The discounted labour savings are £ [   ]

Task 10

HE Ltd has been reviewing the quality of the solar panels that it produces and has engineered two new products, the SP2000 and the SP3000.

The SP2000 is a low quality product with an economic life of 5 years. The SP3000 is a high quality product with an economic life of 20 years.

The Sales Director has provided information about the expected demand and price for the SP2000 and SP3000 for the coming year.

* SP2000 will be priced at £200 per panel and demand is expected to be around 9,000 units per year.

* SP3000 will be priced at £300 per panel and demand is expected to be around 5,000 units per year.

Forecast statement of profit or loss (income statement)

	SP2000	SP3000
Volume	9,000 units	5,000 units
	£	£
Revenue	1,800,000	1,500,000
Cost of production		
Direct materials (glass)	540,000	300,000
Direct labour	126,000	175,000
Fixed production overheads	120,000	120,000
Total cost of sales	786,000	595,000
Gross profit	**1,014,000**	**905,000**
Selling and distribution costs	400,000	400,000
Administration costs	200,000	200,000
Operating profit	**414,000**	**305,000**

Extracts from the forecast statement of financial position

	£	£
Inventory of material (glass)	60,000	60,000
Inventory of finished goods	NIL	NIL
Net assets	2,014,000	1,905,000

(a) **Complete the table to calculate the following performance indicators for BOTH products.**

	SP2000	SP3000
Gross profit margin		
Operating profit margin		
Direct materials cost per unit		
Direct labour cost per unit		
Fixed production overheads cost per unit		
Return on net assets		
Raw materials holding period in days		

(b) **Draft a report for the Finance Director covering the following:**

(i) An explanation of why the gross profit margin is different for each product. Your answer should refer to the following and explain their effect on the gross profit margin:

- Sales price per unit
- Materials, labour and fixed cost per unit

(ii) An assessment of the return on net assets for each product.

From: A Student

To: Finance Director

Sent: 1 December 20X8

Subject: Performance indicators

(i)   **Gross profit margin**

(ii) **Return on net assets**

BPP PRACTICE ASSESSMENT 1
FINANCIAL PERFORMANCE

ANSWERS

Task 1

Standard cost card for production of 250 tonnes of rubberised asphalt:

		Quantity	Unit price	Total cost
			£	£
CR material	tonnes	50	474	23,700
Asphalt	tonnes	200	150	30,000
Direct labour	hours	800	10	8,000
Fixed production overheads	tonnes	250	600	150,000
Standard cost				211,700

Task 2

The standard labour rate per hour is **£8** per hour.

The standard labour hours for actual production is **630** hours.

The direct labour rate variance is **£300 Adverse**.

The direct labour efficiency variance is **£240 Favourable**.

Workings

Standard labour rate per hour	=	Budgeted labour cost/Budgeted labour hours
	=	£4,800 / 600
	=	£8 per hour
Standard labour hours for actual production	=	Standard labour hour per tonne × Actual production
	=	600 hours/200 tonnes × 210 tonnes
	=	630 hours

Direct labour rate variance

	£
600 should have cost (× £8)	4,800
But did cost	5,100
Labour rate variance	300 Adv

Direct labour efficiency variance

210 tonnes should have taken (×3)	630 hours
But did take	600 hours
Efficiency variance in hours	30 Fav
× standard rate per hour	× £8
Labour efficiency variance	240 Fav

Task 3

	Variance £	Adverse/Favourable
Fixed overhead expenditure variance	200,000	Favourable
Fixed overhead volume variance	160,000	Adverse
Fixed overhead efficiency variance	360,000	Adverse
Fixed overhead capacity variance	200,000	Favourable

Workings

Fixed overhead expenditure variance

	£
Budgeted fixed overhead 100,000 units × 8 hours × £10.00	8,000,000
Actual fixed overhead	7,800,000
Expenditure variance	200,000 (F)

Fixed overhead volume variance

	£
Standard hours for actual production @ standard OAR 98,000 units × 8 hours × £10.00	7,840,000
Standard hours for budgeted production @ standard OAR 100,000 units × 8 hours × £10.00	8,000,000
Volume variance	160,000 (A)

Fixed overhead efficiency variance

	Hours
Actual units should take (98,000 × 8 hrs)	784,000
But did take	820,000
Fixed overhead efficiency variance in hours	36,000 Adv
× standard fixed overhead absorption rate per hour	× £10
Fixed overhead efficiency variance in £	360,000 Adv

Fixed overhead capacity variance

	Hours
Budgeted hours of work (100,000 × 8hrs)	800,000
Actual hours of work	820,000
Fixed overhead capacity variance	20,000 Fav
× standard fixed overhead absorption rate per hour	× £10
Fixed overhead capacity variance in £	£200,000 Fav

Task 4

	Favourable £	Adverse £	Total £
Standard cost of actual production (4,850 units × £18.60)			90,210
Variances			
Materials price		600	
Materials usage	500		
Labour rate	200		
Labour efficiency	13,600		
Labour idle time		4,000	
Variable overhead expenditure		200	
Variable overhead efficiency	510		
Total variances	14,810	4,800	10,010 (F)
Actual cost of actual production (9,800 + 67,800 +2,600)			80,200

Task 5

(a)

June cost	103.13
November cost	106.25

$$\text{June} = \frac{£4.95}{£4.80} \times 100 = 103.13$$

$$\text{November} = \frac{£5.10}{£4.80} \times 100 = 106.25$$

(b) January X8 cost $= \dfrac{£4.80 \times 108.25}{100} = £5.20$

(c) Percentage increase $= \dfrac{£5.20 - £4.80}{£4.80} \times 100$

$$= 8.33\%$$

Task 6

REPORT

To: Production Director

From: Assistant Management Accountant

Date: xx/xx/xx

Subject: **Fixed overhead variances**

This memorandum provides information on fixed overhead variances. In particular it covers the similarities between fixed overhead variances and other cost variances, the meaning of the various fixed overhead variances and the ways in which such variances can be of assistance in the planning and the controlling of the division.

Similarities between fixed overhead variances and other variances

The fixed overhead expenditure variance is the difference between the budgeted fixed overhead expenditure and actual fixed overhead expenditure. It is therefore similar to the material price and labour rate variances in that it shows the effect on costs and hence profit of paying more or less than anticipated for resources used.

Material usage and labour efficiency variances show the effect on costs and hence profit of having used more or less resource than should have been used for the actual volume of production. Fixed overheads should remain constant within the relevant range of production, however; they should not change simply because budgeted and actual production volumes differ. Fixed overhead variances similar to material usage and labour efficiency variances (reflecting the difference between the actual fixed overhead expenditure and the fixed overhead expenditure which should have been incurred at the actual volume of production) cannot therefore occur.

The meaning of fixed overhead variances

Whereas labour and material total variances show the effect on costs and hence profit of the difference between what the actual production volume should have cost and what it did cost (in terms of labour or material), if an organisation uses standard absorption costing (as we do), the fixed overhead total variance is the difference between actual fixed overhead expenditure and the fixed overhead absorbed (the under- or over-absorbed overhead).

The total under- or over-absorption is made up of the fixed overhead expenditure variance and the fixed overhead volume variance. The volume variance shows that part of the under- or over-absorbed overhead which is due to any difference between budgeted production volume and actual production volume.

The volume variance can be further broken down into an efficiency variance and a capacity variance. The capacity variance shows how much of the under- or over-absorbed overhead is due to working the labour force or plant more or less than planned, whereas the efficiency variance shows the effect of the efficiency of the labour force or plant.

The volume variance and its two subdivisions, the efficiency variance and the capacity variance, measure the extent of under or over absorption due to production volume being different to that planned. Material usage and labour efficiency variances, on the other hand, measure the effect of usage being different from that expected for the actual volume achieved.

Fixed overhead variances and planning and control

The fixed overhead volume variance and its subdivisions are perhaps misleading as variances for management control, because unlike expenditure variances or variable cost efficiency variances, they are not a true reflection of the extra or lower cash spending by an organisation as a result of the variance occurring. However, the fixed overhead efficiency and capacity variances are of some relevance for planning and control. They provide some measure of the difference between budgeted production volume and actual production volume, and management should obviously be interested in whether budgeted output was achieved, and if not, why not. A favourable efficiency variance might indicate an efficient workforce whereas an unfavourable capacity variance might indicate plant breakdowns or strikes. The existence of a fixed overhead volume variance can therefore be important; it is only the monetary value given to it that can be misleading.

The fixed overhead expenditure variance highlights the effect on costs and hence profit of changes to the level of overheads. For overhead expenditure variances to have any practical value as a planning or control measure, the variance for each overhead cost centre needs to be calculated, and reported to the manager responsible. Within each overhead cost centre, the manager should be able to analyse the total variance into indirect material cost variances, indirect labour cost variances and excess or favourable spending on other items, such as depreciation, postage, telephone charges and so on. Managers can then, for example, consider other suppliers, reconsider pricing structures of products and the like.

Task 7

	20X6	20X7
Gross profit margin	40.1%	39.1%
Operating profit margin	14.1%	13.0%
Return on capital employed	13.3%	11.9%

(**Note**. Total CE used ie share capital and reserves + long term loan.)

	20X6	20X7
Asset turnover	0.95	0.92
Non-current asset turnover	1.29	1.20
Current ratio	3.9	3.5
Quick ratio	3.1	2.6
Receivables' collection period	40 days	46 days
Inventory holding in days	45 days	54 days
Payables' payment period	60 days	62 days

Workings

	20X6	20X7
Gross profit margin	570/1,420	610/1,560
Operating profit margin	200/1,420	203/1,560
Return on capital employed	200/1,500	203/1,700

(**Note**. Total CE used ie share capital & reserves + long term loan.)

	20X6	20X7
Asset turnover	1,420/1,500	1,560/1,700
Non-current asset turnover	1,420/1,100	1,560/1,300
Current ratio	540/140	562/162
Quick ratio	435/140	422/162
Receivables' collection period	155/1,420 × 365	198/1,560 × 365
Inventory holding in days	105/850 × 365	140/950 × 365
Payables' payment period	140/850 × 365	162/950 × 365

Task 8

The breakeven point in units is 100,000 units

The margin of safety in units is 30,000 units

The margin of safety as a percentage of budgeted sales is 23%

Workings

Breakeven point $= \dfrac{£2,000,000}{£56 - £36}$

$= 100,000$ units

Margin of safety (units) = Budgeted sales – breakeven sales

$= (130,000 - 100,000)$ units

$= 30,000$ units

Margin of safety (% budgeted sales) $= \dfrac{130,000 - 100,000}{130,000} \times 100\%$

$= 23\%$

Task 9

(a)

Year	0	1	2	3	4	5
	£'000	£'000	£'000	£'000	£'000	£'000
Purchase price	300					
Running cost		30	30	30	30	30
Residual value	—	—	—	—	—	(50)
Net cost	300	30	30	30	30	(20)
Discount factor	1.000	0.952	0.907	0.864	0.823	0.784
Present cost	300	28.560	27.210	25.920	24.690	(15.680)

Net Present Cost = £390,700

The discounted lifecycle cost of the machine is £390,700.

(b)

Year	0	1	2	3	4	5
	£'000	£'000	£'000	£'000	£'000	£'000
Labour cost Saving (W1)	0	105	105	105	105	105
Discount factor	1.000	0.952	0.907	0.864	0.823	0.784
Present value		99.960	95.235	90.720	86.415	82.320

Net Present Labour Cost Saving = £454,650

The discounted labour savings are £454,650

Working

3 hours saving per unit × 5000 units × £7 = £105,000

··

Task 10

(a)

	SP2000	SP3000
Gross profit margin	56.33%	60.33%
Operating profit margin	23.00%	20.33%
Direct materials cost per unit	£60.00	£60.00
Direct labour cost per unit	£14.00	£35.00
Fixed production overheads cost per unit	£13.33	£24.00
Return on net assets	20.56%	16.01%
Raw materials holding period in days	40.56 days	73.00 days

Workings

	SP2000	SP3000
Note all monetary amounts in '000 for (i) and (ii)		
(i) = Gross Profit/Turnover × 100	Gross profit margin (1,014/1,800) × 100 = 56.33%	(905/1,500) × 100 = 60.33%

	SP2000	SP3000
(ii) = Operating Profit/Turnover × 100	Operating profit margin (414/1,800) × 100 = 23.00%	(305/1,500) × 100 = 20.33%
(iii) = Direct materials cost/Sales units	Direct materials cost per unit £540,000/9,000 = £60.00	£300,000/5,000 = £60.00
(iv) = Direct labour cost/Sales units	Direct labour cost per unit £126,000/9,000 = £14.00	£175,000/5,000 = £35.00
(v) = Fixed prod'n o/hds cost/Sales units	Fixed production overheads cost per unit £120,000/9,000 = £13.33	£120,000/5,000 = £24.00
(vi) = Operating profit/Net assets × 100	Return on net assets £414,000/£2,014,000 × 100 = 20.56%	£305,000/£ 1,905,000 × 100 = 16.01%
(vii) = (Inventory of material/Direct materials) × 365	Inventory holding £60,000/£540,000 × 365 = 40.56 days	£60,000/£300,000 × 365 = 73.00 days

(b)

From:	A Student
To:	Finance Director
Sent:	1 December 20X8
Subject:	Performance indicators

(i) **Gross profit margin**

The gross margin for the SP3000 is higher than the SP2000 by 4%.

This difference can be explained by differences in the selling price per unit and the cost of production of each unit.

The selling price of the SP3000 is £300 per unit whereas the selling price of the SP2000 is £200 per unit. If the cost of production for both products was the same then the SP3000 would have a higher gross margin.

The cost of production of the two products should be compared:

- The direct material cost of glass is constant at £60 per unit and so does not affect the margin.

- The direct labour cost per unit is much higher for the SP3000. This will reduce the gross margin for the SP3000.

- The fixed costs per unit are also higher for the SP3000 because less volume is produced (£24 per unit as opposed to £13.33 per unit for SP2000). Again this will reduce the margin for the SP3000.

The higher unit selling price of the SP3000 more than outweighs the additional costs per unit and hence the SP3000 has a higher gross margin.

(ii) **Return on net assets**

The SP2000 has a higher return on net assets than the SP3000 because its operating profits are larger relative to its net assets. Thus it generates an additional £109,000 but only uses an additional £109,000 of net assets.

BPP PRACTICE ASSESSMENT 2
FINANCIAL PERFORMANCE

Time allowed: 2.5 hours

PRACTICE ASSESSMENT 2

Task 1

The bagging division of a tea company operates a standard costing system. The standard cost card for the coming months is being prepared and you have been provided with the following information.

- Loose tea is expected to cost £5 per kilogram.
- 1,000 tea bags require 3 kilograms of loose tea.
- Tea bags cost 0.6 pence per bag.
- One machine can package 5,000 bags per hour and requires one operator who costs £10 per hour.
- Budgeted labour hours are 4,000 per month.
- Fixed production overheads are £200,000 per month.
- Budgeted production is 20,000 batches of 1,000 tea bags per month.
- Fixed production overheads are absorbed on the basis of direct labour hours.

Prepare the standard cost card for the production of 1,000 tea bags.

Standard cost card for 1,000 tea bags	£
Direct materials	
Direct materials	
Direct labour	
Fixed overhead	
Total standard cost	

....

Task 2

The standard direct materials cost for a business's product is:

14.4 kg @ £5.00 per kg = £72.00

During the month of May production was 9,200 units of the product and the actual materials cost was £671,600 for 135,500 kg. The price of the materials has been unexpectedly increased to £5.70 per kg for the whole month.

The total materials price variance is £ [   ]

The non-controllable element of the materials price variance that has been caused by the price increase is £ [   ]

The controllable element of the materials price variance caused by other factors is

£ [   ]

....

Task 3

A business produces a single product in its factory which has two production departments, cutting and finishing. In the following quarter it is anticipated that 200,000 units of the product will be produced. The expected costs are:

Direct materials	£10 per unit
Direct labour	3 hours cutting @ £8.00 per hour
	1 hour finishing @ £9.00 per hour
Variable overheads cutting	£444,000
finishing	£382,000
Fixed overheads cutting	£240,000
finishing	£110,000

Overheads are absorbed on the basis of direct labour hours.

(a) **The absorption cost per unit is**

£45.65

£46.60

£47.13

£48.88

(b) **The marginal cost per unit is**

£45.65

£46.60

£47.13

£48.88

Task 4

A company budgeted to produce 80,000 of its product with a standard cost of £4.60 per unit but in fact produced 84,000 units.

The actual costs of production were:

Materials	278,850
Packaging	8,800
Labour	17,100
Fixed overheads	85,000

The variances for the period have already been calculated:

Materials price	Zero	
Materials usage	£1,650	Adverse
Packaging price	£400	Adverse
Packaging usage	Zero	
Labour rate	£900	Favourable
Labour efficiency	£1,200	Adverse
Fixed overhead expenditure	£5,000	Adverse
Fixed overhead efficiency	£6,000	Adverse
Fixed overhead capacity	£10,000	Favourable

Calculate the budgeted cost for 84,000 units and then complete the table with the variances to reconcile to the actual cost of production.

Budgeted cost for actual production			
Variances	Favourable	Adverse	
Materials price			
Materials usage			
Packaging price			
Packaging usage			
Labour rate			
Labour efficiency			
Fixed overhead expenditure			
Fixed overhead efficiency			
Fixed overhead capacity			
Total variance			
Actual cost of actual production			

Task 5

(a) Given below are the production cost figures for the last nine months.

Calculate a three month moving average for these figures.

	Production costs	Three month moving total	Three month moving average
	£	£	£
March	226,500		
April	245,300		
May	240,800		
June	231,400		
July	237,600		
August	246,000		
September	241,200		
October	242,300		
November	247,500		
December	249,300		

(b) **The three month moving average represents which of the following?**

Random variations
Seasonal variations
Trend
Cyclical variations

Task 6

You are employed as an accounting technician at BeThere Airlines, a company that operates flights across Europe. The company has several divisions including a catering division operating from Manchester. The catering division produces meals daily for the flights. Currently all meals produced are used only on BeThere flights.

The company operates an integrated standard cost system in which:

- Purchases of materials are recorded at standard cost
- Direct material costs and direct labour costs are variable
- Production overheads are fixed and absorbed using direct labour hours

The budgeted activity and actual results for November 20X6 are as follows:

		Budget		Actual
Production (meals)		112,000		117,600
Direct materials	56,000 kg	£224,000	61,740 kg	£185,220
Direct labour	28,000 hours	£252,000	27,930 hours	£279,300
Fixed overheads		£84,000		£82,000
Total cost		£560,000		£546,520

(a) **Calculate the following information for November (to two decimal places):**

    (i)   Standard price of materials per kilogram
    (ii)   Standard usage of materials per meal
    (iii)   Standard labour rate per hour
    (iv)   Standard labour hours per meal
    (v)   Budgeted overhead absorption rate per hour
    (vi)   Overheads absorbed into actual production
    (vii)   The total standard cost of actual production

(b) **Calculate the following variances for November:**

    (i)   Direct material price variance
    (ii)   Direct material usage variance
    (iii)   Direct labour rate variance
    (iv)   Direct labour efficiency variance
    (v)   Fixed overhead expenditure variance
    (vi)   Fixed overhead volume variance
    (vii)   Fixed overhead capacity variance
    (viii)   Fixed overhead efficiency variance

(c) **Prepare a report to the managing director giving ONE possible reason for each of the following variances you calculated in (b).**

    (i)   Direct material price variance
    (ii)   Direct material usage variance
    (iii)   Direct labour rate variance
    (iv)   Direct labour efficiency variance

REPORT

To: Managing Director

From: Accounting Technician

Subject: Reasons for the variances

Date: 14 December 20X6

Direct material price variance

Direct material usage variance

Direct labour rate variance

Direct labour efficiency variance

....

Task 7

The production figures for January for a factory are as follows.

Budgeted production in units	12,000
Actual production in units	11,250
Labour hours worked	30,000
Standard hours for each unit	2

Calculate the efficiency, capacity and activity ratios for January (give answers to two decimal places).

The efficiency ratio is [＿＿＿＿＿＿] %

The capacity ratio is [＿＿＿＿＿＿] %

The activity ratio is [＿＿＿＿＿＿] %

Task 8

(a) The following information relates to one period for a single product produced by a company.

Expected sales revenue = £400,000
Selling price per unit = £40 per unit
Variable cost = £18 per unit
Fixed costs = £99,000

The breakeven point both in terms of units and sales revenue is:

Breakeven point in units	Breakeven point in sales revenue	
4,500 units	£99,000	☐
4,500 units	£180,000	☐
2,475 units	£99,000	☐
2,475 units	£180,000	☐

(b) Company X sells product Y for £28 per unit. Variable costs of production are £23 per unit. The company has fixed overheads of £440,000 and has budgeted to sell 95,000 units of the product in the next year.

The margin of safety as a percentage (to two decimal places) is [＿＿＿＿＿＿] %

Task 9

(a) A company is developing a new product to monitor energy consumption. There are currently several other companies manufacturing similar products which sell for a price of £25 each. The company wishes to make a margin of 30%.

The target cost of each new product is £ [   ]

(b) Improvements in product design or specification to reduce defective products is an example of which type of quality cost?

Prevention cost	☐
Appraisal cost	☐
Internal failure cost	☐
External failure cost	☐

··

Task 10

Voltair Ltd has developed a domestic wind turbine. A colleague has prepared forecast information based upon two scenarios. The forecast statements of profit or loss (income statements) and statements of financial position for both scenarios are shown below.

- Scenario 1 is to set the price at £1,250 per unit with sales of 10,000 units each year.
- Scenario 2 is to set the price at £1,000 per unit with sales of 14,000 units each year.

Forecast statement of profit or loss (income statement)

	Scenario 1	Scenario 2
	£'000	£'000
Revenue	12,500	14,000
Cost of production:		
Direct (raw) materials	3,000	4,200
Direct labour	2,000	2,800
Fixed production overheads	3,000	3,000
Total cost of sales	8,000	10,000
Gross profit	4,500	4,000
Selling and distribution costs	1,000	1,000
Administration costs	750	750
Operating profit	2,750	2,250
Interest payable	600	600
Net profit	2,150	1,650

Extracts from the forecast statement of financial position

	£'000	£'000
Non-current assets	20,000	20,000
Current assets	5,000	5,500
Current liabilities	4,600	5,800
Long-term loans	12,000	11,300
	8,400	8,400
Represented by:		
Share capital	5,650	6,150
Reserves	2,750	2,250
	8,400	8,400

(a) **Calculate the following performance indicators for each scenario:**

   (i)   Gross profit margin
   (ii)   Net profit margin
   (iii) Direct materials cost per unit
   (iv) Direct labour cost per unit
   (v)   Fixed production cost per unit
   (vi) Gearing ratio
   (vii) Interest cover

(b) **Draft a report for the Finance Director covering the following:**

   (i)   An explanation of why the gross profit margin is different in each scenario. Your answer should refer to the following:

   •   Sales price per unit
   •   Materials, labour and fixed cost per unit

   (ii) An assessment of the level of gearing and interest cover and whether it is a problem for the business.

REPORT

To: Finance Director   **Subject:** Gross profit margin, gearing and interest cover

From: AAT Trainee   **Date:** 16 June 20X8

(i) **Gross profit margin**

(ii) **Gearing and interest cover**

BPP PRACTICE ASSESSMENT 2
FINANCIAL PERFORMANCE

ANSWERS

Task 1

Standard cost card for 1,000 tea bags	
	£
Direct materials – tea (3kg × £5)	15.00
Direct materials – bags (1,000 × £0.006)	6.00
Direct labour $\left(\dfrac{1,000}{5,000 \text{ hours}} \times £10\right)$	2.00
Fixed overhead $\left(\dfrac{0.2 \text{ hours} \times £200,000}{4,000 \text{ hours}}\right)$	10.00
Total standard cost	33.00

Task 2

The total materials price variance is £5,900 Favourable.

The non-controllable element of the materials price variance that has been caused by the price increase is £94,850.

The controllable element of the materials price variance caused by other factors is £100,750.

Workings

Total materials price variance

	£
Standard cost for actual quantity 135,500 × £5	677,500
Actual cost	671,600
	5,900 (F)

Planning variance caused by price increase

	£
Standard cost for actual quantity 135,500 × £5.00	677,500
Adjusted cost for actual quantity 135,500 × £5.70	772,350
	94,850 (A)

Control variance caused by other factors

	£
Adjusted cost for actual quantity 135,500 × £5.70	772,350
Actual cost	671,600
	100,750 (F)

Task 3

(a) £48.88
(b) £47.13

Workings

(a) **Absorption costing**

	£
Direct materials	10.00
Direct labour – cutting (3 × £8.00)	24.00
Finishing	9.00
Variable overheads:	
Cutting (£444,000/600,000) × 3 hrs	2.22
Finishing (£382,000/200,000) × 1hr	1.91
Fixed overheads:	
Cutting (£240,000/600,000) × 3 hrs	1.20
Finishing (£110,000/200,000) × 1 hr	0.55
	48.88

(b) **Marginal costing**

	£
Direct materials	10.00
Direct labour – Cutting (3 × £8.00)	24.00
Finishing	9.00
Variable overheads:	
Cutting (£440,000/600,000) × 3 hrs	2.22
Finishing (£382,000/200,000) × 1 hr	1.91
	47.13

Task 4

	£	£	
Budgeted cost for actual production (84,000 × £4.60)			**386,400**
Variances	**Favourable**	**Adverse**	
Materials price	–	–	
Materials usage		1,650	
Packaging price		400	
Packaging usage	–	–	
Labour rate	900		
Labour efficiency		1,200	
Fixed overhead expenditure		5,000	
Fixed overhead efficiency		6,000	
Fixed overhead capacity	10,000		
Total variance	10,900	14,250	3,350
Actual cost of actual production (£278,850 + £8,800 + £17,100 + £85,000)			389,750

Task 5

(a)

	Production costs	Three month moving total	Three month moving average
	£	£	£
March	226,500		
April	245,300	712,600	237,533
May	240,800	717,500	239,167
June	231,400	709,800	236,600
July	237,600	715,000	238,333
August	246,000	724,800	241,600

	Production costs	Three month moving total	Three month moving average
September	241,200	729,500	243,167
October	242,300	731,000	243,667
November	247,500	739,100	246,367
December	249,300		

(b)   The correct answer is: Trend

Task 6

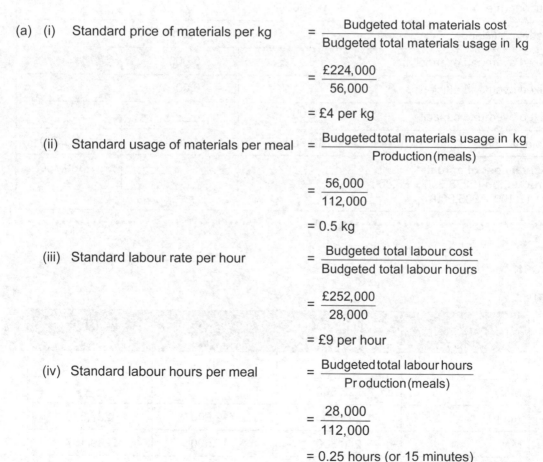

(a) (i)   Standard price of materials per kg $= \dfrac{\text{Budgeted total materials cost}}{\text{Budgeted total materials usage in kg}}$

$= \dfrac{£224,000}{56,000}$

= £4 per kg

(ii)   Standard usage of materials per meal $= \dfrac{\text{Budgeted total materials usage in kg}}{\text{Production (meals)}}$

$= \dfrac{56,000}{112,000}$

= 0.5 kg

(iii)   Standard labour rate per hour $= \dfrac{\text{Budgeted total labour cost}}{\text{Budgeted total labour hours}}$

$= \dfrac{£252,000}{28,000}$

= £9 per hour

(iv)   Standard labour hours per meal $= \dfrac{\text{Budgeted total labour hours}}{\text{Production (meals)}}$

$= \dfrac{28,000}{112,000}$

= 0.25 hours (or 15 minutes)

(v) Budgeted overhead absorption rate per hour $= \dfrac{\text{Budgeted total overhead cost}}{\text{Budgeted total labour hours}}$

$$= \dfrac{£84,000}{28,000}$$

$$= £3 \text{ per hour}$$

(vi) Overheads absorbed into actual production $= 27,930 \text{ hours} \times £3$

$$= £83,790$$

(vii) Total standard cost of actual production $= £560,000 \times \dfrac{117,600}{112,000}$

$$= £588,000$$

Alternatively:

	Standard cost per meal
	£
Direct material (0.5 kg × £4)	2.00
Direct labour (0.25 hours × £9)	2.25
Fixed overheads (0.25 hours × £3)	0.75
	5.00

Total standard cost of actual production   = 117,600 meals × £5 per meal

                                                     = £588,000

(b) Variance calculations:

£

(i) **Direct material price variance**

61,740kg should have cost (× £4)   246,960

But did cost   185,220

                                              61,740 (F)

(ii) **Direct material usage variance**

117,600 meals should have used (× 0.5 kg)   58,800

But did use   61,740

Variance in kg   2,940

at standard cost (× £4)   × £4

                                              11,760 (A)

(iii) **Direct labour rate variance**

27,930 hours should have cost (× £9)   251,370

But did cost   279,300

                                              27,930 (A)

(iv) **Direct labour efficiency variance**

117,600 meals should have taken (× 0.25 hrs) 29,400

But did take   27,930

Variance in hrs   1,470

at standard cost (× £9)   × £9

                                              13,230 (F)

(v) **Fixed overhead expenditure variance**

Budgeted fixed overhead   84,000

Actual fixed overhead   82,000

                                              2,000 (F)

(vi)   **Fixed overhead volume variance**

Actual production volume at standard rate
(117,600 × 0.25 × £3)   88,200

Budgeted production volume at standard rate
(112,000 × 0.25 × £3)   84,000

                                                                4,200 (F)

Tutorial note. This is a favourable variance because a greater production volume has been achieved than was budgeted for. The two variances below are a further analysis of the volume variance and the sum of the two will therefore equal the volume variance. The capacity variance looks at how the actual production hours differ from the originally budgeted hours. The efficiency variance compares actual with the flexed budget, and is the same type of calculation as the labour efficiency variance.

                                                                    £

(vii)   **Fixed overhead capacity variance**

Budgeted hours of work   28,000

Actual hours of work   27,930

                                                                    70

at standard rate   × £3

                                                                 210 (A)

(viii)   **Fixed overhead efficiency variance**

Actual units should take (117,600 × 0.25)   29,400

But did take   27,930

                                                                 1,470

at standard rate (× £3)   × £3

                                                               4,410 (F)

(c)   **REPORT**

To: Managing Director

From: Accounting Technician

Subject: Reasons for the variances

Date: 14 December 20X6

Having investigated the materials and labour variances calculated for November 20X6, I can suggest the following possible causes.

(i)   Direct materials price variance £61,740 (F)

      This variance resulted from the purchase of materials at £3 per kg rather than the standard cost of £4 per kg. This material was cheaper and possibly of a lower quality.

(ii) Direct material usage variance £11,760 (A)

      The actual usage was worse than expected, and this could have been a consequence of buying inferior material.

(iii) Direct labour rate variance £27,930 (A)

      Direct workers were actually paid at £10 per hour, whilst we had only budgeted for a rate of £9 per hour. It is possible that the workers used were more skilled than we planned for.

(iv) Direct labour efficiency variance £13,230 (F)

      Actual production required fewer hours than were expected which is consistent with using more highly-skilled staff.

Tutorial note. There is more than one possible reason for each of the above variances, and marks would have been awarded for any reasonable suggestions.

··

Task 7

$$\text{Efficiency ratio} \quad = \quad \frac{\text{Standard hours for actual production}}{\text{Actual hours worked}} \times 100$$

$$= \quad \frac{11,250 \text{ units} \times 2 \text{ hours per unit}}{30,000} \times 100$$

$$= \quad \frac{22,500}{30,000} \times 100$$

$$= \quad 75.00\%$$

Capacity ratio $= \dfrac{\text{Actual hours worked}}{\text{Budgeted hours}} \times 100$

$= \dfrac{30,000}{12,000\,\text{units} \times 2\,\text{hours}} \times 100$

$= \dfrac{30,000}{24,000} \times 100$

$= 125.00\%$

Activity ratio $= \dfrac{\text{Standard hours for actual production}}{\text{Budgeted hours}} \times 100$

$= \dfrac{11,250\,\text{units} \times 2\,\text{hours}}{12,000\,\text{units} \times 2\,\text{hours}} \times 100$

$= \dfrac{22,500}{24,000} \times 100$

$= 93.75\%$

Task 8

(a) Breakeven point in units: 4,500 units and breakeven point in sales revenue: £180,000

Workings

Contribution per unit = £(40 – 18) = £22

Contribution required to breakeven = fixed costs = £99,000

Breakeven point $= \dfrac{\text{Fixed costs}}{\text{Contribution per unit}}$

$= \dfrac{£99,000}{£22}$

= 4,500 units

Sales revenue at breakeven point = 4,500 units × £40 per unit

$= £180,000$

(b)   Margin of safety = 7.37%

Workings

Breakeven point = $\dfrac{£440,000}{£28 - £23}$

= 88,000 units

Margin of safety = $\dfrac{95,000 - 88,000}{95,000} \times 100 = 7.37\%$

....

Task 9

(a)   Target cost =   Market price – Desired profit margin

=   £25 – (£25 × 30%)

=   £25 – £7.50

=   £17.50

(b)   **Prevention cost**. Prevention costs are the costs incurred prior to, or during, production in order to investigate, prevent or reduce defects in products or mistakes in services.

....

Task 10

(a)

	Scenario 1	Scenario 2
(i) Gross profit margin		
= Gross Profit/ Revenue (turnover) × 100	(4,500/12,500) × 100 = 36.00%	(4,000/14,000) × 100 = 28.57%
(ii) Net profit margin		
= Net Profit/ Revenue × 100	(2,150/12,500) × 100 = 17.20%	(1,650/14,000) × 100 = 11.79%
(iii) Direct materials cost per unit		
= Direct materials cost/Sales units	£3,000,000/10,000 = £300	£4,200,000/14,000 = £300
(iv) Direct labour cost per unit		
= Direct labour cost/Sales units	£2,000,000/10,000 = £200	£2,800,000/14,000 = £200
(v) Fixed production cost per unit		
= Fixed production cost/ Sales units	£3,000,000/10,000 = £300	£3,000,000/14,000 = £214.29
(vi) Gearing		
= Total debt/(Total debt + Share capital + Reserves)	12,000/(12,000 + 8,400)= (0.5882 or 58.82%)	11,300/(11,300 + 8,400)= 0.5736 or 57.36%

Alternative answer for gearing:

Gearing

= Total debt/ (Share capital + Reserves)	12,000/8,400 =	11,300/8,400 =
	(1.4286 or 142.86%)	(1.3452 or 134.52%)
(vii) Interest cover		
= Operating profit /Interest payable	2,750/600 = 4.58	2,250/600 = 3.75

(b)
REPORT

To: Finance Director **Subject:** Gross profit margin, gearing and interest cover

From: AAT Trainee **Date:** 16 June 20X8

(i) **Gross profit margin**

The gross profit margin for scenario 1 is 36% and scenario 2 is 28.57%. Direct materials and labour are the same under both scenarios so that the higher gross profit margin for scenario 1 must be as a result of differences in sales price per unit or fixed production overheads. In fact the fixed costs per unit are higher under scenario 1 because less volume is produced (£300 per unit as opposed to £214.29 per unit for scenario 2). Therefore the reason for the higher gross margin is the higher price per unit (£1,250 and £1,000 respectively).

(ii) **Gearing and interest cover**

The level of gearing for both scenarios is at a similar level and there appears to be reasonable security in the form of non-current assets. Everything else being equal, the higher the gearing ratio the higher the risk. This is because long term loans have interest payments that have to be made from operating profit. However, the gearing indicator cannot be considered in isolation. Voltair's ability to service the debt is also important.

The level of interest cover shows how many times Voltair can pay its interest payable out of operating profit. For scenario 1 the profit is 4.58 times greater than interest payable. This falls slightly to 3.75 times for scenario 2 due to the fall in profits, as the interest payable is constant under both scenarios.

Both scenarios have a relatively high interest cover and this does not appear to be a problem for the business.

BPP PRACTICE ASSESSMENT 3
FINANCIAL PERFORMANCE

Time allowed: 2.5 hours

PRACTICE ASSESSMENT 3

Task 1

A business produces one product which requires the following inputs:

Direct materials	3 kg @ £6.20 per kg
Direct labour	7 hours @ £8.00 per hour
Rent/rates	£24,000 per quarter
Leased delivery vans	£1,000 for every 900 units of production
Warehouse costs	£10,000 per quarter plus £2.00 per unit

Complete the table to show the total cost of production and the cost per unit at each of the quarterly production levels.

Production level – units	Total cost of production – £	Cost per unit – £
2,000		
3,000		
4,000		

Task 2

(a) A company purchases 14,000 kg of material at a cost of £58,000. The standard cost per kg is £4.

The total materials price variance is

£14,000

£2,000

£58,000

£4.14

The variance is [▼]

Picklist

Adverse

Favourable

(b) A company purchases 10,000 kgs of material at a cost of £22,000. The budgeted production was 6,000 units which requires 9,000 kgs of material at a total standard cost of £18,000. The actual production was 6,500 units.

The material usage variance is

500 kg ☐

250 kg ☐

£500 ☐

£250 ☐

The variance is [　　　　　　▼]

Picklist

Adverse
Favourable

(c) Extracts from Drizzle Co' records from last period are as follows:

	Budget	Actual
Production	1,925 units	2,070 units
Variable production overhead cost	$13,475	$13,455
Labour hours worked	3,850	2,990

The variable production overhead expenditure variance for the last period is

£[　　　　　　]

The variance is [　　　　　　▼]

Picklist

Adverse
Favourable

Task 3

The budgeted activity and actual results for a business for the month of May 20X8 are as follows:

		Budget		Actual
Production (tonnes)		200		210
Direct labour	600 hours	£4,800	600 hours	£5,100
Fixed overheads		£90,000		£95,000

Complete the table to calculate the following:

	£
Budgeted overhead absorption rate per tonne	
Overheads absorbed into actual production	
Fixed overhead expenditure variance	
Fixed overhead volume variance	

Task 4

(a) The standard labour cost for one unit of product Z is £24 (3 hours @ £8 per hour). The budgeted level of production is 14,000 units.

Actual results for the period are:

Production   13,200 units

Labour   18,600 hours costing £111,600

Prepare a reconciliation of the budgeted labour cost with the actual labour cost using the labour cost variances.

Standard cost of labour for actual production			
Variances	Favourable	Adverse	
Direct labour rate variance			
Direct labour efficiency variance			
Total variance			
Actual cost of labour for actual production			

(b) **Which variances would not be included in an operating statement prepared under a system of marginal costing?**

Fixed overhead efficiency variance and fixed overhead capacity variance ☐

Fixed overhead expenditure variance and fixed overhead volume variance ☐

Fixed overhead expenditure variance and fixed overhead efficiency variance ☐

Fixed overhead expenditure variance and fixed overhead capacity variance ☐

(c) The standard material content of one unit of product A is 25kgs of material X which should cost £10 per kilogram. In March 20X4, 6,250 units of product A were produced and there was an adverse material usage variance of £7,500.

The quantity of material X used in March 20X4 is ⎡‾‾‾‾‾‾‾⎤ **kg**

Task 5

A material which is derived from soft fruit is either imported or purchased from UK farmers by a company. The price of the material fluctuates month by month depending on the time of year. The cost information for the four months ending August 20X6 is given below.

	May X6	June X6	July X6	August X6
Cost per 1,000 kg	£1,000	£900	£700	£800

The underlying cost does not change during the period May to August. The change in cost over the four months is due only to the seasonal variations which are given below.

	May X6	June X6	July X6	August X6
Seasonal variations	£200	£100	–£100	£0

(a) **Complete the table to calculate the underlying cost per 1,000 kilograms for the period May to August 20X6.**

	May 20X6	June 20X6	July 20X6	Aug 20X6
	£	£	£	£
Cost per 1,000 kg				
Seasonal variation				
Trend				

(b) Indications are that the underlying cost per 1,000 kilograms for the period May 20X7 to August 20X7 will be £850.

The percentage increase in the underlying cost from 20X6 to 20X7 is ⎡‾‾‾‾‾‾⎤ **%**

(c) **Complete the table to calculate the forecast cost per 1,000 kilograms for the period May 20X7 to August 20X7 using the underlying cost and the seasonal variations given above.**

	May 20X7	June 20X7	July 20X7	Aug 20X7
	£	£	£	£
Trend				
Seasonal variation				
Cost per 1,000 kg				

Task 6

Given below is the operating statement for a manufacturing business for the last month:

Reconciliation of standard cost of actual production to actual cost – March 20X9

	Variances		
	Favourable	Adverse	
	£	£	£
Standard cost of actual production			672,500
Variances:			
Materials price		24,300	
Materials usage	6,780		
Labour rate		10,600	
Labour efficiency	10,300		
Fixed overhead expenditure	7,490		
Fixed overhead capacity	4,800		
Fixed overhead efficiency	6,100		
	35,470	34,900	(570)
Actual cost of production			671,930

A number of factors about the month's production have been discovered:

- At the end of the previous month a new warehouse had been purchased which has meant a saving in warehouse rental.

- Six new machines were installed at the start of the month which are more power efficient than the old machines, but also more expensive, causing a larger depreciation charge.

- There was an unexpected increase in the materials price during the month and when other suppliers were contacted it was found that they were all charging approximately the same price for the materials.

- A higher than normal skilled grade of labour was used during the month due to staff shortages. The production process is a skilled process and the benefit has been that these employees, although more expensive, have produced the goods faster and with less wastage. This particular group of employees are also keen to work overtime and, as the business wishes to build up inventory levels, advantage of this has been taken.

Prepare a report for the production director.

Your report should do the following:

(a)   Suggest what effect the combination of the factors given above might have had on the reported variances.

(b)   Make suggestions as to any action that should be taken in light of these factors.

REPORT

To: Production Director

From: Management Accountant

Date: xx/xx/xx

Subject: March 20X9 variances

New warehouse

New machines

Price increase

Skilled labour

Task 7

Given below are the production figures for a factory for the last four months.

	November	December	January	February
Output in units	64,300	68,900	62,100	60,200
Budgeted output	65,000	65,000	60,000	62,000
Hours worked	98,200	107,300	90,200	92,000

The standard time for each unit of production is 1.5 hours.

Complete the table to calculate the following performance indicators for each of the four months.

	November	December	January	February
Actual hours per unit				
Efficiency ratio				
Capacity ratio				
Activity ratio				

....

Task 8

Voltair Ltd has developed a domestic wind turbine. A colleague has prepared forecast information based upon two scenarios. The forecast statement of profit or loss (income statement) for both scenarios is shown below.

- Scenario 1 is to set the price at £1,250 per unit with sales of 10,000 units each year.
- Scenario 2 is to set the price at £1,000 per unit with sales of 14,000 units each year.

Forecast statement or profit or loss (income statement)	Scenario 1	Scenario 2
	£'000	£'000
Revenue (turnover)	12,500	14,000
Cost of production		
Direct (raw) materials	3,000	4,200
Direct labour	2,000	2,800
Fixed production overheads	3,000	3,000
Cost of sales	8,000	10,000

Forecast statement or profit or loss (income statement)		
	Scenario 1	Scenario 2
Gross profit	4,500	4,000
Selling and distribution costs	1,000	1,000
Administration costs	750	750
Operating profit	2,750	2,250
Interest payable	600	600
Net profit	2,150	1,650

The Managing Director has been in talks with a Romanian manufacturer who could produce the wind turbines. You have been asked to analyse the information in order to evaluate whether Voltair should contract out the manufacture of the turbines.

If the turbines are manufactured in Romania the costs and savings would be as follows:

- The cost of each turbine would be £650 including transport costs to the UK.

- The material and labour costs would be saved.

- The fixed production costs consist of £1.95 million of specific costs which would be avoided, and £1.05 million of allocated overheads which would not be avoided.

(a) **Complete the table to calculate the following information for the demand level of 10,000 turbines per annum.**

	£
Full production cost per turbine manufactured by Voltair	
Voltair's unavoidable fixed production cost per turbine if contracted out	
Voltair's avoidable production cost per turbine if contracted out	

(b) **Complete the table to calculate the following information for the demand level of 14,000 turbines per annum.**

	£
Full production cost per turbine manufactured by Voltair	
Voltair's unavoidable fixed production cost per turbine if contracted out	
Voltair's avoidable production cost per turbine if contracted out	

Task 9

A company is reviewing various alternatives to determine whether it is possible to reduce monthly costs. The operations director is considering whether to invest in a new machine which:

- Could either be purchased for £3 million or rented for £50,000 per month
- Is expected to have a life of 10 years and a scrap value of £900,000

It is assumed under both options that:

- The maintenance cost of the machine is £50,000 per annum
- Decommissioning costs will be £100,000
- The machine will be used for 10 years

Calculate the lifecycle cost of the TWO options outlined

Ignore the time value of money and any opportunity costs when calculating the lifecycle cost.

Task 10

A division of Fooddrink Ltd is developing a new supplement and a colleague has prepared forecast information based upon two scenarios. The forecast statements of profit or loss (income statements), statements of financial position and performance ratios for both scenarios are shown below.

- Scenario 1 is to set the price at £10 per unit with sales of 120,000 units each year.
- Scenario 2 is to set the price at £5 per unit with sales of 360,000 units each year.

	Scenario 1	Scenario 2
	£'000	£'000
Budgeted statement of profit or loss (income statement)		
Revenue	1,200	1,800
Cost of production		
Direct (raw) materials	300	900
Direct labour	120	360
Fixed production overheads	360	360
Total cost of sales	780	1,620
Gross profit	**420**	**180**
Selling and distribution costs	74	122
Administration costs	100	100
Operating profit	**246**	**(42)**

	Scenario 1	Scenario 2
Budgeted statement of financial position		
Non-current assets		
Machinery	1,600	1,600
Current assets		
Inventory of raw materials	50	50
Receivables	150	150
Current liabilities		
Payables	75	75
Net current assets	**125**	**125**
Long-term loans	754	1,042
Net assets	**971**	**683**
Represented by:		
Share capital	725	725
Operating profit for the year	246	(42)
Share capital and reserves	**971**	**683**
	Scenario 1	**Scenario 2**
Performance ratios		
Gross profit margin	35.00%	10.00%
Operating profit margin	20.50%	−2.33% (0%)
Direct materials as a percentage of revenue	25.00%	50.00%
Direct materials cost per unit	£2.50	£2.50
Return on net assets	25.33%	−6.15% (0%)

(a) **Draft a report for the finance director giving an explanation of why the following ratios have changed:**

(i)   Gross profit margin
(ii) Operating profit margin
(iii) Direct materials as a percentage of revenue

To: Finance Director

Subject: Differences in key performance indicators

From: Accounting Technician

Date: 18 June 20X7

Gross profit margin

Operating profit margin

Direct materials

You have found that your colleague has made a few mistakes with the figures for Scenario 2. The impact on gross profit, operating profit and net assets for Scenario 2 is shown below.

- Recalculated gross profit = £540,000
- Recalculated operating profit = £318,000
- Recalculated net assets = £1,043,000

(b) **Recalculate the following ratios:**

    (i)   Gross profit margin
    (ii)   Operating profit margin
    (iii) Return on net assets

(c) **Redraft your report for the finance director commenting on the ratios you recalculated in (b) above and recommend whether the price of the product should be set at £10 or £5.**

To: Financial Director

Subject: Differences in key performance indicators

From: Accounting Technician

Date: 18 June 20X7

Gross profit margin

Operating profit margin

Return on net assets

Recommendations

BPP PRACTICE ASSESSMENT 3
FINANCIAL PERFORMANCE

ANSWERS

Task 1

Production level – units	Total cost of production – £	Cost per unit – £
2,000	190,200	95.10
3,000	267,800	89.27
4,000	345,400	86.35

Workings

	2,000 units £	3,000 units £	4,000 units £
Direct materials 3kg × £6.20 × units	37,200	55,800	74,400
Direct labour 7 hours × £8.00 × units	112,000	168,000	224,000
Rent/rates	24,000	24,000	24,000
Leased delivery vans	3,000	4,000	5,000
Warehouse costs £10,000 + £2.00 × units	14,000	16,000	18,000
	190,200	267,800	345,400
Cost per unit	£95.10	£89.27	£86.35

Task 2

(a) £2,000 Adverse

	£
14,000 kg should have cost (× £4)	56,000
But did cost	58,000
Total materials price variance	2,000 A

(b) £500 Adverse

6,500 units should have used × 1.5 kgs	9,750 kg
But did use	10,000 kg
	250 kg
@ standard rate per kg £2	× £2
Materials usage variance	£500 A

(c)   £2,990 Adverse

Standard variable production overhead cost per hour = $13,475/3850 = £3.50

	£
2,990 hours of variable production overhead should cost (× £3.50)	10,465
But did cost	13,455
Variable production overhead expenditure variance	2,990 A

....

Task 3

Budgeted overhead absorption rate per tonne	£450
Overheads absorbed into actual production	£94,500
Fixed overhead expenditure variance	£5,000 Adverse
Fixed overhead volume variance	£4,500 Favourable

Workings

Budgeted overhead absorption rate per tonne	= Fixed overheads/Budgeted output
	= £90,000/200 tonnes
	= £450
Overheads absorbed into actual production	= Actual production × Absorption rate
	= 210 units × £450
	= £94,500

Fixed overhead expenditure variance

	£
Budgeted fixed overhead	90,000
Actual fixed overhead	95,000
Fixed overhead expenditure variance	5,000 Adv

Fixed overhead volume variance

	£
Actual production at absorption rate per unit (210 × £450)	94,500
Budgeted production at absorption rate per unit	90,000
Fixed overhead volume variance	4,500 Fav

Task 4

(a)

Standard cost of labour for actual production			£316,800
Variances	Favourable	Adverse	
Direct labour rate variance	£37,200		
Direct labour efficiency variance	£168,000		
Total variance			£(205,200)
Actual cost of labour for actual production			£111,600

Workings

Standard cost for actual units produced = 13,200 units × 3hrs × £8 = £316,800

Labour rate variance	£
18,600 hrs should have cost (× £8)	148,800
But did cost	111,600
Rate variance	37,200 (F)

Labour efficiency variance	
13,200 units should have taken (× 3 hours)	39,600 hrs
But did take	18,600 hrs
	21,000 (F)
At standard cost	× £8
Usage variance	168,000 (F)

(b) The correct answer is: Fixed overhead efficiency variance and fixed overhead capacity variance.

Neither fixed overhead efficiency variance nor fixed overhead capacity variance (which together make up the fixed overhead volume variance) exist in a marginal costing system.

(c) The quantity used is 157,000kg.

Workings

Let the quantity of material X used = Y

6,250 units should have used (× 25kgs)	156,250 kg
but did use	Y kg
Usage variance in kg	(156,250 –Y) kg
× standard price per kg	× £10
Usage variance in £	£7,500 (A)

$10(156,250 - Y) = -7,500$

$156,250 - Y = -750$

$Y = 157,000kg$

Alternatively:

Standard material cost of actual production	£1,562,500
6,250 × 25kgs × £10	
Usage variance (adverse)	£7,500
So actual material used should have cost (at standard price per kg)	£1,570,000
÷ standard price per kg	÷ £10
Actual material used	157,000 kg

···

Task 5

(a)

	May 20X6	June 20X6	July 20X6	Aug 20X6
	£	£	£	£
Cost per 1,000 kgs	1,000	900	700	800
Seasonal variation	200	100	(100)	0
Trend	800	800	800	800

Tutorial note. The underlying cost is the Trend.

(b) The percentage increase in the underlying cost from 20X6 to 20X7 is 6.25%

$$\left(\frac{(850-800)}{800}\right) \times 100 = 6.25\%$$

Tutorial note. The above calculation is the most normal way of calculating a change from one period to the next, as a percentage of the original figure.

(c)

	May 20X7	June 20X7	July 20X7	Aug 20X7
	£	£	£	£
Trend	850	850	850	850
Seasonal variation	200	100	(100)	0
Cost per 1,000 kgs	1,050	950	750	850

··

Task 6

REPORT

To: Production Director

From: Management Accountant

Date: xx/xx/xx

Subject: March 20X9 variances

New warehouse

This will have the effect of simply reducing the fixed overhead expense (assuming the rent saved exceeds any new depreciation charge) and therefore is part of the favourable fixed overhead expenditure variance. The standard fixed overhead cost should be adjusted to reflect the rental saving.

New machines

The new machines use less power than the old ones therefore reducing the power costs element of the fixed overhead. The additional depreciation charge however will increase the fixed overhead expense. Once the reduction in power costs and increase in depreciation charge are known then the standard fixed overhead should be adjusted.

Price increase

The price increase will be a cause of the adverse materials price variance. The price increase appears to be a permanent one as all suppliers have increased their prices, so the standard materials cost should be altered.

Skilled labour

The use of the higher skilled labour will have been part of the cause of the favourable labour efficiency variance and the favourable materials usage variance. If the fixed overheads are absorbed on a labour hour basis then the efficiency of the skilled labour will also be a cause of the favourable fixed overhead efficiency variance. The additional expense of the skilled labour and the overtime that has been worked will have been causes of the adverse labour rate variance. The overtime may also have led to the favourable capacity variance as actual hours exceeded the budgeted hours. Unless the use of this grade of labour is likely to be a permanent policy, then there should be no change to the standard labour rate or hours.

Task 7

	November	December	January	February
Actual hours per unit	1.53 hours	1.56 hours	1.45 hours	1.53 hours
Efficiency ratio	98.2%	96.3%	103.3%	98.2%
Capacity ratio	100.7%	110.1%	100.2%	98.9%
Activity ratio	98.9%	106.0%	103.5%	97.1%

Workings

		November	December	January	February
(i)		$\dfrac{98,200}{64,300}$	$\dfrac{107,300}{68,900}$	$\dfrac{90,200}{62,100}$	$\dfrac{92,000}{60,200}$
	Actual hours per unit	1.53 hours per unit	1.56 hours per unit	1.45 hours per unit	1.53 hours per unit
(ii)		$\dfrac{64,300 \times 1.5}{98,200}$	$\dfrac{68,900 \times 1.5}{107,300}$	$\dfrac{62,100 \times 1.5}{90,200}$	$\dfrac{60,200 \times 1.5}{92,000}$
	Efficiency ratio	98.2%	96.3%	103.3%	98.2%
(iii)		$\dfrac{98,200}{65,000 \times 1.5}$	$\dfrac{107,300}{65,000 \times 1.5}$	$\dfrac{90,200}{60,000 \times 1.5}$	$\dfrac{92,000}{62,000 \times 1.5}$
	Capacity ratio	100.7%	110.1%	100.2%	98.9%
(iv)		$\dfrac{64,300}{65,000}$	$\dfrac{68,900}{65,000}$	$\dfrac{62,100}{60,000}$	$\dfrac{60,200}{62,000}$
	Activity ratio	98.9%	106.0%	103.5%	97.1%

Task 8

(a)

Full production cost per turbine manufactured by Voltair	£800.00
Voltair's unavoidable fixed production cost per turbine if contracted out	£105.00
Voltair's avoidable production cost per turbine if contracted out	£695.00

(b)

Full production cost per turbine manufactured by Voltair	£714.29
Voltiar's unavoidable fixed production cost per turbine if contracted out	£75.00
Voltaire's avoidable production cost per turbine if contracted out	£639.29

Workings

(a) (i) Full production cost per turbine based upon production of 10,000 turbines = £8,000,000

Therefore cost per turbine = £8,000,000 / 10,000 = £800.00

(ii) Unavoidable fixed production cost = £3,000,000 – £1,950,000 = £1,050,000

Therefore unavoidable fixed production cost per turbine for 10,000 units = £1,050,000 / 10,000 = £105.00

(iii) Avoidable production cost per turbine for 10,000 units = £800 – £105 = £695.00

(b) (i) Full production cost per turbine based upon production of 14,000 turbines = £10,000,000

Therefore cost per turbine = £10,000,000 / 14,000 = £714.29

(ii) Unavoidable fixed production cost = £3,000,000 – £1,950,000 = £1,050,000

Therefore unavoidable fixed production cost per turbine for 14,000 units = £1,050,000 / 14,000 = £75.00

(iii) Avoidable production cost per turbine for 14000 units = £714.29 – £75.00 = £639.29

Task 9

Lifecycle costs of renting the machine:

	£
Rental (£50,000 × 12 months × 10 years)	6,000,000
Maintenance (£50,000 × 10 years)	500,000
Decommissioning	100,000
Total	6,600,000

Lifecycle costs of buying the machine:

	£
Purchase	3,000,000
Maintenance (£50,000 × 10 years)	500,000
Decommissioning	100,000
Scrap value	(900,000)
Total	2,700,000

Task 10

(a) **To:** Finance Director

Subject: Differences in key performance indicators

From: Accounting Technician

Date: 18 June 20X7

(i) **Gross profit margin**

The gross profit margin for scenario 1 is 35% but falls to 10% for scenario 2. There are two causes for this difference. The selling price has been reduced by 50% (from £10 to £5) which will have reduced the margin. The reduction in the selling price has, however, increased the volume produced and sold which has reduced the fixed overhead per unit which will have increased the margin. However, the effect of the decreased selling price in reducing the margin has outweighed the beneficial effect of the fixed overheads.

(ii) **Operating profit margin**

The operating profit margin for scenario 1 is 20.5% and this falls to a loss under scenario 2. The reduction in gross profit margin has fed down to the operating profit margin and the selling and distribution costs have increased due to the higher sales volume.

(iii) **Direct materials**

The direct materials cost as a percentage of turnover has increased from 25% under scenario 1 to 50% under scenario 2. This difference is caused by the 50% reduction in the selling price. Every unit that is sold under the two scenarios has the same direct material cost (£2.50) but the selling price in scenario 2 is only £5 giving a percentage material cost of 50%, whereas the selling price in scenario 1 is £10 giving a percentage material cost of 25%.

(b)

	%
Gross profit margin £ $\left(\dfrac{540,000}{1,800,000}\right) \times 100$	30.00
Operating profit margin £ $\left(\dfrac{318,000}{1,800,000}\right) \times 100$	17.67
Return on net assets £ $\left(\dfrac{318,000}{1,043,000}\right) \times 100$	30.49

(c) **To:**   Financial Director

Subject: Differences in key performance indicators

From: Accounting Technician

Date: 18 June 20X7

(i) **Gross profit margin**

The revised gross profit has increased to 30%. The increase in the gross profit is caused by the reduction in the cost of raw materials per unit.

However, although the reduction in cost per unit increases the gross profit of scenario 2, it is still below the gross profit of scenario 1 because the effect of scenario 2's lower selling price outweighs the advantages of its lower raw materials and fixed cost absorption rate.

(ii) **Operating profit margin**

The revised operating profit for scenario 2 has increased to £318,000 from a loss. The operating profit margin is now improved to 18% which is fed through from the gross margin but this is still less than the 20.5% for scenario 1.

(iii) **Return on net assets**

The revised return on net assets for scenario 2 is 30.5% compared to 25% for scenario 1.

Recommendations

Based purely on the above three indicators, the decision should be to set the price at £5 as per scenario 2 because the higher return on net assets indicates that the return on investment is (pound for pound) better in scenario 2 and therefore will increase shareholder value. The fact that scenario 1 still has better gross and operating margins is not decisive. These margins do indicate that there are better operating efficiencies in scenario 1 compared to scenario 2. However, the fact that the revised figures for scenario 2 show that it has a significantly larger operating profit than scenario 1 with net assets for the two scenarios being almost the same causes the return on investment in scenario 2 to be better.

BPP PRACTICE ASSESSMENT 4
FINANCIAL PERFORMANCE

Time allowed: 2.5 hours

Task 1

The following information has been calculated for one unit of product, Plate.

Each unit requires 2 litres of material at a cost of £3.50 per litre.

Each unit requires 0.5 hours of grade A labour at £15 per hour, and 0.25 hours of grade B labour at £10 per hour.

Fixed production overheads are £100,000 and budgeted output is 20,000 units.

Complete the standard cost card:

Standard cost card for per unit of Plate	
	£
Direct materials	
Direct labour – grade A	
Direct labour – grade B	
Fixed overhead	
Total standard cost per unit	

Task 2

The standard direct materials cost for a business's product is:

3 kg @ £15 per kg = £45.00

During the last month production was 2,600 units of the product and the actual materials cost was £149,910 for 7,890 kg. The market price of the materials unexpectedly increased by 20% for the whole month.

Complete the following sentences:

The total materials price variance is £ [   ] adverse/favourable.

The non-controllable element of the materials price variance that has been caused by the price increase is £ [   ] adverse/favourable.

The controllable element of the materials price variance caused by other factors is

£ [   ] adverse/favourable.

Task 3

A business makes one product. Fixed overheads are absorbed on the basis of machine hours. The standard cost card shows that fixed overheads are to be absorbed on the basis of 3 machine hours per unit at a rate of £6 per hour. The budgeted level of production is 10,000 units.

The actual results for the period were that fixed overheads were £192,000, actual machine hours were 29,000 and the actual units produced were 9,500.

(a) **The fixed overhead expenditure variance is:**

£12,000 Favourable ☐
£12,000 Adverse ☐
£18,000 Adverse ☐
£21,000 Adverse ☐

(b) **The fixed overhead volume variance is:**

£9,000 Adverse ☐
£9,000 Favourable ☐
£6,000 Adverse ☐
£3,000 Adverse ☐

(c) **The fixed overhead efficiency variance is:**

£3,000 Adverse ☐
£6,000 Adverse ☐
£6,000 Favourable ☐
£9,000 Favourable ☐

(d) **The fixed overhead capacity variance is:**

£3,000 Adverse ☐
£6,000 Adverse ☐
£6,000 Favourable ☐
£21,000 Adverse ☐

Task 4

The following budgetary control report has been provided

	Budget		Actual	
Units	1,100		1,240	
Material	5,280 litres	£14,784	5,800 litres	£17,100
Labour	2,750 hours	£23,375	3,280 hours	£27,060
Fixed overheads		£4,400		£4,650
Total cost		£42,559		£48,810

The following variances have been calculated:

Fixed overhead expenditure	£250
Direct materials price	£860 A
Direct materials usage	£426
Direct labour rate	£820
Direct labour efficiency	£1,530 A
Fixed overhead volume	£560 F

Complete the operating statement:

	£	£	£
Budgeted/Standard cost for actual production			
Variances	**Favourable**	**Adverse**	
Direct materials price			
Direct materials usage			
Direct labour rate			
Direct labour efficiency			
Fixed overhead expenditure			
Fixed overhead volume			
Total variance			
Actual cost of actual production			

Task 5

A company has the following historic information about the cost of material.

	May 20X9	June 20X9	July 20X9
	£	£	£
Total cost	£50,000	£52,000	£55,000
Total quantity purchased	5,000 kg	5,100 kg	5,300 kg

(a) **The cost index for July 20X9 based on May 20X9 being the base period of 100 is:**

100 ☐
90.9 ☐
103.8 ☐
96.3 ☐

(b) In August 20X9, the cost index is 110 (where May 20X9 is the base period of 100).

If the total cost is £60,500, the number of kg purchased is:

6,050 kg ☐
6,655 kg ☐
5,500 kg ☐
5,600 kg ☐

Task 6

Rix Limited manufactures one standard product. Rix Limited operates a standard costing system.

Data from the budget and the standard product cost for the last month are given below.

1   Budgeted and standard cost data:

Budgeted sales and production for the month 10,500 units

Standard cost for each unit of product:

Direct material: A   4 kilograms @ £2.50 per kilogram

                                B   6 kilograms @ £1 per kilogram

Labour: 0.5 hours   @ £16 per hour

Fixed production overhead is absorbed @ 300% of direct wages.

2 Actual data for last month:

Production and sales were 11,000 units sold at standard price.

Direct materials consumed:

A 45,000 kilograms, costing £108,000

B 62,000 kilograms, costing £68,200

Direct wages incurred 5,250 hours and cost £94,500.

Fixed production overhead incurred £250,000.

Prepare a report to the finance director, which includes an operating statement reconciling the standard absorption cost of actual production to actual costs for last months, and explain what the fixed overhead variances reveal about last month's production, and the success of the manager responsible for overhead costs.

Report

To: A Finance Director

From: An Accountant

Date: 14 April 20X2

Subject: Last month's variances

I enclose (in the appendix) an operating statement reconciling the standard cost of actual production last month to the actual cost.

Fixed overhead variances

Appendix

Reconciliation statement – previous month			
	£	£	£
Standard absorption cost of actual production			
	(F)	(A)	
Variances			
Material A price			
Material A usage			
Material B price			
Material B usage			
Labour rate			
Labour efficiency			
Fixed overhead expenditure			
Fixed overhead efficiency			
Fixed overhead capacity			
Actual absorption cost of actual production			

Task 7

Given below are production and sales figures for a manufacturing organisation for the last three months:

	January	February	March
Production costs	£552,300	£568,500	£629,500
Production wages	£104,800	£98,300	£110,800
Output in units	8,540	8,670	9,320
Hours worked	8,635	7,820	9,280
Budgeted output	8,500	8,200	9,500
Sales revenue	£916,000	£923,000	£965,000
Number of employees	55	55	58

Production costs are made up of the materials for production and the bought in services required in the month. It is estimated that each unit takes 1.1 hours to produce.

Complete the table to calculate the performance indicators for each of the last three months:

	January	February	March
Productivity per labour hour			
Efficiency ratio			
Capacity ratio			
Activity ratio			
Value added per employee			

Task 8

A company makes three products with the following standard cost information, and predicted maximum sales demand.

The material available in the coming period is 8,000 kg

The labour hours available in the coming period are 2,000 hours.

	Product		
	A	B	C
Direct materials @ £3 per kg	£9	£6	£12
Direct labour @ £12 per hour	£6	£12	£18
Selling price	£20	£30	£40
Maximum sales demand	1,000 units	800 units	600 units

Complete the table to determine the production plan which will maximise contribution.

Product	Units

Task 9

(a) The costs of the maintenance department of a manufacturing business are estimated to be £102,000 for the following quarter. During that period it is estimated that there will be 50 maintenance visits on site. Product X will require 10 maintenance visits during the quarter and Product Y 40 maintenance visits.

Complete the table below using activity based costing to show how much maintenance overhead will be absorbed into Product X and Product Y.

	£
Overhead included in Product X	
Overhead included in Product Y	

(b) A manufacturer, operating in a competitive market, can sell its product at £35 per unit. It wishes to make a profit margin of 40%. Each unit of product requires 1 hour of labour at £6/hour and incurs other overheads at a rate of £7/labour hour. The product requires 4kg of material per unit.

What is the maximum that the manufacturer can afford to pay for each kg of material?

Maximum £ per kg [ ]

Task 10

A company makes and sells a single product. The forecast statement of profit or loss (income statement) and statement of financial position are shown below.

The forecast is based on an assumed sales price of £8 per unit, and anticipated demand of 500,000 units.

	£'000
Budgeted statement of profit or loss (income statement)	
Revenue	4,000
Cost of production	
Direct materials	1,500
Direct labour	500
Fixed production overheads	800
Total cost of sales	2,800
Gross profit	**1,200**
Fixed selling and distribution costs	85
Fixed administration costs	210
Operating profit	**905**
Budgeted statement of financial position	
Non-current assets	
Machinery	1,600
Current assets	
Inventory of raw materials	280
Receivables	800
Current liabilities	
Payables	(150)
Net current assets	**930**
Long-term loans	500
Net assets	**2,030**
Represented by:	
Share capital and reserves	2,030
Net assets	**2,030**

Draft a report to the finance director which

(a) Includes calculations of the performance indicators listed below

    (i)   Gross profit margin
    (ii) Operating profit margin
    (iii) Direct materials cost per unit
    (iv) Receivables' collection period in days

(b) Advises on the following scenarios:

(i) The gross profit margin for the industry is 35%. Advise the finance director, what the selling price would have to be if demand and costs stay the same, in order to achieve this margin.

(ii) The operating profit margin for the industry is 25%. If it is not possible to change the selling price, demand or most costs, but it may be possible to reduce fixed administration costs, what would the percentage reduction in fixed administration costs have to be, in order to achieve a gross profit margin of 25%?

(iii) The average receivables' payment period in the industry is 65 days. If sales are unchanged, advise the finance director by how much (in £) the year-end receivables would have to change, to achieve the industry average payment period.

To: Finance Director

Subject: Key performance indicators

From: Accounting Technician

Date: 26 October 20X2

Gross profit margin – selling price to achieve industry margin

Operating profit margin – percentage reduction in administration costs

Receivables' collection period – change to achieve industry average

Appendix

	£
Gross profit margin	
Operating profit margin	
Direct materials cost per unit	
Receivables' collection period in days	

BPP PRACTICE ASSESSMENT 4
FINANCIAL PERFORMANCE

ANSWERS

Task 1

Standard cost card for per unit of Plate	
	£
Direct materials (2 × £3.50)	7.00
Direct labour – grade A (0.5 × £15)	7.50
Direct labour – grade B (0.25 × £10)	2.50
Fixed overhead (£100,000/20,000)	5.00
Total standard cost per unit	22.00

Task 2

The total materials price variance is £31,560 Adverse.

The non-controllable element of the materials price variance that has been caused by the price increase is £23,670 Adverse.

The controllable element of the materials price variance caused by other factors is £7,890 Adverse.

Workings

Total materials price variance

	£
7,890 should have cost (× £15)	118,350
But did cost	149,910
	31,560 (A)

Non-controllable variance caused by price increase

	£
Standard cost for actual quantity 7,890 × £15	118,350
Adjusted cost for actual quantity 7,890 × £18*	142,020
	23,670 (A)

*Adjusted price is 120% of £15 = £18

Controllable variance caused by other factors

	£
Adjusted cost for actual quantity 7,890 × £18	142,020
Actual cost	149,910
	7,890 (A)

Task 3

(a) £12,000 Adverse
(b) £9,000 Adverse
(c) £3,000 Adverse
(d) £6,000 Adverse

Workings

Fixed overhead expenditure variance

	£
Budgeted fixed overhead 10,000 units × 3 hours × £6	180,000
Actual fixed overhead	192,000
Expenditure variance	12,000 (A)

Fixed overhead volume variance

	£
Standard hours for actual production @ standard OAR 9,500 units × 3 hours × £6	171,000
Standard hours for budgeted production @ standard OAR 10,000 units × 3 hours × £6	180,000
Volume variance	9,000 (A)

Fixed overhead efficiency variance

	£
Standard hours for actual production @ standard OAR 9,500 × 3 hours × £6	171,000
Actual hours @ standard OAR 29,000 × £6	174,000
Efficiency variance	3,000 (A)

Fixed overhead capacity variance

	£
Actual hours @ standard OAR 29,000 × £6	174,000
Budgeted hours @ standard OAR 10,000 × 3 × £6	180,000
Capacity variance	6,000 (A)

....

Task 4

	£	£	£
Budgeted/Standard cost for actual production			47,976
Variances	Favourable	Adverse	
Direct materials price		860	
Direct materials usage	426		
Direct labour rate	820		
Direct labour efficiency		1,530	
Fixed overhead expenditure		250	
Fixed overhead volume	560		
Total variance	1,806 F	2,640 A	834 A
Actual cost of actual production			48,810

Workings

Standard cost of actual production.

Budgeted cost per unit = £42,559/1,100 = £38.69 per unit

Budgeted cost of 1,240 units = £38.69 × 1,240 = £47,976

Fixed overhead expenditure variance – actual overheads larger than budgeted, therefore expenditure variance is adverse.

Direct materials usage variance – budgeted usage = 5,280/1,100 = 4.8 litres/unit

Actual usage = 5,800/1,240 =4.68 litres/unit ie lower usage than budgeted so favourable.

Labour rate variance – budgeted rate = £23,375/2,750 = £8.50 per hour

Actual rate = £27,060/3,280 = £8.25 per hour ie lower rate than budgeted, so favourable.

....

Task 5

(a) The cost index for July 20X9 based on May 20X9 being the base period of 100 is:

103.8

Working

Cost per kg for May = £50,000/5,000kg = £10 per kg

Cost per kg for July = £55,000/5,300kg = £10.38 per kg

Therefore July's index = £10.38/£10 × 100 = 103.8

(b) In August 20X9, the cost index is 110 (where May 20X9 is the base period of 100). If the total cost is £60,500, the number of kg purchased is 5,500 kg.

Working

Cost per kg in May is £10 per kg

So cost in August = £10/100 × 110 = £11 per kg

Therefore, number of kg purchased = £60,500/£11 = 5,500 kg.

Task 6

Report

To: A Finance Director

From: An Accountant

Date: 14 April 20X2

Subject: Last month's variances

I enclose (in the appendix) an operating statement reconciling the standard cost of actual production last month to the actual cost.

Fixed overhead variances

The total fixed overhead variance is a favourable variance £14,000. £14,000 more fixed overheads were absorbed than were actually incurred.

Only £2,000 of this favourable variance is due to the actual fixed overheads being lower than the budgeted fixed overheads (this difference is the fixed overhead expenditure variance). Therefore, a manager responsible for incurring fixed overheads, can only be credited with a saving of £2,000.

The remaining £12,000 variance is caused by the volume of units produced being greater than expected. The volume was greater entirely because of increased efficiency of labour – more units (11,000) were produced in the labour hours available (5,520) than were expected (10,500).

None of the favourable variance was due to the company having greater capacity than expected (nil capacity variance) as the actual hours worked were equal to those budgeted.

Appendix

Reconciliation statement for last month

	£	£	£
Budgeted cost (W)			528,000
Cost variances	F	A	
Material A price	4,500		
Material A usage		2,500	
Material B price		6,200	
Material B usage	4,000		
Direct wages rate		10,500	
Direct wages efficiency	4,000		
Fixed overhead expenditure	2,000		
Fixed overhead efficiency	12,000		
Fixed overhead capacity	0		
	26,500	19,200	7,300 F
Actual cost (£108,000 + £68,200 + £94,500 + £250,000)			520,700

Workings

Standard absorption cost per unit

			£	£
Direct material A	4 kg	@	2.50	10.00
Direct material B	6 kg	@	1.00	6.00
Labour	0.5 hrs	@	16.00	8.00
Fixed overhead	300% of direct labour			24.00
Total standard cost				48.00

Therefore, standard cost for actual production = 11,000 × £48 = £528,000

Cost variances
Material A price variance

	£
45,000 should have cost (× £2.50)	112,500
But did cost	108,000
	4,500 Fav

Material A usage variance

11,000 should have used (× 4 kg)	44,000
But did use	45,000
	1,000 Adv
× standard rate of £2.50	× £2.50
	2,500 Adv

Material B price variance

	£
62,000 should have cost (× £1)	62,000
But did cost	68,200
	6,200 Adv

Material B usage variance

11,000 should have used (× 6 kg)	66,000
But did use	62,000
	4,000 Fav
× standard rate	× £1
	4,000 Fav

Labour rate variance

	£
5,250 hours should have cost (× £16)	84,000
But did cost	94,500
	10,500 Adv

Labour efficiency variance

11,000 should have taken (× 0.5)	5,500
But did take	5,250
	250
× standard rate	× £16
	4,000 Fav

Fixed overhead expenditure variance

	£
Budgeted fixed overhead (£24 × 10,500)	252,000
Actual fixed overhead	250,000
	2,000 Fav

Fixed overhead efficiency variance

Standard hours for actual production at standard absorption rate	
11,000 × 0.5 × £48*	264,000
Actual hours at standard absorption rate	
5,250 × £48	252,000
	12,000 Fav

*£24 per unit is absorbed, or £24/0.5 = £48 per labour hour

Fixed overhead capacity variance

Actual hours at standard absorption rate	
5,250 × £48	252,000
Budgeted hours at standard absorption rate	
10,500 × 0.5 × £48	252,000
	0

Task 7

	January	February	March
Productivity per labour hour	0.99 units	1.11 units	1.00 units
Efficiency ratio	108.8%	122.0%	110.5%
Capacity ratio	92.4%	86.7%	88.8%
Activity ratio	100.5%	105.7%	98.1%
Value added per employee	£6,613	£6,445	£5,784

Workings

		January	February	March
(i)	Productivity per labour hour	$\dfrac{8,540}{8,635}$	$\dfrac{8,670}{7,820}$	$\dfrac{9,320}{9,280}$
		0.99 units per hour	1.11 units per hour	1.00 unit per hour
(ii)	Efficiency ratio	$\dfrac{8,540 \times 1.1}{8,635}$	$\dfrac{8,670 \times 1.1}{7,820}$	$\dfrac{9,320 \times 1.1}{9,280}$
		108.8%	122.0%	110.5%
(iii)	Capacity ratio	$\dfrac{8,635}{8,500 \times 1.1}$	$\dfrac{7,820}{8,200 \times 1.1}$	$\dfrac{9,280}{9,500 \times 1.1}$
		92.4%	86.7%	88.8%
(iv)	Activity ratio	$\dfrac{8,540}{8,500}$	$\dfrac{8,670}{8,200}$	$\dfrac{9,320}{9,500}$
		100.5%	105.7%	98.1%

(v)	Value added per employee	£	£	£
	Sales	916,000	923,000	965,000
	Production costs	(552,300)	(568,500)	(629,500)
	Value added	363,700	354,500	335,500
	Value added per employee	£6,613	£6,445	£5,784

Task 8

Product	Units
A	1,000
B	800
C	466

Workings

1 **Determine the limiting factor**

Material usage per unit of each product:

A   £9/£3 = 3 kg per unit
B   £6/£3 = 2 kg per unit
C   £12/£3 = 4 kg per unit

So maximum sales demand would use:

A   3 kg × 1,000 = 3,000 kg
B   2 kg × 800 = 1,600 kg
C   4 kg × 600 = 2,400 kg

Therefore total materials usage for this demand = 3,000 + 1,600 + 2,400 = 7,000 kg

8,000 kg are available so material is not the limiting factor

Labour hours per unit of each product:

A   £6/£12 = 0.5 hours per unit
B   £12/£12 = 1 hour per unit
C   £18/£12 = 1.5 hours per unit

So maximum sales demand would require:

A   0.5 × 1,000 = 500 hours
B   1 × 800 = 800 hours
C   1.5 × 600 = 900 hours

Therefore, total labour hours for this demand = 500 + 800 + 900 = 2,200 hours
Only 2,000 hours are available so labour hours is a limiting factor.

2 **Contribution per limiting factor:**

A   (£20 – £9 – £6)/0.5 = £10 per labour hour
B   (£30 – £12 – £6)/1 = £12 per labour hour
C   (£40 – £12 – £18)/1.5 = £6.67 per labour hour

Therefore, rank B, A and then C.

3 **Production to maximise contribution**

B   800 units use 800 hours
A   1,000 units use 500 hours, so 1,300 hours used so far
C   Remaining 2,000 – 1,300 = 700 hours can be used for product C. Makes 700/1.5 = 466 units.

Task 9

(a)

Overhead included in Product X	£20,400
Overhead included in Product Y	£81,600

Workings

Maintenance cost per visit =   £102,000/50   =   £2,040

Product X   =   10 × £2,040   =   £20,400

Product Y   =   40 × £2,040   =   £81,600

(b)   Maximum £ per kg = £2.00

	£
Selling price	35.00
40% margin	14.00
Target cost	21.00
Less	
Labour 1 hr @ £6/hr	(6.00)
Overheads 1 hr @ £7/hr	(7.00)
Available for 4kg material	8.00
Maximum price per kg	£2.00

Task 10

(a)

Gross profit margin	30%
Operating profit margin	22.63%
Direct materials cost per unit	£3 per unit
Receivables' collection period in days	73 days

Workings

Gross profit = $\frac{£1,200,000}{£4,000,000} \times 100 = 30\%$

Operating profit margin = $\frac{£905,000}{£4,000,000} \times 100 = 22.63\%$

Direct materials cost per unit = $\frac{£1,500,000}{500,000} = £3$ per unit

Receivables' collection period in days = $\frac{£800,000}{£4,000,000} \times 365 = 73$ days

(b) **To:** Finance Director

Subject: Key performance indicators

From: Accounting Technician

Date: 26 October 20X2

(i) **Gross profit margin – selling price to achieve industry margin**

The current gross profit margin is 30% but the industry margin is 35%. Therefore, for the same level of costs, the sales price would have to increase to £8.62 per unit.

(ii) **Operating profit margin – percentage reduction in administration costs**

For an operating profit margin of 25% when the only cost/revenue that can change is administration costs, these would have to decrease by 45.24%

(iii) **Receivables' collection period – change to achieve industry average**

Receivables would have to reduce by £87,671 to achieve the industry average of receivables' days of 65, for this level of revenue.

Workings

(i) Gross profit margin of 35%

Cost of sales = £2,800,000

Revenue would have to be £2,800,000/65% = £4,307,692

Sales price per unit would have to be £4,307,692/500,000 = £8.62

(ii) Operating profit margin of 25%

Operating profit/revenue = 25%

Revenue would be unchanged, so operating profit would be 25% × £4,000,000 = £1,000,000 ie an increase of £95,000.

Therefore, fixed administration overheads would have to decrease by £95,000.

Percentage reduction in fixed administration overheads = £95,000/£210,000 = 45.24%

(iii) Industry receivables' days are 65 days

Revenue × 65/365 = receivables

£4,000,000 × 65/365 = £712,329

Reduction in receivables = £800,000 − £712,329 = £87,671